Sex and the Slayer

Sex and the Slayer

A GENDER STUDIES PRIMER FOR THE *Buffy* FAN

LORNA JOWETT

WESLEYAN UNIVERSITY PRESS MIDDLETOWN, CONNECTICUT

Published by Wesleyan University Press
Middletown, CT 06459
www.wesleyan.edu/wespress
Copyright © 2005 by Lorna Jowett

Printed in the United States of America
♾ The paper used in this publication meets the
minimum requirements of the American National
Standard for Information Sciences—Permanence of
Paper for Printed Library Materials, ANSI Z39.48-1992.

Library of Congress Cataloging-in-Publication Data
Jowett, Lorna, 1971–
Sex and the slayer : a gender studies primer for the Buffy
fan / Lorna Jowett.
        p. cm.
Includes bibliographical references and index.
ISBN 0-8195-6757-4 (cloth : alk. paper) —
ISBN 0-8195-6758-2 (pbk. : alk. paper)
1. Buffy, the vampire slayer (Television program)
2. Sex role on television. I. Title.
PN1992.77.B84J69   2005
791.45'72—dc22
                    2004043120
05 06 07 08 09   5 4 3 2 1

TO CHARLOTTE AND JAMIE

"You think you know. What's to come,
what you are. You haven't even begun."
— *"Restless"*

contents

ACKNOWLEDGMENTS

The first part of my title is taken from a panel discussion on *Buffy* at Wis-Con 25. When I attended WisCon 27 I asked around to find out who came up with "Sex and the Slayer," but no one could remember. Whoever it was, thanks for a great title.

This book would never have been completed without assistance from many different people. Thanks are owed to those who supported me at University College Northampton, particularly the Cultural Studies research cluster, which provided money for what was optimistically called a "partial sabbatical," and the American Studies division. Brian Caldwell and Nick Heffernan deserve special mention for reading parts of the manuscript and giving helpful suggestions for revision and new approaches, as does Sue Donnelly for enduring many excited *Buffy* conversations in our shared office. Those conversations have been going on for some time, and I would like to thank all the students who talked *Buffy* with me. Ben Crook and Mark Rowe made sure I saw season 7 in good time, and Mark, Andy Cassidy, and other media staff from the library also provided invaluable technical help.

Thanks to all those who shared ideas. Stevie Simkin discussed masculinity. Bronwen Calvert carried out reading above and beyond the call of duty and offered much-needed general support. Audiences at conference papers also provided insights and suggestions.

I must also thank the readers employed by Wesleyan University Press for their helpful and constructive suggestions, editor Leonora Gibson for answering all my questions and believing in the book, and Suzanna Tamminen for stepping in and taking over as editor at the eleventh hour.

Thank you to family and friends who believed in me. Special thanks to Gavin for going to Sunnydale with me the first time and for seeing it through to the end.

The basis for chapters 4–6 appeared as "Masculinity, Monstrosity and Behavior Modification in *Buffy the Vampire Slayer*" in *Foundation, the International Review of Science Fiction* 31.84 (Spring 2002): 59–73.

Sex and the Slayer

Introduction

As I begin, I am tempted to paraphrase Angela McRobbie (1994: 18) and say that it would be difficult not to know about Sarah Michelle Gellar but impossible not to know about *Buffy the Vampire Slayer* (1997–2003). Initially I started watching *Buffy* because it appeared to be a genre I enjoy and because the trailers were intriguing. Like many other viewers, I continued watching because the show used and played with genre, because it was funny and had great dialogue, and because of its representation of gender. Until *Buffy* I would never have described myself as a real fan of a television program. I quickly realized that it wasn't just me— *Buffy* was being discussed in the academy too.[1] *Buffy* was my favorite television show, but that didn't mean I was entirely uncritical of it. It might even be true that fans are more likely to be critical, not less, since they regularly engage in discussion and analysis.

As a fan, a feminist, and an academic, I have always found watching popular television and film problematic because their texts offer varying and often contradictory sources of viewing pleasure. *Buffy* is no exception, and this raises several points that shape my analysis. First, as a feminist viewer I both enjoy and critique the show. Second, given that different viewers read the show differently, it is possible to read *Buffy* as a "feminist" show, to read it "simply" as a supernatural fantasy that has nothing to do with real life, or to read it as a heroic story about universal values (that is, detached from any social or gendered context). What I aim to demonstrate in this book is not how "feminist" or "progressive" the show is but how it represents femininity, masculinity, and gendered relations, including sexuality, and how this relates to the context of genre. This book aims to draw out what I see as patterns of gender representation and to relate these to relevant contexts. How do gender and genre work together, clash with each other, and interact?

I believe that *Buffy* presents neither a "subversive" nor a "conservative" view of gender but, rather, a contradictory mixture of both. The ambivalences that mark the show's representation of gender are typical of contemporary television and especially of what is now called "quality" television. That *Buffy* is both subversive of and complicit in dominant culture and ideologies marks it as a key example of such popular culture products. These ambivalences and the apparent contradictions in representing gender (both feminine and masculine) expose a complex negotiation and mediation of gender located within a particular social and historical context that I identify as postfeminist and postmodern. The show's negotiation allows viewers to recognize the difficulties of constructing and maintaining gender identities. This in turn affords a kind of "use value": in discussion viewers might compare situations in the show with situations in their own lives, and as I write, one of the most recently published books on *Buffy* is called *What Would Buffy Do?* (Riess 2004). I see *Buffy* as an ideologically and formally ambiguous postfeminist artifact, one that is characteristic of postmodern cultural production. It is both a product of and a response to our postfeminist and postmodern society.

Buffy, Feminism, and Cultural Studies

When I first envisaged this book, it seemed to me that the obvious focus to adopt for analysis of *Buffy* was the show's representation of gender, including its constructions of sexuality, and I wondered why nobody else had done so in detail. Having embarked on this project, I realized that discussing gender in *Buffy* or in any other contemporary cultural product is far more complex and difficult than it might seem. I have already suggested that *Buffy* emerges from a particular historical moment: here I sketch out how the changes of recent decades have produced that moment and how it has been theorized in cultural studies.

Many discussions of gender highlight the distinction between biological sex and gender as a social construction. Thus sex is male or female, while gender is masculine or feminine (and many readers will have noticed immediately that my title blurs this distinction). In treating gender as what he calls a "sign system" or "code," Brian Attebery defines gender as "a way of assigning social and psychological meaning to sexual difference, insofar as that difference is perceived in form, appearance, sexual function, and expressive behavior" (2002: 2). Postmodernism and postfeminism have changed the way we think about gender, representation, and identity, even if "we" are not academics. *Buffy*'s creator, Joss Whedon, describes himself as a feminist, but *Buffy* has been read in different ways. What I offer in this book could broadly be described as a feminist cultural studies reading of gender in *Buffy* (that is, one inflected by postmodernism), and it is useful to outline this approach and its value.

Cultural studies has been shaped by thinking about postmodernism. Although there is no real consensus about what postmodernism "is," postmodern theory has changed how we think and speak about identity. While others have argued that it relates primarily to the aesthetic and the cultural, McRobbie suggests that postmodernism is a "concept for understanding social change" (1994: 62). In the United States the latter half of the twentieth century has often been designated as a period of late corporate capitalism and has seen many changes. Since the 1950s the dominant position of white heterosexual middle-class American males has faced a series of challenges from the civil rights movement, the women's movement, and the gay rights movement, altering the way people think about race (and ethnicity), gender, and sexuality. In simplistic terms, being identified as of a particular race, gender, or sexual orientation is no longer a guarantee of dominance or superiority. Women, people of color, and gays and lesbians argued that they were just "as good as" white heterosexual men and demanded to be treated equally at work, at home, and at leisure. This had widespread effects. To offer only a couple of minor examples, discrimination because of race, gender, or sexuality is no longer considered acceptable, and our everyday language is now judged against standards of "political correctness." Shifts in industry and employment and what is often referred to as "the standard of living" in the Western world have altered the way we think about social class, and for some, class is no longer a key identifier. The construction of families and relationships has also changed in relation to some of these other factors.

The result is that the ways we think about, discuss, and represent identity, and therefore gender, have changed to accommodate these developments. Representations of women are no longer focused on marriage, the domestic, and motherhood, for instance, but might now include working women, single mothers, and lesbians. Feminism is seen to have been succeeded by postfeminism, and even the name *postfeminism* implies that feminism has had its day, although the nature of that succession and links between the two are not always clear-cut, as I outline below. The terms *postmodern* and *postfeminist* do not just exist in the vacuum of academic debate—they are intended to refer to actual social contexts.

One "drawback" of a postmodernist approach is that it might seem to preclude any certainty at all about identity: we can no longer say who "we" are, "I" am, or "you" are, or that a person or a character is "feminine" or "masculine." More usefully, it might be argued that postmodernism has questioned the ways in which the subject is constructed and has thus opened up debates about power, representation, diversity, and difference. This means in part that race, gender, class, and ethnicity are seen to impact on identity, but also that these factors intersect and impact on each other and mean different things to different people. Via postmodernism, popular culture has come to be seen as a "site of struggle" wherein "[g]endered identities and cultural forms are produced, reproduced and negotiated in specific historical contexts within specific and shifting forms of power relations" (Hollows 2000: 27). Since *Buffy* is a pop-culture product, my analysis regards it as just such a site of struggle. *Buffy* treats identity as inherently unstable. Its characters often talk about being or not being "themselves"; they shift from being "good" to being (perhaps temporarily) "bad," from being "bad" to being "good," from being straight to being gay, from being stiff to being loose, from being teens to being adults. This is perhaps the one point on which *Buffy*'s categorization as postmodern television stands: in the show identity is always being constructed, reconstructed, and negotiated, and for many viewers there is a sense of recognition in that. This means that gendered identity is also constantly being negotiated.

There is little real consensus about what "feminism" and "postfeminism" are. Many of our ideas about feminism derive from what is often called the "second wave" of feminism in the 1960s and 1970s. The feminist ideas that came out of this period have been criticized from various standpoints, not least as being ideas that focused on and were of most significance to white middle-class academic feminists and as such did not bear much relation to the lives of working-class women or women of color. The label *feminism* is now unappealing to many women, in part because it symbolizes such exclusivity. Current thinking assumes that "even within specific historical contexts, there is no single feminine identity, but multiple feminine identities" and that "feminine identities are also cross-cut by class, sexual, 'racial,' ethnic, generational and regional identities" (Hollows 2000: 34).

At this stage it may be necessary to explain some of the "commonsense" aspects of feminism, especially the use of terms that I adopt here. In 1991 McRobbie made the passing comment that *patriarchy* is "a word rarely used these days" (1994: 35), yet many feminist discussions of cultural studies continue to use the term. From a sociological point of view, Vicki Coppock, Deena Haydon, and Ingrid Richter suggest that patriarchy

> defines the personal, physical and institutional power that men exert over women. Through the process of hegemony the dominance of men over women is achieved and maintained. This takes the form of social arrangements, cultural traditions and political management. Through these, personal relations are contextualised and accepted as "normal" and "right." Thus, patriarchy maintains and sustains structures of male dominance through systems of ideas, beliefs and shared assumptions about gender, sexuality and reproduction, material subordination and coercion. (1995: 18)

Joanne Hollows observes that in "feminist cultural studies the term is often taken for granted: a system of male domination is assumed to exist and used to identify and explain different instances of women's oppression," while noting that for "many feminists, patriarchy may not be a perfect concept but it remains the best tool for understanding women's subordinate position" (2000: 8). Like previous feminist scholars, I have adopted the concept of patriarchy as a necessity in discussing some aspects of representation, though I acknowledge that "patriarchy" is not an unchanging and inflexible system.

The second wave of feminism and some of its ideas have permeated our culture, its construction of femaleness and femininity, and its representation of women. As my analysis demonstrates, shows like *Buffy* carry the marks of feminist history and cultural change, and in this way, cultural studies argues that feminism or some feminist ideas have been incorporated into hegemony. *Hegemony*, a term adopted by cultural studies from the work of Antonio Gramsci, denotes how dominant ways of seeing and understanding (ideologies or discourses) are presented as reasonable and "commonsensical," the "only" way to see. Yet hegemony is never "complete"; it changes and adapts to the historical moment. "Hegemony also accommodates contradiction," state Coppock, Haydon, and Richter. "It is precisely the *illusion* of 'freedom,' 'choice' and 'opportunity' which remains fundamental to the political management of conflict and resistance" (1995: 183). Within hegemony, ideology is "continually reproduced, which is to say internalised in some degree by subjects whose consciousness it never exhausts, who may resist or contest it in various ways" (Traube 1992: 14). My discussion throughout this book and particularly in chapters 1 and 2 will show how this argument is relevant to *Buffy* and shows like it.

Another term I employ in my discussion is "the Other." This alludes to oppositional or binary ways of thinking about identity. That is, we identify ourselves in relation to others, and often in opposition to other categories. This applies to gender, but also to race, ethnicity, and sexuality. The usual construction is that of Self and Other, the Other being anything that is not Self. Gender in particular is often seen having two polar categories, male and female, the former being the "default norm" and the latter therefore equating to not-male. In such a binary model, "one gender is meaningful only to the degree that it differs (or is treated as if it differs) from another" (Attebery 2002: 3), and this can be seen in the way people commonly talk about "the opposite sex." Clearly such definitions of "self" or "norm" are constructed by dominant groups and work to exclude characteristics or identities that do not match those of the dominant group, and the "default norm" is generally white, middle class, and often male and/or heterosexual. While *Buffy* uses various strategies for disrupting or destabilizing gender binaries and those related to sexuality (hetero/homosexual), it tends not to question racial or ethnic binaries.

I have already suggested that "female" is often taken to denote sex, "femininity" to refer to gender. While it is acknowledged that being female (or male) will mean different things to different people, there is another set of issues relating to the way "femininity" has been understood and used in analysis. Feminist cultural studies has focused on images of women, women viewers, and women's genres (primarily soap and melodrama). Within these discussions several critics have noted a tendency to create an opposition between feminism and femininity and a tendency to fall into a "feminism good, femininity bad" polarization of "positive" and "negative" images of women (Brunsdon, McRobbie). In her recent analysis *Feminism, Femininity and Popular Culture*, Hollows describes the "ways in which feminist critiques of femininity are often dependent on creating an opposition between 'bad' feminine identities and 'good' feminist identities" (2000: 9). This is almost exactly the reverse of how popular versions of postfeminism have positioned feminism as "bad" because it is seen to be hostile toward conventional femininity.[2] Previous drafts of this book exhibited this oppositional tendency, and I have tried in my revisions to steer away from it, instead emphasizing the ambivalence that characterizes both the form and the "message" of *Buffy*. This collapsing of boundaries is also characteristic of postmodern thinking. In 1993 McRobbie suggested that "the old binary opposition which put femininity at one end of the political spectrum and feminism at the other is no longer an accurate way of conceptualizing young female experience (maybe it never was)" (1994: 158); in fact, the "postfeminist" conjunction of feminism and femininity in *Buffy* may be one reason why the show is often seen as particularly useful to its audience, as representing "real" issues.

Discussing gender in *Buffy* is also more complex from a feminist cultural studies approach in that the show is not from a traditionally "female" genre, though it is inflected by soap and melodrama, especially in its narrative form and its privileging of emotion. The fact that *Buffy*'s creator, Joss Whedon, describes himself as a feminist has led to some discussion about whether *Buffy* is a "feminist show," and I examine the intersections of genre and representation in terms of gender in the course of the book. Furthermore, although feminist cultural studies has tended to focus on images of women, I discuss masculinity as well. In 1995 Lyn Thomas used the British detective show *Inspector Morse* to demonstrate how feminism influenced representations of masculinity on television (in Brunsdon, D'Acci, and Spigel 1997). Likewise, Attebery suggests that feminism and its advances meant that "males too become gendered," with the result that men "are forced to reexamine themselves" and dominant notions of masculinity (2002: 7). To me, "postfeminist" representations of the female or feminine must effect changes in representation of the male and masculinity, and I discuss these representations as complementary.

Cultural studies and feminist cultural studies has also been concerned with audiences, and I refer here and subsequently to fans, viewers, subject positions, and *Buffy* as a "polysemic" text, that is, a text open to many interpretations. The substantial following the show has acquired means that there are established fan communities and that many instances of fan as well as academic dialogue and discourse surround the show. Changes in viewing practice (video and DVD releases as well as reruns) and fan communities (especially Internet use) have made such analysis easier and more accessible, and further audience studies on *Buffy* would be useful. *Buffy* is not what would normally be considered a "woman's" show; it can fall into several genre categories that are traditionally "male." Perhaps this is why it has attracted a mixed audience.

Given the perceived limitations of second-wave feminism and the new ways of thinking about identity offered by postmodernism, it is now commonplace for critics to describe their own specific identities as a way of alerting readers to possible bias. I have already stated that I am an academic and a fan, two positions which do not necessarily sit comfortably together (it is not always acceptable to admit in academic circles to being a "fan," and academics are often greeted with some suspicion in fan communities or discussions). I have suggested above that there is no general agreement on what "feminism" is, and therefore to identify myself as a "feminist" may mean different things to different readers (another reason to outline my general approach). My position as a British viewer of *Buffy* also inevitably affects my viewing practice and my perception of the show.[3]

Recent debates about "quality television" (for example, Jancovich and Lyons 2003) only complicate matters. One of the most frequently used definitions of "quality television" I have encountered in academic circles comes from Robert J. Thompson's *Television's Second Golden Age: From* Hill Street Blues *to* ER (1997). Thompson set out various criteria that can be used to identify "quality television," and these range from formal features to aspects of production and reception. In Thompson's theorization "quality television" distinguishes itself from other television, it is produced by experienced professionals or what are sometimes called television "auteurs," it attracts a particular (educated, professional) audience, and it may initially be unappreciated or struggle for success. Formal identifiers include an ensemble cast allowing for multiple plot lines, a "memory" enabling plot lines or characters to develop over time (what I later refer to as serial form), a mixture of genres, a more literary style than other television shows, self-conscious references to culture and popular culture, incorporation of controversial subjects, and aspirations to realism. The final identifier is that all of the above result in achievement and critical appreciation (Thompson 1997: 13–16).

Thompson suggests that by 1992 the "innovative elements" that identified "quality television" had "become more and more predictable" (1997: 16), and some of these elements are now common in shows (especially serial drama) that may not generally be recognized as "quality." Part of the problem with the term *quality television* is that no one can really agree what it means. Thompson's criteria are useful in identifying particular features, but the values inherent in the categorization "quality" are always problematic. When I tell people I am working on *Buffy*, they often react with disbelief or dismissal (though, to be fair, some say, "Cool!"). *Buffy* has not won critical acclaim in terms of mainstream awards, and its generic positioning as fantasy may automatically downgrade it for some, but its popularity in academic circles demonstrates a critical appreciation. *Buffy* is often included in discussions of "quality television," and here I surround the term with quotation marks to indicate its contested nature.

It may be flattering to think that one's favorite television shows are "quality," but it would be naive to overlook the commercial basis of television programming. Other "quality" television shows are marked by similar characteristics and demonstrate the same contradictions as *Buffy*, especially tensions involving narrative and closure, romance and friendship, and gender and the family. My identity as a white middle-class academic inevitably positions me in particular ways, both as a viewer and as a critic. Mark Jancovich and James Lyons observe that quality television is marketed at "affluent, highly educated consumers who value the literary qualities of these programs,"[4] and they suggest that the "overwhelming preoccupation with the white, affluent, urban middle classes" such shows display is actually a consequence of their "celebrated formal features" which "work to exclude sections of the viewing public" (2003: 3). Following this logic, it is hardly surprising if shows like *Buffy* are more preoccupied with issues such as gender and sexuality rather than race and class, since the former are of more significance in the lives of its consumers. It is also hardly surprising that I should enjoy the show, since Jancovich and Lyons' description of the quality television market identifies me as part of the target audience.

Throwing Away the Handbook

Giles tells Buffy in the subtitle to this introduction that "the handbook" is not appropriate for her because she is not like other Slayers; she does not fit the template. Similarly, I suggest here that "the handbook," the usual rules, do not work for *Buffy* the show because it cannot be read as having one particular narrative form, one particular set of generic conventions, or one set of representations. Joss Whedon has suggested that "[o]ne of the things TV is about is comfort, is knowing exactly where you are," but he goes on to state, "I'm very much committed to keeping the audience off their feet. It's sort of antithetical to what TV is devised to do" (in Longworth 2002: 211). Whether this is "what TV is devised to do," it is clear that in *Buffy* Whedon wants to throw away the handbook, and one way of doing this is to offer a mixture of genres.

From the outset the show's title, *Buffy the Vampire Slayer*, suggests an unsettling of generic conventions and unexpected juxtapositions. The show mixes action, horror/vampire, comedy, science fiction, the gothic, teen drama, and melodrama. As Whedon implies, this mixture can upset the audience's expectations, but it could not succeed if audiences were not familiar with the conventions of those genres and therefore able to identify how they are subverted by these juxtapositions (viewing competence). This kind of self-conscious play with genre and format is one of the formal features of postmodern and contemporary popular culture,[5] so that in this sense *Buffy does* follow the handbook, *is* a typical example. The show's "use value," in other words, is that it deals as much with television itself as with the "real world," and this is a further postmodern dimension. Different genres offer particular roles and narratives, and it follows that a hybrid of genres allows scope to highlight or play with such roles and narratives. Throughout I seek to demonstrate how certain genres affect gender and what this blurring of genres does to gender representation. As its title shows, part of what *Buffy* does is to reverse roles in terms of their gender, so that the female is not victim but slayer, not passive but active.

Genre is not the only significant factor that affects gender in *Buffy*. Form also has an important impact on the representation of gender and sexuality. *Buffy* is a prime-time series, but over its seven-year run it increasingly took on aspects of serial form, and I discuss this as the soap or serial element of the show. A brief word on the terms *series, serial,* and *soap* may be necessary here. *Buffy* is a series with seven seasons: season 1 consisted of twelve episodes; every other season has twenty-two episodes. Various commentators have set out different definitions of *series* and *serial*. Graeme Turner summarizes: "One of the key differences, it seemed then, was the series' use of self-contained episodes with relatively autonomous plotlines as against the serial's use of continuing storylines with characters who learned from episode to episode." He then suggests that "[t]oday, there are elements of the serial in many of what the industry would regard as series," citing "US sitcoms such as *Friends*, hospital dramas such as *ER*, and cop shows such as *NYPD Blue*" (2001: 6), and I would add teen drama. Adopting this terminology, then, *Buffy* is a series with elements of a serial. This brings into play a variety of narrative and formal elements, including the deferral of resolution, the use of "backstory" by dedicated viewers, and the juxtaposition of pattern/familiarity and disruption/change.

Although it can be argued that *Buffy* is a standard series in that each episode resolves a problem (the defeat of the "monster of the week") and thus offers weekly closure of a linear narrative, the narrative form of the show is a little more complicated. Another longer-running linear narrative can be identified in terms of the season: there is generally a season villain (the "big bad") who recurs and is defeated at the end. This allows ongoing story arcs but also a resolved linear narrative contained within each season. As the show developed, so did other narratives. John Corner has observed that "[s]eries have become flexible in their employment of single episode and multi-episode strands and, following American precedents, they have often developed complex, multi-strand narratives, switching to and from concurrent lines of action during the course of an episode" (1999: 58). From season 2 of *Buffy*, ongoing story arcs also include the development of relationships and characters, and these narratives are nonlinear in that they do not offer closure and continue to develop over several seasons. The linear narrative itself may be familiar and predictable (a mythical story of good and evil), but it will never have real closure partly because of the renewal of the show into another season (though the final seventh season offers closure of Buffy's story) and also because of the cyclical nature of its basic premise, the Slayer (Buffy's story is only part of the history of the Slayer).

Strongly developmental relationship arcs allow the show to diverge from the resolved linear narrative to dwell on continually changing relationships between its characters. In her introduction to *Reading the Vampire Slayer*, Roz Kaveney observed that *Buffy*'s "emotional structures have more in common with soap opera relationships than with most genre series" (2001: 5). This variation or tension between forms is also related to gender in my reading. Robyn Warhol (1999) argues that serial form both resists the traditional marriage plot of much nonserial fiction and enables the construction of nontraditional and nonnuclear families (see also Nochimson 1992). Thus I suggest that serial form in *Buffy* is a factor in its representation of gender.[6] The serial nature of *Buffy*'s narrative and its juxtaposition of resolvable (action plot) and open-ended (relationship arcs) narrative strands potentially allow it to resist both the closure of heterosexual romance (traditionally leading to marriage) and the patriarchal structure of the traditional family. Furthermore, linear narrative is seen as masculine and is often related to "high" forms of art such as literature or cinema. The continuous narrative of the soap or serial is seen as "low" art and as feminine both in terms of production and in terms of address and audience (see Modleski, Ang). *Buffy* uses both types of narrative.

Perhaps narrative and genre seem less important than my argument that *Buffy* is the product of a particular cultural moment, but it is useful to lay out how the show uses genre and narrative. Generic and narrative forms have evolved over time and under different social conditions that have undoubtedly affected their ideological textures. I suggest that *Buffy* uses genres and mixes or revises them to fit its own context and ideology and that the way it uses them can be identified as postmodern and postfeminist. Judith Mayne has argued that

> television narrative has relied centrally on principles of multiple identification and of narrative structure in which there is a fine line, if any line at all, between irony and rhetoric, between critique and celebration. Indeed, one of the most distinctive characteristics of contemporary television narrative might well be the breaking down of familiar boundaries — between fiction and non-fiction, between transparency and self-reflexivity, between progressive and reactionary vantage-points. What is particular to the narrative ambiguity of *L.A. Law* is its constant return, not only to issues of gender — which is not so uncommon in television narrative — but also to the ways these issues have been raised in feminist discourse. (1997: 86–87)

A similar ambiguity is at work in *Buffy* and its use of both "progressive and reactionary vantage-points" is indicative and characteristic of its attempt to negotiate gender identities for the late twentieth and early twenty-first centuries.

Buffy's Binaries

The following chapters make reference to *Buffy*'s binaries. *Buffy* makes much play with the binary oppositions invoked by the various generic conventions it uses. These include masculine/feminine, human/monster, active/passive, strong/weak, good/bad, teen/adult, and power/powerlessness. The show attempts to destabilize binaries through ambivalence and ambiguity and through the multiple intersections of its generic hybridity. In reversing, subverting, or blurring boundaries between these binaries, *Buffy* potentially opens up an arena for alternative representations of gender and sexuality. It offers postfeminist and postmodern representations of gendered identity in that the identities of its main characters are shifting, in that the ensemble cast offers multiple versions of gender and sexuality, and in that its mixture of fantasy and reality allows it to be self-conscious and to offer some sense of estrangement from social "norms." The show's polysemic nature is acknowledged by its creators, most clearly in Joss Whedon's "Bring Your Own Subtext" comment. Whedon has suggested, "Part of the attraction of the Buffy-verse" is that it "lends itself to polymorphously perverse subtext. It encourages it. I personally find romance in every relationship [with exceptions], I love all the characters, so I say B. Y. O. Subtext!" (in Saxey 2001: 208; parentheses in original). Thus resistant readings are in some sense "authorized" and celebrated.

However, generic metanarratives and constructions may prevail for some viewers, and the use of fantasy elements means that it is easy to dismiss some of the more subversive elements of the show as "pure fantasy." In this sense *Buffy* may be too neatly tailored for a "quality television" audience who have the cultural capital and viewing skills to negotiate the different readings and subject positions the show has to offer. In season 7 the good-prevails-over-evil metanarrative reinscribes the good-versus-evil binary, and previously ambivalent characters such as Spike and Faith are rehabilitated as "good." Moral ambiguity also relates to the disruption of traditional gender binaries. The meanings of "good" and "bad" shift according to context and perspective. In *Buffy* this serves to demonstrate how gendered identities (especially for females) have changed over time: behavior once seen as "bad," particularly violent action or overt sexuality, are no longer labeled this way, as I discuss in chapters 2 and 3. Although I show that in many ways identity in *Buffy* is seen to be relational, I explore how this can mean that identity is often oppositional—that is, identity is defined in relation to others, who are often Others.

The majority of *Buffy*'s characters, male and female, are white, middle class and heterosexual and this becomes more noticeable because other "quality" television shows attempt to reflect the diversity of British and American society, and daily serial soaps (like the British *EastEnders*) represent a range of ages, races, ethnicities, classes, genders, and sexualities. It has been noted that in the United States' history of representing itself, "being white became synonymous with being American" (Babb 1998: 2), and *Buffy*'s white, middle-class, heterosexual "norm" is rarely named and remains largely invisible even as it influences constructions of identity and gender. As Richard Dyer points out, *race* is often a term "only applied to non-white peoples," and "as long as white people are not racially seen and named, they/we function as a human norm" (1997: 1). Some difference on *Buffy* is given a subject position and point of view (sexuality) but other differences are not (race and class). Although the show opens up possibilities for alternative sexualities, heterosexuality as a predominant "norm" in *Buffy* is contradictory, just as the negotiation of heterosexuality becomes increasingly complex in the "real" world. I discuss heterosexual romance in particular as problematic for the show's negotiation of "feminist" identities for both male and female characters.

The structure of this book entails rather mechanical divisions into sections on masculinity and femininity and a final chapter on parents, with some obvious overlap in discussion. This structure has been adopted to help address some key issues surrounding gender and genre, while the overlap arises inevitably from an attempt to compare and contrast issues, characters, and themes in text and context. Analysis of *Buffy*'s representation of femininity and masculinity and its constructions of sexuality is achieved not only through analysis of popular main characters but also by examining shorter-running characters, many of whom have not been covered in critical discussion to date.

Since I began writing this book, I have struggled with the first two chapters. On reflection and in undertaking my revisions, I believe that my difficulty with these chapters lies not so much in the impossibility of covering so much material, such long-running characters, and so much existing scholarship (though these were undoubtedly factors) as in my own resistance to some of *Buffy*'s "postfeminist" aspects and in my reluctance to appreciate ambivalences in the representation of female characters. The "problems" that I identified in the show—the conventional femininity (in terms of appearance) of most female characters; the insistence on heterosexual romance; my judgment that ideas of "good" and "bad" are more strict for female characters than for male; and issues of power and agency in female characters—may be apprehended differently by other viewers. More constructively, it could even be argued that the "problems" as I saw them are actually the "problems" that real women now face and that viewers can recognize them as "real" issues.

At the end of the opening episode of season 7, the First Evil tells the resouled Spike, "It's about power." Power and powerlessness has always been an underlying binary in *Buffy*. Tanya Krzywinska has argued that the horror genre has traditionally played with and even created enjoyment from feelings of powerlessness as well as power (2003). In my first chapter, "Girl Power," I address *Buffy*'s initial role reversal of male hero and female victim and Buffy as a powerful female protagonist. In examining representations of female power I also discuss how the show presents its female characters as attempting to incorporate both "feminist" and "feminine" qualities. Some are more successful in doing so than others, demonstrating that there are still difficulties in constructing a postmodern female identity. In allocating fantasy rather than "real-world" power to its female characters, *Buffy* both allegorizes and avoids the issue of women "having it all."

The division of my discussion into chapters highlights divisions that still hold sway over gender representation. Chapters 2 and 3, "Good Girls" and "Bad Girls," work to further expose the mediation between "feminism" and "femininity" in terms of social judgments that relate gender and morality. *Buffy* demonstrates that being too "good" a girl is no longer a viable strategy in our postfeminist society, yet the show cannot quite avoid matching gender hybridity with moral ambiguity in characters like Buffy and Willow. "Good Girls" also deals with appropriate sexuality as part of acceptable (good) feminine behavior, and thus it discusses how heterosexual romance is presented as problematic for powerful and independent females. The behavior of the bad girls can offer viewing pleasure and may be read as "feminist," but I suggest that their representation causes a clash between genre (most of them are vampires or otherwise inhuman) and context (they share postfeminist characteristics such as strength and independence with the good girls). The bad girls are vastly enjoyable, yet the show's moral framework cannot allow them to be "better" than the good girls, as demonstrated in the development of a character like Faith.

Chapters 4 and 5, "Tough Guys" and "New Men," discuss the ways in which the postfeminist context of *Buffy* affects its representation of masculinity as in crisis. Thus chapter 4 argues that the tough-guy model of masculinity is consistently shown to be redundant, partly because the old-style action hero is replaced by Buffy in a genre and gender reversal, but also because these characters refuse to adopt the new behaviors required to deal with powerful females. Even an apparently "good" character like Riley bears this out. New men like Xander and Giles demonstrate the problems in combining new and old versions of masculinity (in a similar way to Buffy and Willow's negotiation of femininity), and my analysis again highlights heterosexuality as a stumbling block. In chapter 6, "Dead Boys," the representation of male vampires is discussed in terms of the show's manipulation of generic conventions but also as a strategy for further iteration of conflicted masculine identity. Vampires are outside society and therefore need not maintain gendered identities, yet male vampire characters, even more than other males on *Buffy*, show how conflicted gender representation can be. Film theory is applied here to examine how the split between generic roles and viewer perception becomes a split between "masculine" and "feminine" identities, particularly for the key characters of Angel and Spike.

The emphasis on cooperation in *Buffy* fits into the formation of an alternative family among the ensemble cast, something that can work to subvert gendered roles within the family but that also reproduces gendered functions and behaviors. The alternative Scooby family is situated on the crossover of genres and arises from the characters' wish for "normal" lives as opposed to their extraordinary fight against supernatural evil. This family aspect is related to the show's development as a serial text, since it is part of the teen characters' growing up. Parental roles are specifically discussed in chapter 7, "Parental Issues," and are complicated by the show starting out as a teen drama/teen horror inflected with generational conflict and its subsequent movement toward a format more like that of a domestic melodrama, foregrounding emotion and relationships. Characters like Giles and Joyce play out and play with the late-twentieth-century conflict in representation between the working mother and the nurturing father. This too is situated firmly in a postfeminist context where the traditional family is no longer the norm, where roles within the family are changing to match social shifts.

Meanings in television are contingent, and multiple readings of a television text are always possible. The dominant or preferred reading of *Buffy* may be that its representation of gender is "progressive," but my study shows that the contexts of television form, serial narrative, and genre work in different ways simultaneously to allow potentially new representations of gender and sexuality and to limit these. The adoption of serial form (as in soap or contemporary teen drama) privileges emotion (which has been called a feminine address) and enables some subversion of (masculine) narratives of resolution and closure in which divergence from traditional gender roles is often a problem to be solved. But this works alongside identifiable enclosed season and episode narratives and, perhaps, a "master" narrative from the show's creator. Other genres are subverted by separating roles or behaviors from gender (I mention in particular horror and action), something the show consistently tries to do. Fantasy thus works to liberate characters and viewers from received constructions or representations of gender and sexuality, but "reality" also inflects such representations: the show is always a product of and a response to its social context.

In bringing together my knowledge of the show as a fan and my background in academic analysis with perspectives on *Buffy*, gender, genre, and television form, I hope that this study will provide new and valuable insights. This book seeks to present its arguments about the show in a clear and accessible fashion, offering a general case study with transferable arguments or applications. I intend that it will offer something for those with some familiarity with *Buffy* and for more knowledgeable viewers and fans. Throughout, theories, concepts, and ideas from the study of cinema and television, psychoanalytic theory, and cultural studies will be applied where they seem useful in discussion, though I hope to keep them accessible to a less academic audience. Of course, this will be only part of an ongoing dialogue about *Buffy* and these contexts—there will never be a handbook with all the answers.

1 *Girl Power*

As I indicated in my introduction, *Buffy* and other contemporary tele-vision shows have been shaped by the history of feminism. Elizabeth Traube has noted that the new screen woman became "defined by her refusal to be contented with an exclusively domestic function and by her pursuit of the culturally masculine goals of independence and career achievement," pointing to "sources in the feminist movement and in the middle-class ideology of success through individual initiative, which lib-eral feminism helped extend to women" (1992: 126–127). Similarly, Ien Ang observes that contemporary "popular television offers an array of strong and independent female heroines, who seem to defy—not with-out conflicts and contradictions, to be sure—stereotypical definitions of femininity" and who "do not fit the traditional ways in which female characters have generally been represented in prime-time television fic-tion: passive and powerless on the one hand, and sexual objects for men on the other" (1997: 155).

2nd wave

Joss Whedon considers himself a feminist. He envisaged *Buffy the Vampire Slayer* the movie (1992) as "a serious look at violence and women's empowerment" (in Olsen 1999: 79) and says of the television show that its "very first mission statement . . . was the joy of female power: having it, using it, sharing it" (in Miller 2003: 35). Frances Early and Kathleen Kennedy describe Buffy as "a 'girl power' hero" (2003: 3), but 1990s "girl power" has been disparaged, even, as Spike's comment from "Something Blue" (4009) in my title shows, within *Buffy* itself. Girl power has been interpreted as a media construction (it was associated with 1990s British pop stars The Spice Girls) and is described by Imelda Whelehan as

> play[ing] on the illusion of contemporary culture full of ready choices
> and opportunities for self-expression available equally to all women.
> Girl power adds fuel to the myth that young women are "in control"

2nd wave

of their lives and as such offers a more positive liberatory message to young women than contemporary feminism ever could. (2000: 38)

Arising from a postfeminist era, girl power seems to be a contradictory notion: it can be "more positive" for younger women, yet it is based on an "illusion" of freedom.

Buffy has likewise been read in various, even oppositional ways. Sue Tjardes sums up what she calls dominant readings of *Buffy*, "Buffy the vampire slayer as warrior or 'grrl' hero," and oppositional readings, "*Buffy the Vampire Slayer* as heteronormative, unself-consciously white, commodified text," suggesting, as others have, that *Buffy* is "largely a polysemic, open text, available for a variety of readings by a variety of active readers" (2003: 66). Certainly the show "draws on popularized conceptions of feminism" and "concerns itself with white, middle-class, individualist, and ostensibly pleasurable notions of female identity, most of them produced by commercial enterprises," as Kent A. Ono observes (2000: 165). There has been substantial discussion of Buffy's role as a woman warrior, but Buffy is not the only "girl" on the show. The four female characters I look at here display different kinds of power, and the show challenges gender constructions by reversing generic (and gendered) roles or by allocating characteristics regardless of gender. I suggest that *Buffy*'s female characters embody tension between "feminism" and "femininity," yet the show presents this as relatively normal for young women.

Action and Power: The Slayer

The basic premise of *Buffy the Vampire Slayer* is that Buffy Summers appears to be a regular high school girl but is actually the Chosen One, the latest in a line of female Slayers fated to fight vampires and demons. *Buffy* is set in Sunnydale, California, which appears to be a regular small town but is built on a Hellmouth and is a focal point for supernatural activity. An institution called the Watcher's Council has developed to support the Slayer, and each Slayer is appointed a Watcher as mentor, trainer, and researcher. Buffy is helped by her Watcher Rupert Giles and by her friends, Willow Rosenberg and Xander Harris, as well as others who drop in and out of a core group that became known as the Scooby Gang. (Less predictably, the team has included two vampires, a werewolf, and an ex-demon.) From the outset, then, *Buffy* plays with role reversal: the female is vampire slayer, not victim.[1] Whedon is often quoted as saying that he grew tired of horror films in which "bubblehead blonds wandered into dark alleys and got murdered by some creature," remarking, "I would love to see a movie in which a blond wanders into a dark alley, takes care of herself and deploys her powers" (in Bellafante 1997: 82). The character of Buffy subverts the male power embodied in the traditional vampire and its slayer, and Vivian Chin interprets this as using "an antifeminist model, the helpless blond, to present an alternative, feminist possibility" (2003: 94).

Established film and television genres (largely American, though also Japanese animé)[2] serve to inform the show. Second-wave feminism claimed that girls and boys were socialized into values and behavior associated with either "feminine" (passive, submissive) or "masculine" (active, heroic) values and behaviors and that these gender roles were mapped onto biological sex, making them appear "natural" rather than socially constructed (Hollows 2000: 10). Archetypes such as the warrior hero and genres like horror, action, and science fiction are gendered masculine because they are products of patriarchal culture designed to valorize "masculine" qualities and/or they are seen as largely produced and consumed by males. When Sherrie A. Inness suggests that "tough women . . . are being depicted more frequently than in past decades" (1999: 4), it is in these "masculine" genres that they are found. Following the success of 1980s cinematic action heroines like Ripley of the *Alien* movies or Sarah Connor of the *Terminator* films, the 1990s brought television protagonists such as Dana Scully in *The X-Files*, *Xena: Warrior Princess*, or *La Femme Nikita*.[3] Few of these are exclusively mainstream or "realist," and a speculative setting allows more leeway for alternative constructions of gender.

Yet drawing on patriarchal archetypes and myths means that recent female heroes often adopt "masculine" behavior and values. Furthermore, protagonists like Clarice Starling in *Silence of the Lambs* (1990), Scully in *The X-Files*, or Sydney in *Alias* are women operating in a man's world, working to prove themselves to male colleagues (to be "as good as" men); fighting with masculine weapons (guns, science, technology), they must adopt masculine values to succeed. Science fiction characters like Ripley or Sarah Connor are similarly masculinized, and in taking such protagonists as a sign of progress, "masculine" attributes come to be seen as heroic or "universal" (Marshment in Hollows 2000: 194). Television shows like *Star Trek: Deep Space Nine* and *Farscape* have strong female characters operating in a futuristic and potentially nonpatriarchal system, but all of these characters are alien rather than human. These powerful female protagonists can thus be read as exceptional. In my reading, Buffy cannot entirely escape the masculinization of the female action hero or the exceptionalism of the female protagonist.

The initial horror role reversal puts Buffy in the traditionally male role of vampire slayer. As the show often points out, Buffy is not a passive damsel in distress—she is the action hero. Both reversals potentially award Buffy the traditionally masculine characteristics that accompany those roles. Yet the power of the Slayer is passed down through generations of young women, and it brings supernatural strength, mystical prophecy, and vision.[4] Buffy is thus one in a line of female warriors, and the aspect of mysticism feminizes the role. (Sara Buttsworth [2002: 191] notes a similarity with Joan of Arc.) I argue that the show works to hybridize Buffy's "masculine" aspects in various ways.

As McRobbie observes, the fact that

> feminist topics are now a standard part of the staple of "sitcom" material, soap opera, plays and series . . . does not mean that younger women identify themselves as feminist. They are more likely to resist such a label and assert, at least as an image, an excessively conventional femininity. At the same time they frequently express strongly feminist views in their day-to-day discussions. (1994: 158)

Buffy the character embodies this contradiction. She is a "typical" white middle-class high school girl, style conscious and "feminine." "I've patrolled many times in this halter," she tells the Initiative, resisting the idea of a "Private Benjamin" look ("The I in Team" 4013; see figure 1). Whedon has argued, "If I made 'Buffy the Lesbian Separatist,' a series of lectures on PBS on why there should be more feminism, no one would be coming to the party, and it would be boring. The idea of changing the culture is important to me, and it can only be done in a popular medium" (in Lavery 2002b: 15). Yet the popular medium of television inevitably shapes how femininity and feminism are represented, not least because of its context of material production and its commercial funding. Buffy joins femininity and feminism in particular postfeminist ways, offering different kinds of viewing pleasure and recognition. Zoe Williams states that "Buffy's hair is not the point. The point is that she fights huge demons" (2001: 34), but I would suggest that Buffy's hair *is part of* the point. In my own experience both male and female viewers enjoy commenting on hairstyles or outfits ("What have they done to Buffy's hair in this episode?" or "Why is Angel wearing that blue shirt?"). Viewers engage readily with these aspects, making judgments about the charac-

FIGURE 1: *"I've patrolled many times in this halter,"*
Buffy tells the Initiative ("The I in Team").

ters ("X would never wear that," "What was Y thinking?") from prior
knowledge but also recognizing that these images are consciously manufactured ("What have *they* done to Buffy's hair?"). Sections such as "It's a
Designer Label!" in Keith Topping's episode guide *Slayer* acknowledge
evaluation of style and appearance as part of the viewing process.

The conventionally "feminine" appearance of *Buffy*'s "girls" led some
to dismiss it as a standard display of the female body, objectifying women
through the "male gaze" (Mulvey 1989). The term *scopophilia* describes
the pleasure of looking at another person as an object, and Laura Mulvey
argued that in film the (passive) female functions as the object, for the
(active) male gaze of spectator and camera. In chapter 6 I argue that the
show displays male bodies as objects of desire and that male bodies are
as sexualized as females on *Buffy*. The idea of the "male gaze" is predi-
cated on cinema, and it has been suggested that television, in contrast,
has a female address. The mixture of "feminine" soap/melodrama and

"masculine" action or horror in *Buffy* further confuses this issue: *Buffy* offers female bodies as spectacle, but their primacy and activity means that they are not simply passive objects. Whedon, himself a film studies graduate, demonstrates this contradiction in his comment, "I definitely think that a woman kicking ass is extraordinarily sexy" (in Udovitch 2001: 165).

Any association between physical ("butch") toughness and homosexuality is refuted by Buffy's insistent "femininity" and heterosexuality. A common strategy used to neutralize female action heroes' transgressive masculine behavior is to balance it with recognizable femininity and underline its exceptionalism (Tasker 1993a: 20). For Buffy, a "feminine" appearance positions her as a "normal girl" despite her exceptional Slayer power. Applying Dyer's ideas about whiteness and heroism, Buffy's "normality" offers a "foundation of both psychological realism—when we don't get superheroes or obvious stereotypes, we feel we're getting the real—and of novelty and transgression, where the bounds of the typical are exceeded." Yet Dyer also notes that "the right not to conform, to be different and get away with it, is the right of the most privileged groups in society" (1997: 12), and Buffy's ability to blur the boundaries of "appropriate" gendered behavior can be read as another consequence of her privilege as a white middle-class American.

In conjunction with her masculine role as an action hero, Buffy's conventionally feminine appearance can be interpreted as "ironic distancing" from gender stereotypes (Early 2003: 58). The show's self-conscious play with generic and gender conventions means that Buffy is marked by excess in contradictory ways: she is hyperfeminine as well as exceptionally strong and heroic, "Barbie with a kung-fu grip" (Whedon in Nazzaro 2002: 223). While the "final girls" of slasher movies (Clover 1992) tend be androgynous and have names to match (Laurie, Sidney), even Buffy's name is indicative of her femininity, and its inclusion in the show's title underlines its irony. Excessive gender coding points to *Buffy*'s playful postmodern elements and also highlights the constructed nature of gender representation.

Other "masculine" characteristics include the way Buffy defines herself by her role/profession, her individualism in season 4, and her use of violence. Yet these are hybridized by their representation. Only females can be Slayers, but Buffy's dedication to work seems traditionally masculine—professional life is more important than domestic life. At times Buffy defines herself wholly as the Slayer, and she frequently complains that she cannot have a normal life. *Buffy* has been described as "a wry, ongoing parable of the modern woman's greatest conflict: the challenge to balance personal and professional life" (Bellafante 1997: 83). Thus the double life of the superhero becomes the bind of the contemporary professional female, who can never "have it all," despite the notion of the postfeminist "superwoman" balancing career, family, and social life. The show's season 1 opening sequence states, "In every generation there is a Chosen One. She alone will stand against the vampires, the demons and the forces of darkness. She is the Slayer." Buffy is *chosen* to be Buffy the Vampire Slayer (fairly typical for action heroes or superheroes); she does not have the power to make her own choices. The Watcher's Council controls Buffy's power through Giles, who directs its use and can even remove it. Toward the end of season 3, Buffy begins to realize her lack of agency, leading to her "graduation" from the Council.

Given the increasing anonymity of postmodern society, Susan Jeffords suggests that in action films of the 1990s the "power of individual decision-making and individual action" is valorized (1993: 257) and many male heroes are presented as individuals who neither wish nor need to be part of a team. Similarly, the lauded ability of young women today to make individual choices is conflated with liberation, and achieving equality becomes an individual struggle, backgrounding collective struggle or a wider social context (Woloch 2000: 573). Early seasons of *Buffy* emphasized collectivity as key to Buffy's success, but during season 4 she takes on most of the action herself. One obvious reason for Buffy's individualism here is to contrast the "bad" team of the Initiative. Having recently escaped the control of the Council, Buffy questions orders and decides to act alone ("The I in Team") like the (usually male) maverick hero of action or cop films. The Initiative is clearly presented as a patriarchal institution, and this adds a gender spin to the individualist hero: rather than a male standing out against a threat to individualism, Buffy is a woman resisting patriarchy.

The use of violence is a contested aspect of female action heroes and leads to complaints that shows like *Buffy* "tout themselves as feminist as long as the young girls beat people up" (Pasley 2003: 254). Feminists have critiqued this kind of representation because it suggests that women can be heroes only through masculinized aggression. Yet part of the show's attraction for viewers is watching Buffy defeat male enemies in an "unfeminine" display of physical power, just as Carol Clover argues that 1970s horror films successfully positioned male audiences to identify with and applaud female heroes (1992). Whedon articulates such viewing pleasure when he admits that he "never loved [Buffy] more"

FIGURE 2: *Rocket-launcher Buffy provides viewing pleasure through role reversal ("Innocence").*

than when she used a rocket launcher in "Innocence" (2014) (in Lavery 2002a: 47; see figure 2). Willow tells Buffy in "Phases" (2015), "Don't forget, you're supposed to be a meek little girlie-girl like the rest of us," pointing out Buffy's variance from traditional gender norms, while Buffy's answer, "Spoil my fun," highlights the pleasure to be had from seeing those norms transgressed.

The premise of *Buffy* and its use of horror and action means that violence is an integral part of a fight between good and evil, and some have argued that Buffy's Slayer power is equated with physical prowess (Abbott 2001: 11), another way of universalizing "masculine" attributes. Buffy uses phallic, penetrative weapons (these also relate to the sexual subtext of the vampire myth), but they are generally archaic, and she rejects technological weapons and guns in particular (see Simkin 2004a). Subsequent female heroes, such as Max from *Dark Angel*, consciously reject guns in an assertion of "feminine" resistance to technological (masculine) weapons. Hong Kong–style techniques are also used for visual appeal. Dave West notes that in the movie *Buffy the Vampire Slayer*, "Kristy Swanson [playing Buffy] . . . was very visibly performing her own martial arts" (2001: 183), yet it is equally clear that body doubles are used in the television show. Thus while *Buffy* shows women's bodies as physically powerful (Owen 1999: 25), viewers are also aware that this power is an illusion manufactured by television.

Lisa Parks notes that violence adopted by women can be recontextualized as self-defense (2003), and others have observed that Buffy responds to violent acts that are themselves gendered or sexualized (Marinucci 2003: 69). Certainly Buffy often fights oppressive patriarchal figures or institutions. The Council is easily read as "a male-dominated hierarchy" (J. P. Williams 2002: 62), and Early takes Buffy's rejection of it to imply that she "will no longer accept uncritically authoritarian patriarchal rule" (2002: 26). The final season furthers this notion when Buffy discovers that the Slayer was created through demonic "violation" of a young woman, orchestrated by three older men. Buffy rejects this violation, even when told it will give her more power ("Get It Done" 7015). A few episodes later she clashes with ex-Watcher Giles and tells him conclusively, "I think you've taught me everything I need to know" ("Lies My Parents Told Me" 7017). Buttsworth notes that the soldiers of the Initiative "are threatened by the feminine identity of the Slayer," and this fourth season deliberately sets the female Slayer against the largely male Initiative (2002: 188). Similarly, the "real-world" villains of season 6—Warren, Jonathan and Andrew, "the Trio"—are a homosocial group viewing women primarily as sexual objects, and season 7's Caleb is one of Buffy's most overtly misogynist adversaries. From this angle, Buffy's use of violence is "justified" as a reaction to physical and institutional violence against women.

Buffy may be the action hero, but she is not always the leader (as an alpha male would be), nor is she a loner like most mavericks. At various times different members of the Scooby Gang lead so that Giles may plan strategy, Willow take charge in the use of magic, or Xander lead the campaign on the Mayor. This underlines that *Buffy* is not about solitary heroics but about a communal effort from a mixed-gender group. A key moment is in season 4, when the core elements of the Scooby Gang form a "combo-Buffy" to defeat Adam, the ultimate Initiative soldier ("Primeval" 4021). Combo-Buffy is a paradox. She is shielded from Adam's bullets and shells—at one point she touches a shell and it turns into three white doves. Yet she also rips Adam's power source from his chest barehanded. This moment recalls that Buffy is the "hand" (Willow is the spirit, Xander the heart, and Giles the mind) of the group; she is the one who takes action. Combo-Buffy's power is coded as feminine, magical, and "good" in opposition to Adam's masculine, technological "evil," while the allocation among the Scoobies subverts traditionally gendered characteristics. The group's power is the complementary sum of their attributes. Similarly, at the end of season 6, other members of the team defeat Warren and save the world.[5]

Inness suggests that tough women display "the tight emotional and physical control that has been traditionally associated with men" (1999: 13). Although Buffy proves herself capable of such control, she argues that emotions "give [her] power" ("What's My Line? Part 2" 2010). Farah Mendlesohn has observed that the Scoobies make emotional demands on Buffy and thus restrict her autonomy as an action hero (2002: 47). This is not necessarily presented negatively. *Buffy* valorizes emotion and its articulation as equal to action narrative and closure, and characters such as Kendra, Faith, Riley, and even Willow are used to show the negative side of refusing emotional connections. Buffy also displays ("feminine") weakness, whether emotional or physical. The other Scoobies sometimes complain that Buffy cuts herself off, and at these points her role as the Slayer is presented as forcing Buffy to act rationally rather than emotionally. In other words, she struggles to balance "masculine" and "feminine" behaviors.

Both Inness (1999) and Yvonne Tasker (1993a) point out that a common strategy used in presenting female heroes is to have them protecting others, particularly children, because this is seen as "natural" feminine behavior (obvious examples are Ripley in *Aliens* 1986 and Sarah Connor in the first two *Terminator* films). Similarly Jessica Prata Miller suggests that *Buffy*'s "care perspective, with its contextual focus on personal relationships, including feelings and emotions, fits with ideals of femininity" (2003: 37). Thus the Slayer and even Buffy's high school mantle "class protector" ("The Prom" 3020) can be interpreted as traditionally feminine roles. This is enhanced when Buffy agrees to protect Dawn (a mystical energy disguised as her younger sister) and fights to keep her own family and the Scooby family together. The show implies that Buffy has lived longer than other Slayers because this "feminine" investment in family connects her to life, resisting the death wish that Spike tells her all Slayers have ("Fool for Love" 5007). Notably, the alternate Buffy of "The Wish" (3009) lacks such support and dies.[6]

The show uses Buffy to question the "universal" nature of white

male heroism. Miller's comment that "there is something uniquely feminine" in Buffy's presentation (2003: 48) demonstrates that in the process *Buffy* runs the risk of presenting "essential" female attributes as
an alternative form of heroism. The culmination of the group's collective action comes in the final season, when Buffy is voted out as
leader of the Scoobies and the potential Slayers in the battle against
the First Evil ("Empty Places" 7019). Faith, the returned and redeemed
"rogue Slayer," questions Buffy's primacy; Anya articulates the feeling
that Buffy assumes her "superior" Slayer power fits her for leadership;
and every core Scooby rejects Buffy as leader. Although she said herself
that the team has to "be together on this," Buffy leaves because she cannot cooperate as part of the group. When she is allowed to lead again
she does so in a recognizably different fashion and this group rejection
of Buffy's claim to leadership through her exceptional power culminates
in her plan to defeat the First through collective action. An extended
group cooperates to prevent the final apocalypse, the isolation and exceptionalism of the Chosen One is mitigated if not erased when Willow
magically enables all potential Slayers to access Slayer power (they are
asked to *choose* it), and Spike is the sacrifice that closes the Hellmouth
("Chosen" 7022). This highlights the group as a collective heroic agent,[7]
and Buffy is rewarded for her struggle to integrate her contradictory
roles by the chance to live a more "normal" life.

Normal Girls?

At first glance Cordelia seems to have the "normal life" Buffy
often longs for. She is a familiar character from teen drama: popular, a
cheerleader, the center of cliques (power as status). Furthermore, Cordelia's exceptionalism is based on "real" material privilege rather than
supernatural power. She represents in more exaggerated form the unnamed white middle-class heterosexual "normality" (read privilege) of
the other characters (to the point that it becomes visible). Cordelia functions recognizably as the typical female victim of horror, often screaming and running away, and this makes her a perfect contrast for other
female characters. It is common currency that her character was intended
to be a short-running foil for Buffy.[8] Her character moved to L.A. and to
the spin-off series, *Angel*, at the end of season 3, but I restrict my analysis
here to *Buffy*.[9]

Anya's identity is obviously unstable: sometimes human, sometimes
demon; sometimes "feminist," sometimes "feminine." As a demon made

human, she could be said to perform gender (in the way I suggest Spike does in chapter 6)—it does not come "naturally" to her because she has not been part of human society for hundreds of years. Anya is both exceptional (demon) and normal (human). Arguably her character displays a tension between "femininity" and "feminism" but here a combination of the two is not sustained.

Both Cordelia and Anya show how romance can be problematic for young postfeminist women. McRobbie suggests that feminism has effected some changes in how romance is presented, and in girls' magazines "the conventionally coded meta-narratives of romance which . . . could only create a neurotically dependent female subject, have gone for good," while there "is more of the self in this new vocabulary of femininity, much more self-esteem, more autonomy" (1994: 164, 165). Similarly, Nancy Woloch reports a young female professional stating that women can now "get so much satisfaction from other parts of their lives that they don't rely so heavily anymore on the man in their life" (2000: 579). In *Buffy* the teen characters still desire romance relationships but also demonstrate this shift. Changing relationships are an important part of *Buffy*'s serial element. The show's continuous narrative works to undercut the closure of stable relationships, and Esther Saxey has noted "the focus of impossible romance in establishing the series" (2001: 202).

Perhaps because of its origin as teen drama,[10] *Buffy* has been described as "one of the most sexually blunt shows on the air in the US" (Udovitch 2001: 118). Referring to the traditional "rules" of slasher movies, Whedon mentions "the blond girl in the alley in the horror movie who keeps getting killed," saying, "I felt bad for her, but she was always more interesting to me than the other girls. She was fun, she had sex, she was vivacious. But then she would get punished for it" (in Udovitch 2001: 118). Thus *Buffy* presents us with sexually active characters who are not punished for their behavior partly because of its postfeminist context but also because sexually active "girls" are "more interesting." This might suggest that the show advocates a liberated sexuality, but *Buffy*'s girls generally only have sex within serious (heterosexual) romance relationships.

Because romance, love, and sex are generally seen as "personal" or "private" parts of our lives, they are relatively easy to detach from social context. This tends to obscure the relationship between heterosexuality, romance, and patriarchy—that is, the domination of men and the subordination of women. From one point of view heterosexuality "is a patriarchal narrative told about bodies and desires which polices women's and men's adherence to proper gender and erotic behaviors and makes women's liberation unimaginable" (Wilton 1996: 127). Further, as Stevi Jackson observes, there is "considerable ambiguity surrounding the words 'sex' and 'sexual,' which slip and slide between gendered and erotic meanings," so that sex, gender, and sexuality are bound together by language (1999: 6), as in the title of this book.

Like style and appearance, the use of romance and sex in *Buffy* can afford contradictory viewing pleasures. It offers the comfort of a familiar narrative. It may allow an escape into fantasy or the opportunity to occupy a fantasy subject position (one a viewer would not occupy in his or her own life). It demonstrates how heterosexual love, romance, and sex can be a site of simultaneous complicity in and resistance to patriarchal structures (Jackson 1999: 114). And it can offer a recognition of how women negotiate the problems of romance in a postfeminist era.

CORDELIA

From a feminist point of view, Cordelia's power is entrenched in patriarchy: her power is privilege based on her father's wealth and the ability to manipulate her own image to gain (sexual) power over males. Karen Sayer sees her character as having "an almost masculine drive" (2001: 112) because she actively seeks status. Cordelia embodies the contradictions between "feminism" and "femininity." She seems independent and strong-minded, but her hyperfeminine appearance and behavior undercut this. Cordelia is successful because she adheres to social norms; like many soap "bitches," she works within the system, manipulating it and her femininity to her own advantage. The personalized (vanity) plate of Cordelia's car reads "Queen C," a title combining femininity and power, and the car itself is a visible sign of her wealth (initially she is the only student to have one).[11] Her independence is an individualism that verges on selfishness, and Cordelia's transformation involves the loss of her privilege and wealth and an increasing care for others, "feminine" unselfishness.

Following traditional generic conventions, Cordelia shows her fear, has no special supernatural power (noted in relation to Xander but rarely about Cordy), and often requires rescuing or has to flee. On the basis of season 1, viewers might expect that sooner or later Cordelia would end up a "dead ditz," but she survives (alternate Larry calls her this in "The Wish"—in the parallel universe she does die). Detailing a hero-fantasy of Xander's, S. Renee Dechert tellingly describes him as having "the confidence reserved for rock stars, professional athletes, and Cordelia" (2002: 221), and Cordelia's wealth and status provide the foundation for this assertive confidence. In "Homecoming" (3005) it enables her to face down a vampire alone and unarmed. Lyle Gorch has just seen his wife staked by Buffy, who now lies unconscious. Cordelia tells him, "Buffy and I have just taken out four of your cronies. . . . The point is, I haven't even broken a sweat. See, in the end, Buffy's just the runner up, *I'm* the queen. You get me mad, what do you think I'm gonna do to you?" Viewers may assume that Gorch thinks Cordelia is a Slayer, and he has fled before ("Bad Eggs" 2012), yet, intimidated, he simply runs away.

Mary Alice Money sees Cordelia as a transformed or redeemed *Buffy* character. Such characters, she argues, "reveal a previously unsuspected vulnerability that nullifies some of their less attractive traits" (2002: 99). Certainly Cordelia's soaplike transformation from bitchy Queen C to member of the Scooby gang exposes such vulnerability, though I would point out that a character's "less attractive traits" can offer viewing pleasure. Bitchiness enhances Cordelia's comic appeal and her attraction to regular viewers, who relish her comments. The function of truth telling (shared with other comic characters like Spike and Anya) can contribute to this typical bitch persona,[12] though arguably Cordelia's privilege is what enables her to get away with this apparently transgressive behavior. The "vulnerability" of Cordelia's character is first hinted at in "Out of Mind, Out of Sight" (1011) when Cordelia asks Buffy, "You think I'm never lonely because I'm so cute and popular?" As the camera tracks between the two with close-up shots that display both Cordelia's sincerity and Buffy's acknowledgement, the music sets a pensive tone (an early example valorizing the articulation of emotion). Things are not quite so simple, however. Marcie, the invisible girl who attacks Cordelia in this episode, mockingly parodies this speech, and the episode demonstrates the consequences of Cordelia's clique-building behavior.

Cordelia can be read as a typical soap bitch who manipulates her image and uses her gender/sexuality to control men rather than challenging male supremacy. Mendlesohn offers an initially convincing description of Cordelia as someone "whose friendships with women are constructed around status seeking and competition in a game in which points are scored through the attraction of the male gaze" (2002: 53). Yet although Cordelia is sexualized and feminized in some ways, viewers never see her have sex. Furthermore, her representation encompasses the awareness that this *is* a game and that she succeeds by playing the role men want. Thus she is not entirely taken in by the social norms she seems to represent. Cordelia consciously adapts her behavior for success in the social world, dismissing high test scores and Xander's comment that he is "dating a brain" with, "Please, I have *some* experience in covering these things up" ("Lover's Walk" 3008). In this sense, like Buffy, Cordelia is shown as negotiating an individual postfeminist identity: she chooses to present herself in a particular way, but her ability to make such a choice is based on her privilege as a wealthy white girl.

Cordelia is assimilated largely through her relationship with Xander. Although she initially rejects him because of his lack of social status, she eventually casts off peer pressure. "Here I am scrambling for your approval when I'm way cooler than you are because I'm not a sheep," she declares to Harmony and the other Cordettes. "I do what I want to do and I wear what I want to wear and you know what, I'll date whoever the hell I want to date," adding characteristically, "no matter how lame he is" ("Bewitched, Bothered and Bewildered" 2016). Cordelia's vulnerability is shown as she walks away stammering, "Oh god, they're never going to speak to me again." This scene is clearly part of Cordelia's redemption, as close-ups cutting from Cordelia's conviction to the other girls' stunned looks show, while the rising swells of indie guitar in the background indicate approval and induction into a less mainstream clique.[13] One possible interpretation is that Cordelia saw through romance but cannot resist "real" love that goes beyond image. A more critical reading might note that Cordelia's "choice" and assertion of independence is actually an affirmation of heterosexuality and romance. Xander's subsequent betrayal of Cordelia with Willow ("Lover's Walk") is designed to award Cordy further sympathy (her pain is shown only to the viewer). Yet it simultaneously presents her as passive and not in control. Given their relative positions in the Scooby Gang, there is inevitably more emphasis on Xander and Willow. But while Willow and Oz are eventually reunited, Cordelia never returns to Xander; she regains her autonomy.

At the end of season 3 Cordelia loses her privilege when her father is caught in nonpayment of taxes. "I have nothing," she admits to Xander, "no dresses, no cell phone, no car. . . . I can't go to any of the colleges that accepted me and I can't stay home because we no longer have one" ("The Prom"). As with Buffy, external factors restrict the choices Cordelia can make for her future. The show allows Cordelia to save face among her peers by wearing the expensive dress she desires at the prom, but it is donated to her by Xander, and she has to acknowledge his help. Sayer has noted that "[o]ver the course of the show it is primarily the men (Angel,

Oz, Riley and to some extent Spike) who have left, suggesting a higher degree of activity on their part" (2001: 112). Cordelia also leaves, though without the clear farewell accorded the male characters Sayer cites. In *Buffy*, Cordelia is as close as it gets to a normal girl: she is often represented as powerless in the other side of Sunnydale, but her power is that of a soap queen, the (limited) power to play the "real" world.

ANYA

Of all the versions of femininity on *Buffy*, I judge Anya the least likely to offer a sympathetic subject position for viewers, for two reasons: first, Anya is used as a device to make our world seem strange, because she is the alien with a new perspective; second, Anya's comic function is as the butt of jokes, not (like Cordelia) the scathing wit. Anya is one of the first "younger" characters to have a job and her own living space, but this does not earn her recognition, as it does when Xander and Buffy take on these responsibilities. In "I Was Made to Love You" (5015) she tells Tara that she tripled her wages by speculating, but rather than presenting her money-making as a skill that could benefit the group (given Buffy's dire financial situation in season 6), Anya's "greed" makes her an object of ridicule. Unlike Oz and Tara, Anya never forms strong bonds with other Scoobies, and with a few exceptions, she rarely shows affection or emotion, being mainly restricted to impatience, irritation, confusion, or pettiness. Since *Buffy* increasingly valorizes emotion and its display, Anya is effectively set apart by this.

For Anya especially, heterosexuality complicates her independence and her ability to construct an independent identity. Power and heterosexual romance seem to be incompatible in Anya but are intimately related through her character's storylines. Anya became a demon and thus acquired her supernatural power because of the failure of one romance. When she loses that power, she engages in a romance with Xander and, after that breaks down, becomes a demon again. Yet the reacquisition of her demonic power is not a success, and Anya always fails to "measure up" to the other young female Scoobies.

"Selfless" (7005) gives Anya's backstory, and the title alludes to her lack of an independent identity or self. As Aud, she is the lover of Olaf, and thereafter Anya is always presented as defined by someone or something else. Olaf's unfaithfulness and her revenge for it bring Aud to the attention of demon D'Hoffryn, and she becomes a vengeance demon because she was crossed in love (a traditional motive for female rage). As demon Anyanka, she creates a parallel universe when the betrayed Cordelia wishes that Buffy had never come to Sunnydale and is described here as "a sort of patron saint of scorned women" who grants wishes ("The Wish"). Her power is highlighted by the dark contrast between the two Sunnydales: Willow and Xander are vampires, and most of the other Scoobies, including Buffy, die in the alternate version. The patriarch-faces-young-powerful-girl scenario is repeated, highlighted by jump cuts between the two narrative strands—the Master kills Buffy in the alternate world, but Giles saves the day by destroying Anyanka's power. Giles suggests that without her power source (an amulet) Anyanka would "just be an ordinary woman again."

In a follow-up episode, "Doppelgangland," (3016) the now-ordinary Anya tries unsuccessfully to retrieve the amulet after D'Hoffryn refuses to give back her power. When D'Hoffryn initially empowered her ("Selfless"), he renamed her Anyanka, redefining her as his (he calls his vengeance demons "my girls"). Thereafter she is defined by her role: "Vengeance is what I am," she tells Halfrek, in an echo of Buffy's definition as the Slayer. Yet Anyanka's revenge does not destabilize gender relations; she merely punishes their inequalities, reinscribing masculine/feminine binary opposition and heterosexuality. Anya never retrieves her amulet and is forced to live as a powerless teenage girl, reversing Buffy and Willow's acquisition of power. Part of Anya's early comic appeal is this dramatic change. "For a thousand years I wielded the power of the Wish," she says in "Doppelgangland." "I was feared and worshipped across the mortal globe. Now I'm stuck in Sunnydale High. Mortal. A child. And I'm flunking math."

Like Cordelia, Anya is both normalized and redeemed by her relationship with Xander, the very "man" she was called to curse with vengeance. Powerful Anyanka becomes "feminine" Anya. Early on Anya is presented as a parody of the man-hating feminist who only needs the love of a good man to bring her round. During "The Prom" she tells Xander, "I have witnessed a millennium of treachery and oppression from the male of the species and I have nothing but contempt for the whole libidinous lot of them," but she finishes, "I don't have a date for the prom." Anya's "greed" is also underlined and gendered by interactions with Xander: she pressures him to get his own apartment, seems set on a life of material comforts, and complains when she cannot show off her ring because he refuses to announce their engagement. (A feminist reading might suggest that the linkage of romance and economics is not coincidental.) Anya is thus positioned as the nagging girlfriend—

fine if the viewer sympathizes with Xander, but less comfortable from Anya's subject position.

This is complicated by the introduction of Halfrek, a female friend from Anya's demon days. Halfrek offers the emotional support and understanding Anya does not get from the Scoobies. The two are shown chatting over tea or coffee, in a typically "feminine," even ladylike, situation (one flashback in "Selfless" shows them sipping wine while wearing white gloves).[14] Halfrek provides a new perspective on Anya's relationship with Xander, suggesting that *his* behavior rather than *hers* may be "inappropriate" ("Doublemeat Palace" 6012), a resistant reading introduced (and therefore authorized?) by the show itself.

Money suggests that Anya too is "rehabilitated" through her relationship with Xander (2002: 104). Anya's comments indicate that their sex life is extremely active. This is the first time "good" characters are represented as having (hetero)sex that is neither entirely romanticized nor completely vanilla (Anya mentions role playing and spanking and is excited at the prospect of two Xanders in "The Replacement" 5003). Saxey notes that Xander and Anya are "the only couple to engage in kink unproblematically" (2001: 206), and arguably the show uses them to represent a plurality of heterosexualities rather than one "normal" set of sexual relations. Anya initiates both the relationship and sex within it, demonstrating some assertiveness and agency. Yet while for Buffy and the others sexual activity marks their postfeminist independence, Anya's frank discussion of sex makes her an object of ridicule because she cannot distinguish what is "appropriate" to air in public. This reinforces how sexual relations are deemed "personal" and kept separate from the public sphere and their larger social context.

Anya and Xander's engagement and wedding provides further contradictions. On the one hand it is presented traditionally: Xander proposes; Anya has a ring; she reads bridal magazines (under cover of research books in "Wrecked" 6010) and makes wedding plans, exhibiting "feminine" excitement. Yet Anya's draft wedding vows include "feminist" lines like "But not to obey you, of course, because that's anachronistic and misogynistic" ("Hell's Bells" 6016). This may match the awareness of a heterosexual feminist viewer like myself that while compulsory heterosexuality is a way of maintaining control over women, and the myths of romance make this palatable, this does not necessarily negate the desire for a(n equal) sexual and companionate relationship. Yet to me there is still a tension between Anya's "choice" of marriage and her willingness to carry out domestic tasks "for" Xander while she anticipates being "Mrs. Anya Harris" ("Selfless").

When Xander leaves Anya at the altar, she is passive and powerless, and this is a typical *female* tragedy ("Hell's Bells"). Furthermore, it is presented as a direct consequence of her previous power: one of her victims comes back for his revenge by discouraging Xander with "a couple of phoney visions." Christine Geraghty has observed that in soap, "[e]ven apparent narrative closures such as a wedding or a death merely offer the opportunity for more problems to fuel the narrative" (1991: 12). A similar strategy can be identified in *Buffy*: the wedding and episodes leading up to it offer disruption rather than closure, and this story-arc underlines the series' negative presentation of marriage and family life (see chapter 7). Jilted, Anya is briefly allowed subjectivity and sympathy, but even this is mitigated by her role as Xander's partner. At the end of the wedding episode D'Hoffryn tells Anya, "You let him domesticate you. . . . It's time to get back to what you do best," and Anya becomes a vengeance demon again.

This does little to empower her. Although she regains her physical demon strength, Anya cannot measure up to the other young women. She is "converted" to human ideas such as romance and morality, but this only complicates her identity as a demon, and Anya is now reluctant to exact the gory vengeances she once enjoyed. Giving in to pressure from her fellow demons, Anya summons a Grimslaw demon to rip out the hearts of twelve fraternity boys at U. C. Sunnydale in an over-the-top "feminist" revenge ("Selfless"). Anya's subsequent fight with Buffy echoes the fight between Dark Willow and Buffy in season 6 and positions Anya as "bad." Here Anya wears her demon face: like Dark Willow, she is visually distinguished from her regular "human" self, another way the show indicates that identity is never stable. The fight ends not with one version of femininity defeating another but with Willow summoning D'Hoffryn. Anya asks to undo the vengeance, stating that she will pay the price (the death of a vengeance demon)—she is now willing to sacrifice herself for others, like Buffy. Instead, D'Hoffryn destroys Halfrek. Thus benevolent paternalism is revealed as violent controlling patriarchy: Anya loses her demonic power and her one female friend.

Following this, the gap between Anya and the other Scoobies is never closed. During "Get It Done" Buffy challenges her worth and Anya can only respond, "I contribute much needed . . . sarcasm," and even then Xander replies, "That can be my job, actually." In season 7, Anya is most often associated with another marginal Scooby, Andrew. She has a vague (largely sexual) reunion with Xander, and the fact that she dies in the season finale underlines her status as a minor (disposable) character as well as her powerlessness.

Will Power

Willow has received more critical attention since she went "dark" at the end of season 6 and Jes Battis notes "the oppositional binaries of her character" (2003: 3). Unlike the characters discussed above, Willow is never really a "normal girl" because she does not construct a conventionally feminine identity that allows her to fit in. Willow's power and her awareness of it make her different. Whedon complained that the network wanted a "supermodel in horn rims" to play Willow (in Lavery 2002a: 15), though admittedly "none of the actors looks like the kind of kid who does not fit in at high school" (Larbalestier 2002: 234). Mendlesohn suggests that Willow "could have been preselected to play the loveless but funny best friend against whom Buffy's status is measured" (2002: 49), another recognizable character from teen drama, but Willow was immediately popular with audiences.

Willow's character offers a different subject position to the viewer from that of Buffy, the conventionally attractive, confident, and assertive young woman. Anecdotal evidence indicates that male and female viewers find Willow less threatening and more sympathetic than Buffy. When I ask my female students to name their favorite character on the show, they often select Willow. Willow is presented as shy, insecure, and awkward, a social misfit lacking self-confidence (perhaps *because* she is not conventionally "feminine"). She is intellectual and enjoys study, valuing academic success and thus identifying with "masculine" rationality and status (and, like Cordelia, showing masculine drive); it is therefore hardly surprising that female college students might take up Willow's subject position. Willow is also shown initially to lack female friendship structures (her best friend is male), but she is empowered by her new relationship with Buffy and her inclusion in the Scooby Gang. Willow and Buffy are supportive of each other in a way that is common in television soap or melodrama, especially in British soaps, if not in film (Cordelia takes on the more "typical" bitch role). The fact that female relationships empower her is key to Willow's representation as relatively free from male influence.

Willow is further empowered by the acceptance and value placed on her special talents as they contribute to the group effort. David Lavery notes that when Whedon "learned that [Alyson] Hannigan [who plays Willow] was especially masterful at exhibiting pain and fear. . . . putting her in danger became a staple of the show" (2002a: 15), so that Willow, like Cordelia, is positioned as a typical female horror victim. Yet as early as "Halloween" Willow becomes a leader, and during the season 2 finale, she takes charge again. In "Primeval" she is designated the animus or spirit of the group, but she is also (the) Will, and as a leader she imposes her will on the others. This leadership position allows Willow to display behavior and skills traditionally coded masculine. Just as two male heroes might compete for leadership, tension arises between Willow and Buffy. This was articulated first when Willow told Buffy, "I'm not your sidekick" ("Fear, Itself" 4004). When she faces off with Buffy in season 6, Dark Willow claims: "This is a huge deal for me. Six years as a sideman, now I get to be the slayer" ("Two to Go" 6021). Ang suggests that viewers may "alternate between positions of identification and positions of distance, and thus inhabit several, sometimes contradictory imaginary structures at the same time" (1997: 158, note 7). In this case viewers may find themselves identifying with Willow, their favorite character, but distanced from her by unfamiliar "bad" behavior and the desire to identify with the "hero," Buffy. I have already argued that *Buffy* does not necessarily privilege its title character, that the ensemble cast are all major players, and that there is no one protagonist or hero. Dark Willow's resistant reading reflexively highlights the way that dominant readings persist, since conventional structures tend to reassert themselves.

Willow's "power" in early seasons is her skill with computers and her knowledge of technology and science, both "masculine" fields. Brian Wall and Michael Zryd complicate this when they observe that "hard knowledge exists alongside the 'soft knowledge' of computers, which is associated with modernity and with young female characters like Willow, Cordelia and Miss Calendar" (2001: 54). J. P. Williams further suggests that Ms. Calendar's familiarity with computers "is employed for political ends" and forms a critique of Giles (2002: 70). Willow's technological competence is similarly contrasted with Giles and subsequently finds another, darker comparison with Warren, the season 6 villain.

Later Willow acquires another skill—she becomes a powerful witch or, as the show calls it, Wicca. Although Battis suggests that Willow's rejection of the university Wicca group implies that she has "no particular desire for feminine empowerment through Wicca" (2003: 24), I read the show as refeminizing Willow by the shift to witchcraft, a traditionally female power even in contemporary teen movies like *The Craft* (1996) or television shows like *Charmed*. This positions Willow, like Buffy, in a female line. Willow's early mentor is Ms. Calendar, she later shares a reciprocal mentoring of her girlfriend and fellow witch Tara, and she supports Dawn. While she enjoys praise from Giles, Willow rarely actively tries to please him and does not need male approval. The lack of a real mentor might demonstrate Willow's independence and agency—*she* is in charge of her developing powers. Yet the show simultaneously presents her power as uncontrollable and chaotic ("feminine"). Furthermore, the way Willow views and uses her power is often typically "masculine."

The show makes it clear that Willow's talent for magic is innate and exceptional, and many characters (especially villains) can sense it. Battis argues that Willow has no real identity and quotes her comment, "I *am* the magic" from "Grave" (6022). Despite her central place in the group, Willow seems to identify herself through her role, in a typically "masculine" way, rather than through relationships. Her rejection of the Wicca group hinges on their reluctance to use magical power, something she is keen to do. Her ("masculine") strength enables her to keep pushing her magical ability, as when she is "tested" in "Bargaining Part 1" (6001). Although Krzywinska noted that "Willow does not use her magic to conjure self-gratifying wishes and is not in the thrall of a demonic masculine force" (2002: 188), both of these caveats eventually disappear. Even in season 4, Willow uses her power to ease her pain and ends up hurting her friends. When D'Hoffryn offers her a job as a vengeance demon, she refuses his patronage ("Something Blue"), but in season 6 she becomes temporarily dependent on male power "dealer" Rack. The lies Willow tells are a further individualist betrayal of the Scooby family.

Long-term viewers are aware that Tara and Giles are the characters most qualified by experience to comment on Willow's use of her power. She rejects their warnings, interpreting them as "masculine" competition rather than "feminine" care. She twists Tara's caution about using magic around to be Tara's "problem" (implicitly jealousy) and later accuses her of taking Giles' side ("All the Way" 6006). Tara points to Willow's arrogance when she correctly interprets Willow's discomfort after Buffy's resurrection: "You thought she'd say thanks" ("After Life" 6003). Finally Willow turns on Tara in the kind of jealousy and competition Mendlesohn attributes to characters like Cordelia and Faith. One reading could be that Willow is not prepared for the ambivalent reactions produced when such power is wielded by a previously overlooked young woman, and arguments with Giles highlight this, offering contradictory subject positions. Willow is eager to talk with Giles about her success in resurrecting Buffy and is shocked when he calls her "a very stupid girl" ("Flooded," 6004; note the diminutive). Willow frames Giles' reaction very clearly as jealousy that the female "amateur" has succeeded in outstripping an experienced male, and her realization that she now outranks Giles is articulated specifically in terms of power—"You're right. The magics I used are very powerful. *I'm* very powerful and maybe it's not such a good idea for you to piss me off." Although Willow backs down here, the threat is acted upon in "Grave," when Dark Willow taunts Giles using language that underlines gendered relations ("Uh oh! Daddy's home, I'm in wicked trouble now"). Arguably Willow employs "feminist" rhetoric here, in a more convincing because less parodic way than Anyanka, and her comments point to the way patriarchal structures keep power exclusively for men.

It has been suggested that Willow's arc here mirrors that of season villain Warren, in that they both seek revenge for being the geek (Aloi 2002). Willow turns "dark" after Warren kills Tara, and although I discuss this in other chapters, it is worth noting how Dark Willow exercises her power. In "Two to Go" she tells Buffy, "I get it now. The Slayer thing really isn't about the violence. It's about the power," relating power and violence. She uses power to dominate in a "masculine" way. Despite the "feminine" aspect of witchcraft, Dark Willow has more in common with the tough guys discussed in chapter 4. She has several action scenes: she pursues Warren through the woods; breaks into the town jail to try and reach Jonathan and Andrew; fights anyone in her way; and rides a truck in a car chase (a scene reminiscent of *The Terminator* with Dark Willow as the "male" terminator). These involve Dark Willow in aggressive physical (masculine) manifestations of her (feminine) power. Another obvious masculinization of Dark Willow is her killing of Warren, and Stevie Simkin likens their final encounter to a "rape" (2004a: 26). Dark Willow tortures Warren with the bullet he used to kill her (female) lover, penetrating his male body with a phallic weapon ("Villains" 6020). After reducing Warren to a hysterical, pleading (feminized) state, she first flays and then incinerates him, not as part of the fight against larger evil but out of personal revenge.

Yet Willow's revenge, like Buffy's use of violence, could be read as specifically female (even "feminist") in that it is "justified" retaliation for an act of male-on-female violence (see Clover 1992 on rape-revenge films and male audiences). However, the show's moral framework situates this as the biggest moral dilemma in *Buffy* and Dark Willow as "bad." In season 3 Slayer Faith killed a human, and the rest of the season was devoted to working out the consequences. Willow takes this a step further—she is ready to destroy the world. Dark Willow is countered by Giles and Xander so that it may seem that "good" male characters overcome "bad" female power. An alternative reading is that Willow's destructive power trip is "masculine," as the parallel with Warren and even the phallic thrust of the emerging tower suggest, and Giles and Xander represent "feminine" virtues or powers (earth magic, emotion) in what Thomas Hibbs describes as "a systematic reversal of conventional gender roles" (2003: 55). According to Giles, Dark Willow acts out of "rage and power and vengeance" rather than the "the true essence of magic" (earth/female) ("Grave"). Dark Willow is finally defused by a declaration of love from Xander (the "heart" of the group). "You're not the only one with powers," he tells her, and this resolution emphasizes the importance of emotional ties (Willow and Xander's friendship is the longest-lived of the group). It is not Willow's power that is masculinized here, but how she uses it. Reacting from emotion, she denies emotion (she specifically says that she does not want to feel; again like the tough guys), and then uses her power for her own satisfaction, without due consideration for others (individualism, not cooperation). The confusion between Warren and Willow shows that boundaries between "masculine" and "feminine" and between "goodies" and "baddies" blur easily, while the contradictory genderings of Willow and her magical power highlight the difficulty she has in negotiating a way to be a powerful young woman.

In the early episodes of season 7 Willow's rehabilitation takes place in a pastoral environment with a coven of female witches. But this all-female coven is never seen, and Giles acts as Willow's mentor here (she says he has "gone all Dumbledore" on her, invoking the image of a benevolent paternal teacher ["Lessons" 7001]). Willow is convinced the other witches fear her power and worries about the uncontrollable nature of that power. On her return to Sunnydale there are even a number of false alarms. Yet her relationship with potential Slayer Kennedy is further proof of Willow's redemption (the "reward" of romance), and her fleeting transformation into "Willow the White" during the season finale validates this.[15] Buffy's assertion that "this woman" is more powerful than the men who created the first Slayer reinforces Willow's position as the *most* powerful female character on *Buffy*. This also maintains the tension between young female power and old patriarchal structures designed to keep women under control. Operating outside such structures, Willow creates multiple Slayers from the female line of Potentials using magic handed down by a group of women (the Guardians). Her power and its use are refigured as emphatically female.

The *Grr* in *Girl*?

Buffy's characters "choose" conventionally feminine appearances, something second-wave feminism might interpret as being solely to please men or to attract (male) partners. Buffy's "femininity" makes her acceptable on network television and offers a kind of recognition to viewers—she is not "Buffy the Lesbian Separatist" (because everyone knows that lesbians and feminists don't look "girlie"), she *is* a "girlie-girl" because she looks like one, even if her actions are read as "feminist." Cordelia demonstrates a more traditional "feminine" power of manipulation and/or wealth (but she is effectively dependent on her father for the latter). Anya moves between parodic "feminism" and exaggerated "femininity," making both "alien" (compared with the way Buffy makes these positions "normal"). It has been argued that "female audiences are not only capable of making distinctions between femininities, but [also] understand that femininity is a 'masquerade' produced through the use of clothes, interiors, and so on" (Partington in Hollows 2000: 60). While Anya and Cordelia offer different "masquerades" of femininity, Willow has problems reconciling her "feminine" power with her strength and independence. Arguably such representations afford "a powerful recognition of the contradictions of living under patriarchy" (Hollows 2000: 56), at least for the female viewer. It may also be clear to some that the ability to choose or to rebel against social norms is itself a sign of privilege; borrowing Whelehan's words from the beginning of this chapter, power "available equally to all women" is an "illusion" fostered by popular constructions of postfeminism as white and middle class.

The series finale mitigates Buffy's mutually exclusive roles; she retains her power but seems to have a chance at being a "normal girl." This tension between exceptional power and "normal" life can be read as another variant of the public/private tension faced by women who try to "have it all." As Coppock, Haydon, and Richter observe, film and television texts often focus "on women's personal relationships as wives, mothers, girlfriends, mistresses," and thus "women's economic exploitation is conveniently side-stepped, neglecting all recognition of women's potential as a powerful, political force within society" (1995: 133). Although *Buffy* focuses on personal relationships, all the powerful girls discussed here identify themselves by what can be read as a public or professional role (Buffy is the Slayer, Cordelia is Queen C, Anya is vengeance, and Willow is magic), and their power lies in that role. These roles and their power are not easily maintained in the "real" world.

Buffy, Willow, and Anya have supernatural power; Cordelia has real-world power based on wealth and privilege. Buffy's stint as a fast-food worker may be read as part of the overall gloominess of season 6, but it is also an indication of her lack of real-world economic power. She is stuck in a poorly paid job that renders her vulnerable to threats not commonly associated with the middle class (homelessness, Dawn's removal by social services). Dyer has noted that despite their comparative privilege, white women's "occupation of the position of power" is "always temporary" (1997: 30), and what happens to Cordelia, Anya, and Buffy demonstrates this. It could be argued that Buffy's supernatural power reinforces (even causes) her lack of "real" power, since her position as the Slayer precludes her completing a college education or entering a profession. Only Willow retains her power, and it is seen to be essentially female, just as Willow herself often seems to be positioned somehow outside patriarchy.

The show tries to offer its young female characters postfeminist identities that break down gender boundaries and hybridize gendered characteristics to produce new versions of power and heroism. The contradictions that arise can enhance recognition of the problems involved in negotiating such identities. Ang suggests that being a woman "can now mean the adoption of many different identities, composed of a whole range of subject positions, and not predetermined by immovable definitions of femininity. . . . being a woman involves *work*, work of constant self-(re)construction" (1997: 164). *Buffy*'s female characters are represented as always working in this way, whether to come to terms with power, or to maintain a successful "good-girl" identity, as I discuss in chapter 2.

2 *Good Girls*

Blurring of moral boundaries is one way that *Buffy* presents identity as unstable, but the terms *good* and *bad* are complex and shifting in relation to gender and genre. Female characters might be "good" in the sense that they are on the side of "right" in the fight against "evil." *Buffy*'s good girls negotiate their gendered position in a postfeminist though still patriarchal society by acting in ways that might once have been branded "bad" (inappropriate for young women) but now mark them as assertive or independent. The terms *good girl*, *bad girl*, and *bad boy* mean different things because they can refer to morality as well as to gendered identity and "norms" ("boys" are expected to be "bad," while "girls" are expected to be "good"). In my reading, the show demonstrates that being *too good* a girl (too traditionally gendered) is no longer a strategy for success. The quotation from "Hush" (4010) in my title indicates that *Buffy* attempts to undercut stereotypes through its female characters, but I suggest that they retain some traditionally feminine aspects.

I use the term *good girl* to indicate an *ideal* of female behavior. The good girl is the female constructed in relation to others, a construction encompassing emotion and communication, sexual behavior, nurturing, and familial caring. Coppock, Haydon, and Richter describe the policing of gendered behavior thus: "Women are instructed that conformity to weakness, passivity and self-sacrifice will encourage male love/approval but that independence, strength and self-confidence will be punished by castigation, desertion and physical abuse" (1995: 110). The former behavior is therefore seen as "good," the latter as "bad." Good-girl behavior remains an ideal despite clashing with postfeminist aspirations. Although Miller concludes that female autonomy "requires rejecting the stereotype of the selfless giver" (2003: 40), *Buffy*'s good girls are unselfish—they support and help others and are prepared for self-sacrifice. (All the "good" characters do this: perhaps the show in this way tries to universalize "feminine" virtues rather than "masculine" ones.) Good girls take on the traditional female role of civilizing masculine wildness (see Modleski on romance); they allow (male) authority to dictate their behavior; they are more passive than active. *Buffy* modifies "natural" female talents in nurturing and communication through its valorization of emotion and its presentation of responsibility as a key virtue: its good girls have a responsibility to the group, which is designated as an alternative family. Good girls must have a good man, participating in compulsory heterosexuality and romance, as described in the previous chapter. As well as Buffy and Willow, Kendra the second Slayer, April the robot, Tara, and Dawn are examined as good girls in this chapter.

Really Good Girls

KENDRA

Leaving Willow aside for the moment, Kendra is an early example of what I call a really good girl in *Buffy*. Kendra is also the first — and, until the advent of Principal Wood in season 7, the only — "good" nonwhite character[1] and has thus been the subject of some discussion in *Buffy* studies. She is introduced in "What's My Line? Part 1" (2009) when Spike contracts the assassin Order of Teraka to kill Buffy. At the end of the episode the (so far unnamed) Kendra and Buffy fight. Realizing that Kendra is no ordinary young woman, Buffy asks who she is, and the reply, "I am Kendra, the vampire slayer," sets Kendra directly in opposition to Buffy, destabilizing Buffy's identity as *the* Slayer. When Kendra's credentials are verified, the Scoobies conclude that she must have been called after Buffy's momentary "death" at the hands of the Master in season 1.

Kendra's treatment of vampire Angel in this episode (she attempts to kill him) proves that she takes her Slayer duties very seriously. Lynne Edwards suggests that in this way "Kendra becomes more legitimate and thereby a greater threat to Buffy's slayer identity. Slayers are supposed to kill vampires, not fall in love with them" (2002: 93). In denying the strongly romanticized Buffy/Angel relationship, Kendra comes across as hard and unemotional. She later argues, "Emotions are weakness, Buffy. You shouldn't entertain them" ("What's My Line? Part 2"). Since the show increasingly valorizes emotion, this makes Kendra, like Anya in later seasons, an outsider because she does not express or value it. As a Slayer, she functions mainly in the public ("masculine") sphere, and her unfamiliarity with emotions and relationships can be read as an absence of "natural" female skills.

Kendra is presented as almost entirely subsumed within her role as the Slayer, in contrast with Buffy, who tries to integrate her two lives. "My mother and father gave me to my Watcher because they believed they were doing the right thing for me—and for the world," she tells Buffy. "Please, I don't feel sorry for myself. Why should you?" ("What's My Line? Part 2"). In this self-sacrifice (Buffy calls it "personality-removal") Kendra is the ideal good girl, giving herself up to duty and putting others before herself. She also accepts without question the guidance of her Watcher, and thus of the patriarchal Council, and she studies "because it is required. The Slayer handbook insists on it" ("What's My Line? Part 2"). Kendra seeks and wins approval from her male mentors by doing what she is told, following the rules. She does not make her own choices or resist the control of her power by those in authority. In the end she proves she is a good Slayer by dying fighting vampires. Although West suggests that "Kendra's death in battle is as inevitable as it was heroic" (2001: 168), he sees it as a direct result of her submission: "She succumbs to Drusilla's hypnosis, where the more will-ful Buffy was ultimately able to resist that of the Master and Dracula" (171).[2] This exposes the ambivalence of Kendra's "heroism," and Ono cites her as "one more instance of a woman (of color) who cannot be a hero" (2000: 174).

Kendra is gendered through sexualization, and this is complicated by race. *Buffy* has been criticized for its lack of racial diversity[3] and for its demonization of racialized characters (see Ono), since Buffy, Willow, and others are presented as the (white middle-class) "norm." Edwards cites the introductory script description from "What's My Line? Part 1": "an ethnic young woman (seventeen), her *feline, feral eyes* getting used to the sudden light. She's *a predator, a hunter*, and her name is Kendra" (2002: 91; emphasis mine), and this description engages cultural and racial stereotypes (animalistic) as well as stereotypes of "bad" women (feline, predatory). Both Elyce Rae Helford (2002) and Edwards argue that Kendra's race is integral to her gendering; they list out cloth-ing, makeup, jewelry, and speech (accent) as contributing factors to an exoticized racial difference. Yet despite her exotic sexiness, Kendra is innocent. When Xander is appreciative, she lowers her eyes and ad-mits that she is "not permitted to speak with boys" ("What's My Line? Part 2"). This can also be read as characteristic of a good girl—she is attractive without being experienced and follows the rules for appropriate behavior, in contrast with Buffy and other young female characters. Their white middle-class postfeminism, including an interest in "boys"—that is, an investment in heterosexual romance—is upheld here as the "norm."

Characters differing from the norm can be fairly easily integrated into the core group of a soap or series because such shows operate on distinctions between outsiders and insiders. Yet this means that racial or other diversity tends to be subsumed into the "dominant" culture (Geraghty 1991: 144). Following this pattern, Kendra assimilates into the predominantly white middle-class culture of the Scoobies and takes on some of the independence and emotion of the other young women. Kendra's assimilation is largely facilitated through Buffy's realization that another Slayer may not be so bad, and a compromise results in buddy-movie-style bonding. Like Faith in subsequent seasons, Kendra serves largely to illuminate the role of the Slayer and Buffy's negotiation of it. Both Kendra and Faith are Other Slayers; Faith, discussed in the next chapter, is "other" than Buffy because she is coded as working class. Neither fits the white middle-class "norm" of Buffy (the character and the show), and both serve more as foils for Buffy than as fully developed subjects. I argue in the next chapter that Faith's presentation as a "bad girl" makes her more attractive to viewers, and because her character ran longer and was more fully developed, she offered a more viable subject position than Kendra.

Kendra cannot hope to survive because Buffy is *the* Vampire Slayer; it is her show, after all. Unfortunately Kendra stands first in a line of nonwhite Slayers whose function is to die (like the Chinese Slayer and the black New York Slayer, Nikki Wood, in "Fool for Love");[4] notably, Buffy and Faith survive. Kendra's difference to Buffy is exaggerated to enhance her role as a foil. Certainly she does nothing to contradict Candra K. Gill's assessment of "those few characters [of color on *Buffy*] with substantial speaking roles" who "could expect to die, be evil, be marginalized/exoticized, or all three" (2003). Her example proves that being a "good" Slayer and a good girl only gets you killed.

APRIL

In the season 5 episode "I Was Made to Love You" a young woman called April arrives in Sunnydale seeking "true love." Subsequent scenes reveal that she is looking for her "boyfriend" Warren. When Spike hits on her at a U. C. Sunnydale party, April responds by throwing him through a window, and a few moments later she throws Buffy across the room. The Scoobies agree that April must be a robot. April's representation incorporates themes common to (female) robots in science fiction: she is created by a male, has enormous physical strength, and conflicts with her creator over her purpose. April is also, as Zoe Jane Playden notes (2001: 143), a prime example of "objectified woman." She is built to be the perfect girlfriend: Warren explains, "She cares about what I care about and she wants to be with me. She listens to me and supports me." Xander clarifies her other attractions: "She's a sexbot. . . . I mean, what guy doesn't dream about that? A beautiful girl with no other thought but to please you, willing to do anything." April tells Buffy, "Crying is blackmail. Good girlfriends don't cry," and she is the ultimate submissive female, created by Warren for Warren, her sole purpose to "please" him. She says only what he has told her to say, does only what she has been programmed to do (compare the "rape" scene between the android Rachael and Deckard in *Blade Runner* [1982]). Even not answering when he calls her causes her pain, or "feedback," as Warren describes it.

This "perfect" girlfriend is superficially attractive (as both Xander and Willow attest) but ultimately unsatisfying. When Buffy asks Warren if he is in love with her, he replies, "I guess it was too easy and predictable, you know, she got boring." Warren rejects his creation for a fellow student, Katrina. Katrina clearly does not fit Warren's definition of the perfect girlfriend: she walks out on him when both April and Buffy come looking for him and later refuses to speak to him on the telephone. Arguably she is a young woman raised in a postfeminist society, expecting a more equal relationship. In showing Warren to prefer Katrina over April, *Buffy* appears to demonstrate that active, independent young women are more attractive than passive good girls (though this is complicated by the context of heterosexual romance).

April's constant concern resembles the theme displayed in 1950s B-movies like *The Attack of the 50 Foot Woman* (1958): smothering femininity as a threat to male independence. Warren complains to Buffy that April's batteries should have run down days ago—his creation is out of control and more powerful than he anticipated. April defends her position as Warren's "girlfriend" by attacking Katrina and later Buffy (her "combat mode" is "enabled"). The fact that April is a robot rather than a real "girl" is announced in different ways. Her *Terminator*-style visual display implies the unthinking programmed violence of that machine, as does the exposure of metal parts during the fight, and it is almost chance that Buffy is able to defeat April. Yet the visual display also gives April's point of view. As she and Buffy sit together, the pattern of shadow over April and light over Buffy adds poignancy to her situation and the show delivers another "feminist" message: defining herself through heterosexual relationships leaves April vulnerable, articulated by her question, "If I can't do that [love Warren], what am I for?"

This episode might imply that gender is a construction, that the right moves and responses can create gender. Yet although April superficially passes for a real woman, she cannot do so for long. She is a boy's version of a perfect girlfriend—just too much of a good girl to be true. In the end, she is so good that she's bad, so she "dies." Ultimately April embodies extremes of power and powerlessness, emphasizing how romance can be used to subordinate women. She contrasts Buffy and Buffy's subject position (Riley has recently left Buffy), and at the end of this episode Spike orders a Buffy robot from Warren (featuring in seasons 5 and 6, the Buffy-bot is also too good to survive). This contrast again suggests that sticking too closely to outmoded ideas of being a "good girl" is self-destructive but also points out that strong and independent Buffy is still prey to doubts and fears about romance and her responses to male partners.

TARA

Tara enters *Buffy* when she and Willow strike up a friendship after a university Wicca group meeting ("Hush"). Tara is introduced to the other Scoobies in a pivotal episode, "New Moon Rising" (4019), when Willow's werewolf ex-boyfriend Oz returns. Willow is shown overcompensating for Tara's unfamiliarity with Scooby meetings, and when Oz arrives Tara tells her, "You should be with your friends and I should go," articulating her understanding of her place as an outsider while at the same time briefly offering a new subject position to re/view the Scoobies. Tara's sensitivity to atmosphere, ability to read complex situations, and willingness to allow others space are the first indications of her personality and remain strong characteristics. Notably, these relate largely to emotion and help define her as a good girl, that is, a "naturally" emotional or communicative female with the skills to manage relationships.

Tara is willing to let Willow make her own decision about Oz and their relationship. Oz grasps the nature of Tara and Willow's relationship early on. Aggressively asking, "Are you in love with her?" he changes into the wolf and attacks Tara after a chance meeting. Tara is positioned here as a victim of male sexual jealousy and as a helpless female who requires strong men to rescue her: the Initiative stun wolf-Oz and take him away, suspecting that he has killed some of their men. Attacked by a rival for Willow's affections and seeing him removed, Tara tells Willow, knowing that she and the Scoobies can help Oz and proving herself a really good girl by apparently sacrificing her own chance with Willow. However, on being rescued, Oz leaves, and Willow tells Tara she wants her, not Oz: being a good girl can be rewarded.

Played by Amber Benson, an actor with a larger frame than the petite and slim Gellar and Hannigan, Tara's appearance contrasts conventional media femininity. Not since Veruca the female werewolf ("Wild at Heart" 4006) had the show presented a character so divergent from the ultra-slim "norm." Benson responded defensively to viewers' online comments about her size, emphasizing how different the "norms" of network television are from the "norms" of real life (see Topping 2002: 311–312); and for some viewers Benson's casting was a source of pleasure, offering a more realistic female image. Where Veruca was both more masculinized and more sexualized,[5] Tara is always presented as "feminine," visualized by a wardrobe of skirts and dresses. Tara operates almost exclusively in female company: she meets Willow at the all-female Wicca group, she mentions her mother as a guiding influence, and when she does form bonds with the Scoobies they are with other females. Her presentation as witch and lesbian also code her as emphatically female. She is an interesting exception to the other good girls in that she has no "masculine" qualities (one of the reasons she is so good?), and her operation in a largely female sphere directly contradicts what Mendlesohn calls *Buffy*'s heterosocial model for relationships (2002: 49). Willow is later positioned in a similar way.

It has been noted that although "the subtext of much horror/gothic is anxiety about homosexuality . . . , *Buffy* offers a sensitive portrayal of a same-sex relationship" in Willow and Tara, the first lesbian (and the first homosexual) couple on the show (Jarvis 2001: 259). Yet the relationship is figured primarily as romantic. Whedon stated early on, "This story line will not focus on sexuality as a theme but on the intense emotional bond between the characters" ("Buffy's Willow" 2000: 24), and *Buffy* tends to displace Willow and Tara's sexuality onto shared magic use. This allows the show to represent a lesbian relationship with some delicacy. It avoids titillation of the type Xander so often desires, but on the other hand lack of sexual activity renders invisible a large part of lesbian identity. As Tamsin Wilton notes, "It is precisely by our sexual desires and practices that we gain access to the name 'lesbian'" (1996:

134). Whedon reportedly had to argue with the network for a first kiss between the two (see Kaveney 2001: 33). In subsequent seasons more explicitly sexual scenes are included, though the most erotic scene between Tara and Willow is displaced onto magic in a musical number ("Once More with Feeling" 6007). Later scenes showing Willow and Tara in bed together are "normalized" and further de-eroticized through their new role as Dawn's "parents" (after Joyce and Buffy's deaths), discussing the "family" or the day's activities.

As in many other television serials with ensemble casts, *Buffy*'s characters form a supportive group that has been read as an alternative family, both within and without the text. This shifts as the show develops and the core cast changes, while connections between group members can seem as complicated as those in soap opera (as shown by Nancy's comment in "Beneath You" 7002: "Is there anyone here who hasn't slept together?"). I suggested in the introduction that the serial nature of *Buffy*'s narrative potentially allows it to resist the closure of heterosexual romance and the traditional patriarchal family. This is demonstrated in "Family" (5006), which focuses on Tara and opens by reminding viewers that she is not yet part of the group.[6] The arrival of Tara's "real" family, the McClays, increases her isolation. Her father is formal and stern; addressed as "sir," he brings out Tara's stammer. Ominous hints abound: Mr. McClay disapproves of Tara's witchcraft and tells her she must return home because "You can't control what's going to happen. You have evil inside of you and it will come out."[7] Tara is desperate enough to cast a spell on the Scoobies, but it backfires and the Scoobies are attacked by demons that they cannot see. In the nick of time Tara lifts the spell, telling Willow, "I didn't want you to see what I am," while her father explains, "The women in our family have demon in them." Female power is seen by Tara's family as something that needs to be contained in a patriarchal family environment: "She belongs with us. We know how to control her problem."[8]

Here Tara's involvement with the group changes. She does not want to leave, and Buffy steps up to support her decision, followed by all the Scoobies until Buffy concludes, "We're family." Spike puts the final piece in the picture: "It's just a family legend, am I right? Used a bit of spin to keep the ladies in line." Thus the show offers a "feminist" explanation of how potentially powerful females are subordinated and "bad" women are demonized. Tara is accepted into the Scooby family, and this entails a rejection of her real family. Willow reassures her about her choice: "I think about what you grew up with and then I look at what you are, it makes me proud, it makes me love you more." Her comment affirms Tara's ability to transcend her family's limitations and, by implication, the limitations of heterosexuality and a traditional patriarchal system that sees powerful women as bad.

Tara becomes the moral and nurturing center of the Scooby family. She upholds moral values without judging individuals and supports others in their choices. In this way she adopts a typical female role often found in soaps—the matriarch who holds together the extended "family" of the show—but with the spin of being a young woman (rather than a mother) and a lesbian. The matriarchal role is reinforced by Tara's "replacement" of Buffy's mother, Joyce. Tara and Willow are living in the Summers house in season 6, occupying Joyce's old room, and Tara supports Willow, the leader of the Scoobies since Buffy's death. In the private space of their bedroom Tara tells Willow, "It doesn't all have to be good and fine. This is the room. You don't have to be brave, I still love you" ("After Life"), recalling Joyce's declarations of love for Buffy. After she breaks up with Willow, Tara continues to see Dawn, speaking to her like a parent in a divorce: "My moving out had nothing to do with you and I will never stop loving you" ("Smashed" 6009). She also remains a friend and confidante to the others. When Buffy finds out that she has "come back wrong" because Spike's chip does not prevent him from hurting her, it is to Tara that she turns for help, and she ends up crying in Tara's lap ("Dead Things" 6013; another parallel with Joyce; see figure 3). The gradual shift in Tara's presentation from shy and insecure to stable matriarch is a source of pleasure for viewers like me, who identified her as potentially feminist. Tara also acts as a moral guardian in warning Willow about her use of magic,[9] and her motivation characterizes her as a good girl; she is concerned about Willow, and Willow's irritation only evokes affirmations of love.

Since Willow is a focal character, Tara sometimes tends to lack subjectivity, functioning simply as an adjunct to her partner, as Anya does to Xander. Her relationship with Willow is figured as a rerun of Willow's empowerment through her friendship with Buffy, particularly in Tara's song from "Once More with Feeling":

> I lived my life in shadow
> Never the sun on my face
> It didn't seem so sad, though
> I figured that was my place
> Now I'm bathed in light

FIGURE 3: *Tara takes over Joyce's role as "mother" ("Dead Things").*

> Something just isn't right
> I'm under your spell,
> How else can it be
> Anyone would notice me
> It's magic I can tell
> How you've set me free
> Brought me out so easily.

The song could also suggest that Tara accepts her "place" as subordinate in the relationship. However, a more confident Tara begins to assert her right to agency: "You don't get to decide what is better for us, Will. We're in a relationship, we're supposed to decide together." Tara even implies that Willow is selfishly trying to change her ("Tabula Rasa" 6008). It is Tara who suggests a separation and she who returns when Willow seems to be "cured" of her magic addiction.

Tara is not only the most consistently good girl; in addition, she does not operate under male authority or in a male sphere (although she can hold her own at U. C. Sunnydale and in the otherwise all-male poker game in "Older and Far Away"), her power is female, she does not seek male approval or company, and she has no "masculine" characteristics. As such she is an unusual example of a female character on *Buffy*, though she is normalized through her typical nurturing role and eventually somewhat marginalized by being relegated to the domestic. Tara is killed by one of the most anxious male villains, Warren, with a "masculine" weapon, a gun, and in death Tara furthers Willow's development (just as Kendra did for Buffy). Her good influence is turned to bad as Willow goes dark and hunts for revenge.

Virtual Good Girl

Dawn's introduction as Buffy's younger sister in season 5 seemed to be a huge continuity error. Later episodes revealed that Dawn was imported into the lives and memories of Buffy and the others by Dagon monks, who wanted to protect an artifact called the Key from Glory, a hell-god seeking to return to her own dimension. The monks transformed the Key into a human being and sent it to the Slayer, knowing she would "protect it with her life" ("Blood Ties" 5013). Therefore Dawn is not really a girl at all, and Mendlesohn calls her "Buffy's virtual sister" (2002: 52). Dawn allowed the series to refocus on a teen character after its original teens had grown up: themes of generational conflict and responsibility were revisited, with the original characters on the other side of the generation gap. In seasons 5 and 6 Dawn displays mostly "bad" behavior, but this is largely ascribed to typical teen rebellion, and I read her primary characteristic as innocence, so she is always a good girl.

Dawn is initially presented as alienated because she is both a typical teen and the Key, a mystical energy not of this world. Even before she discovers the latter, Dawn feels that no one understands her, as articulated in "Real Me" (5002), her first episode and one that gives her a voice of her own (and potentially a new subject position for viewers). Since the show focuses on the Scoobies and their activities, Dawn's life is not painted in detail, and she often seems to be alone. This offers an immediate bond with Tara, another "newbie," but may prevent regular viewers from taking Dawn's position seriously. Later Willow tells Buffy, "I just have all this involuntary empathy for Dawn because she's, you know, a big spaz" ("No Place Like Home" 5005), adding to the impression of Dawn as an awkward misfit (like the Scoobies in earlier seasons) but also underlining Dawn and Willow's bond. Dawn's two roles, Key and little sister, make her an object of protection to Buffy and the other Scoobies and allow her to function as a symbol of the people the Slayer must keep safe, of what Buffy is fighting for (her family and friends), and later as integral to Spike's redemption. Yet this renders her somewhat passive. Buffy complains, "She has to be protected and coddled from the big bad world. Well, you know what? We are doing nothing but turning her into a little idiot who's going to get us all killed" ("Real Me") — pointing out Dawn's generic function as typical screaming horror victim, or damsel in distress.

When Buffy entered a trance in "Blood Ties," she saw Dawn's image appear and disappear from family photographs. A prime example of unstable identity, Dawn asks, "What am I? Am I real? Am I anything?" The crisis is resolved by Buffy, who affirms that Dawn is her sister, sharing "Summers blood" with her after being injured saving Dawn from Glory (a foresight of the season finale). Dawn is thus integrated into the Summers family and the larger group, finding her identity through the typically "feminine" mechanism of familial relationships. The importance of the family and the emotional bonds that tie Dawn to it are reiterated at many points, as when Dawn lies down beside the Buffy-bot for comfort in "Bargaining Part 1."

Acceptance into the Summers family brings about another identity crisis: Dawn is the little sister of the Slayer and has a lot to live up to. This, and Joyce's illness and death, initiates some of her "bad" behavior (sneaking out of the house to meet friends, shoplifting), coded clearly as teenage rebellion or a cry for help rather than as morally "evil" (in the overall good-versus-evil metanarrative). "All the Way" conflates different kinds of innocence in Dawn, proving she is really "good": she does not realize that her date is a vampire, and she has never kissed before. Although she has crushes, she never has a boyfriend. Both Buffy and Willow are positioned as "role models" for Dawn, and her admiration for them is reiterated frequently. Their mixture of postfeminist independence and more conventional "femininity" are replicated in Dawn, and her model for an ideal relationship is that of Willow and Tara, the lesbian couple. As Dawn matures she accepts her responsibility to the two families she is part of. Early in season 6 she manages to persuade the newly resurrected Buffy to come home by telling her, "I'm your sister," and she later risks herself with Rack to help Willow ("Two to Go"). During the finale Dawn helps Buffy in physical slaying ("Grave") and the first episode in season 7 presents the two patrolling and training together. In a tongue-in-cheek scene Dawn confronts a male vampire and Buffy, the girl power hero, asks, "Who's got the power?" until Dawn is forced to admit, "He does": even in the fantasy world of Sunnydale, male power

is the norm, and "little girls" have to be taught to stand up to it.

Dawn is now presented as capable and survives a visitation by the First Evil and her dead mother Joyce in a test of her strength that is as much emotional as it is physical ("Conversations with Dead People" 7007). Dawn also accepts that despite her involvement in exceptional activities, she is not exceptional herself (her supernatural origin is conveniently forgotten here). In "Potential" (7012) a spell to locate more potential Slayers seems to identify Dawn, but the Sunnydale potential turns out to be a classmate, Amanda. At the end of the episode Xander points out "how tough it is . . . to be the one who isn't Chosen" and concludes, "You're not special, you're extraordinary." On the one hand this emphasizes an underlying message of the show: despite many characters' longing for a "normal" life, no one is normal or ordinary. On the other hand, what Xander tells Dawn sweetens a subordinate position: women make ordinary contributions of domestic or relational work every day, and their reward is simply to be told that they are special, they are extraordinary.

Dawn continues to work as part of the team. She even stands up to Buffy and asks her to leave when the group rejects her leadership ("Empty Places"). This is Dawn at her most mature, calmly telling her sister, "Buffy, I love you. But you were right. We have to be together on this. You can't be a part of it. So I need you to leave. I'm sorry but this is my house too." That Dawn's love is meant to be genuine is underlined by her sharp response to Rona, but she puts the "mission" first. When Buffy tries to send Dawn away before the final battle, she resists and returns to fight with the others. Dawn remains a good girl despite her bad behavior because this is presented as just a teenage phase. Her work with and for the group expands to take in school misfits and the potential Slayers. In my reading, Dawn's primary function is as a symbol of emotion and family relations, but she also negotiates a gendered identity based on the role models available to her.

Good Girls Go Bad

WILLOW

Willow seems to be *Buffy*'s ultimate good girl. Mendlesohn suggests that her "sexuality is muted by its cuddliness, signified by her choice of pink, of cuddly sweaters and dungarees" (2002: 54), and this is not the "sexy" femininity of postfeminism or girl power, as with Buffy. In early seasons Willow wears childish or androgynous clothes that imply innocence rather than sexuality, but the colors (especially pink) and fabrics (fluffy) underline conventional femininity too. Later Willow's dress sense becomes more mature and idiosyncratic, reflecting the fact that she is not a slave to fashion (making choices is conflated with independence).

Willow is further gendered through her relationships, whether her childhood longing for Xander or her new, empowering friendship with Buffy. Both gain from the latter, and both describe the other as their "best friend" (though Xander also calls Willow this). This reinforces Buffy and Willow's "natural femininity": good girls are expected to have close female friends, and the resulting emotional support is seen to be a particularly female mechanism. It is Buffy to whom Willow turns for affirmation (as in "I Robot, You Jane" 1008), and later she berates Buffy for running away: "I didn't have anyone to talk about all this scary life stuff. And you were my *best friend*" ("Dead Man's Party" 3002). Willow puts her friendships first and often makes sacrifices, as when she refuses places at prestigious universities to remain in Sunnydale and help the Scoobies. She takes all her responsibilities seriously and reminds others of theirs. Since responsibility is valorized in *Buffy*, Willow appears as the moral center of the group in earlier seasons, and James B. South observes that she "is repeatedly seen as the best of the Scooby gang" (2003: 133). Thus goodness and female-ness are equated in the good-girl Willow of early seasons.

Willow is "rewarded" with at least two long-term relationships, but these are presented as romantic rather than sexual, and cuddles and handholding replace erotic tension and sexual activity (Mendlesohn 2002: 59). Willow's sexual activity tends to be displaced or projected elsewhere. In her relationship with Oz, sexuality is figured through Oz as werewolf (another example of female influence civilizing wild masculinity, see chapter 5), while in her relationship with Tara it is coded through the use of magic, as discussed above. On the basis of season 5 Mendlesohn argues that this displacement "actually undercuts a queer reading of Willow at all, first by neutralizing her sexuality and then by rechanneling thoughts of lesbian relationships in a safe direction" (2002: 59).

Other television shows with regular gay characters faced similar problems. The portrayal of Jack McPhee in *Dawson's Creek* won a Gay and Lesbian Alliance Against Defamation Media Award in 2000, and some Web sites credit the show with "primetime television's first romantic gay kiss" ("*Dawson's Creek*," www.planetout.com). Yet I have heard teenage viewers disparaging the way Jack's sexuality is coded through changes in costume (style) and only rarely through visual sexualization (the TelevisionWithoutPity.com episode guide [Morgan] refers to "The Annual Gay Kiss"). Rosanne Kennedy describes *L.A. Law*, an earlier show aimed at an older target audience, as having paradoxically "achieved so much credibility, in terms of maintaining a 'lesbian' presence, with so little representation of lesbian sexuality, or even of lesbian issues" (1997: 318). *Dawson's Creek* dealt with Jack "coming out" and encountering resistance from his family before he eventually found "love." In contrast, Willow rarely has to deal with resistance to her sexuality (only in "Smashed" is she shown experiencing any homophobic hostility), but arguably this prevents her sexuality from becoming simply an "issue." Kennedy suggests that in *L.A. Law* lesbian sexuality "is repeatedly displaced onto a series of political and ethical issues" and points out that the "representation of lesbian and gay sexuality as an 'issue' confirms the 'normality' of heterosexuality; heterosexuality only becomes an issue when it is excessive and transgressive, as in cases of incest and rape" (322).

Whedon has related Willow's Jewish identity and her sexuality in comments he made when fan speculation was rising about the latter (in Nazzaro 2002: 154), yet neither Willow's ethnicity nor her sexuality has been a visible issue in the show. Willow's Jewishness is rarely named as a difference, while her sexuality is often named: sexuality seems to be considered a more important identifier than ethnicity. Dyer suggests that "Irish, Mexicans, Jews and people of mixed race" have been ambivalent in racial history since they are at times "assimilated into the category of whiteness, and at others treated as a 'buffer'" (1997: 19). In Willow's case, her ethnicity is neither an issue nor a difference—her Jewishness is assimilated into the middle-class whiteness that is *Buffy*'s norm.

Kennedy notes the *L.A. Law* lesbian character C.J.'s appeal "to all women, regardless of sexuality" (321) and argues that "C.J. embodies queer by refusing to be identified as heterosexual, lesbian, or bisexual" (323). Willow's sexual difference is generally identified (named) as "gay" rather than "lesbian." She is never identified as bisexual, and her sexual identity is constructed within and upholds the binary opposition between hetero- and homosexuality and thus between the gender categories "male" and "female." Given that the sexual element of this identity is largely removed, I am almost tempted to suggest that Willow is a

political lesbian. Arguably she is "removed" from complicity in patriarchal relations when she becomes a lesbian, and both Willow and Tara as
lesbians become more female rather than more hybrid in gender terms.
The conflation of sexual activity and Wiccan magic merely reinforces
this feminization. Hilary Hinds observes that viewers often demonstrate an ability to read televisual texts about lesbian relationships as
"essentially about all (or other) human relationships, rather than about
the specificities of lesbian ones" (1997: 208). Thus Willow the lesbian
may be universalized, just as I have suggested Buffy the character can be
read as a "universal" hero rather than a female or feminist protagonist.

Willow's subsequent relationship with Kennedy *is* eroticized (especially by the "my girlfriend has a pierced tongue" comment in "Chosen")
but I suggest that this is owing to the tension Willow's power creates.
Willow's power and her relationships are closely linked, and viewers
may recognize the way she negotiates power and agency in her relationships. Despite apparent equality in her relationship with Oz, he
leaves Willow twice, and Mendlesohn observes that he denies Willow
agency (2002: 55). The "same-sex" relationship with Tara might promise
equality, though I have already noted a struggle for agency and a negotiation of terms on both sides. Willow is shown as both emotional and
valuing relationships but also as sometimes unwilling to do the work
(traditionally female) of managing and maintaining them. Her emotional state is closely related to the use of her power, and both are often
figured as out of control. In "Something Blue" Giles warns Willow that
using magic when she is emotionally in turmoil (here because Oz has
left her) may be a bad idea. When Glory mind-sucks Tara, Willow sets
out for revenge and foreshadows Dark Willow ("Tough Love" 5019).
Later, when Tara leaves her, Willow becomes "addicted" to magic (her
increasing reliance on magic was a cause of tension between them, and
one of the reasons Tara left), and when Tara dies, full-blown Dark Willow threatens to end the world simply to stop her from feeling.

Willow's use of power is also presented as a rebellion against her reliable good-girl persona. Responding to Buffy's typical comment, "It's
Willow, she of the level head," Anya points out, "Those are the ones you
have to watch out for the most. . . . Responsible people are always so
concerned with being good all the time that when they finally get a taste
of being bad they can't get enough" ("Smashed"). Any viewer might
find this an attractive subject position, a way of acting out being "bad"
in a character so often constrained by what others think. Willow's interactions with Amy and Rack are governed by this rebellion. Given Wil-

low's de-eroticization, her meeting with Rack ("Wrecked") is notable for its sexual undercurrents: "It's all right, it's over fast" and "You taste like strawberries." In this way Willow's shift to being morally "bad" is gendered through (hetero)sexualization, and despite blurring morality elsewhere the show makes strict distinctions between good and bad, white and black magic.

Another characteristic of Willow's rebellion is that she increasingly abandons her duty, especially her responsibilities to the group. She becomes isolated and competitive, as shown in her night out at The Bronze with Amy, and less concerned about what is happening to others than what she wants for herself. Her defensive response, "But I just want to help people" leads to Tara's perceptive dismissal: "Maybe that's how it started but you're helping yourself now, fixing things to your liking" ("Tabula Rasa"). This is presented as a threat to the group, first articulated by Anya and then realized by Willow's endangering Dawn, the object of protection ("Wrecked"). Thus Willow exchanges her "good girl" virtues for more traditionally "masculine" behavior.

Lidia Curti has suggested that soap in particular deals with the process of identifying and threats to identity, pointing to the use of narrative strategies like loss of memory, adoption, the use of doubles, and the use of close-ups that invite viewers to "lose themselves" in characters they identify with (in McRobbie 1994: 51). Almost all of these strategies have been used in *Buffy*, and McRobbie notes that they "comprise forms of self-interrogation about who I am and how I want to be, or how I expect to be" (1994: 51). Despite Buffy's superhero-style "secret identity," it is Willow who most often asks these questions, and her identity is exposed as unstable and fractured. While torturing Warren she uses Vamp Willow's words, "Bored now," and both Vamp Willow and Dark Willow appear to be Willow's antitheses. Masquerading as Vamp Willow, Willow railed against her own reliable persona, "It's pathetic—she lets everyone walk all over her and then she gets cranky at her friends for no reason" ("Doppelgangland"). Dark Willow does the same: "Let me tell you something about Willow. She's a loser. And she always has been. People picked on Willow . . . with her stupid mousy ways. And now—Willow's a junkie" ("Two to Go"). Willow even linked Tara's love to her powerful self, asking Buffy, "If you could be the plain old Willow or Super Willow, who would you be?" and insisting, "Buffy, who was I? Just some girl. Tara didn't even know that girl" ("Wrecked"). When Xander tries to stop Dark Willow, she tells him not to call her Willow. If "Willow" is not a feminized good girl, it seems she is a masculinized bad girl, and she finds it difficult to integrate these competing and oppositional identities.

In season 7 Willow still has difficulty seeing her power as part of her "good" identity, trying to repress it and refusing to use it. It erupts at points of high emotion, as when she returns to Sunnydale feeling nervous of her reception, discovers the massacre Anya facilitated in the fraternity house, or starts a physical relationship with Kennedy. This emotion can itself be read as a sign of "natural" femininity. The reassertion of Willow as a good girl comes in the series finale, when she fulfills Buffy's trust by magically enabling all the Potential Slayers to become Slayers. When she uses magic, she does not turn dark but glows with white light, and Kennedy tells her, "You're a goddess." Her power is not only emphatically female, as I concluded in chapter 1; it is also controlled (by Willow), "white" and good.

BUFFY

Buffy strives to be "normal," but her (morally) good role as the Slayer leads her to be (socially) bad. She disobeys her Watcher, falls in love with a vampire, and eventually quits the Council. She is also a problem teenager who gets into trouble at school, is a suspect in at least three murders, runs away from home, and has an older boyfriend. Buffy's school record notes "[a]ggressive behavior, run-ins with the 'authorities,' about a screenful of violent incidents" ("Phases"). In later seasons Buffy still exhibits "bad" behavior: she uses alcohol irresponsibly, drops out of college, cannot hold down a job, neglects her sister, and has a deadbeat boyfriend. This kind of "bad" behavior is not necessarily gendered, but Buffy's relationship with Spike (the culmination of her "bad" behavior) genders her through sexualization, and having violent kinky sex with a vampire is clearly not the sort of thing a "good girl" should do. In narrative terms, Buffy is "excused" by a series of personal crises (her mother's death and her own death and resurrection), and here I identify other strategies used to keep Buffy a good girl.

For Buffy, sexual purity is not essential, and her power is not dependent on retaining it.[10] When Early suggests that Buffy's role as the Slayer "exists in tension with her own desires, including erotic desires, and her longing to enjoy a normal life" (2003: 59), this points to sexual desire as a normalization of Buffy and links to her more conventional "femininity." Her early relationships are inflected by teen drama and concentrate on the experiences of falling in love, dating regularly, having sex for the first time, and breaking up. When Buffy and Angel have sex, it is he who changes; however much she may be affected emotionally, she loses none of her power.

Following a different (horror) convention, Buffy is bitten (penetrated) by the Master, Angel, and Dracula. The scene when Angel feeds on Buffy ("Graduation Day Part 2" 3022) has even been described as "the most sexual of the season" (Tjardes 2003: 76) in the way it displaces sex onto vampiric feeding. Angel needs the blood of a Slayer to save his life after being poisoned, so Buffy offers herself to him. The other Scoobies see this as a betrayal, if not a violation: Angel has taken advantage of Buffy. Dracula's bite too is sexualized and he is presented as a seducer of women (see chapter 6). Buffy's abilities are not affected[11] in any of these cases, and she is unmarked by her sexual liaison with Spike because it is seen as aberrant. Underscoring this innocence, Buttsworth notes that "Buffy, although 'sexy,' does not use her sexuality as an artifice or a weapon" (2002: 190). When she does, as in "When She Was Bad" (2001) and "Bad Girls" (3014), this is presented as unusual, and the episode titles label it "bad."

I discuss Angel, Riley, and Spike in subsequent chapters, but here I draw attention to certain aspects of Buffy's relationships with them and how these affect her representation as a good girl. Buffy's sexual activity is inflected by gendered constructions, especially of blame and shame. "I'm a slut," she tells Xander after her brief liaison with college student Parker Abrams, for example ("Beer Bad" 4005, see chapter 5 for more on Parker). As early as the first episode, Buffy's verbalizing her two outfits as "Hi! I'm an enormous slut!" and "Hi! Would you like a copy of the Watchtower?" signals the show's (and the character's) awareness of how clothes and appearance can construct gendered and sexualized identities (Whedon [Lavery 2002a: 26] notes that the first line "caused a bit of consternation for the network").

Buffy's first major relationship is with Angel, the vampire with a soul, and this is highly romanticized, perhaps because of the excessive gender coding of both characters. Angel, as I argue in chapter 6, is presented as hypermasculine and hyperheroic and initially appears in stock male roles such as the mysterious stranger—"you know, dark, gorgeous in an annoying sort of way" ("Welcome to the Hellmouth" 1001). The relationship is always coded as a doomed romance: he is a 250-plus-year-old vampire with a history of demonic evil; she is the teenage Slayer, fated to fight evil; yet against the odds they fall in love.[12] Angel's soul was returned as a punishment by a gypsy curse, but the curse stipulated that if he ever experienced a moment of true happiness he would revert to evil soulless Angelus. That this happens when Buffy first has sex with him is the ultimate teen allegory in early seasons, reflecting girls' real anxieties about the value of sex in relationships.

Angel's vampire nature and the curse work to maintain the romantic ideal—it can never be a "normal" relationship—and Buffy's youth positions it as a first love that subsequent relationships cannot match. The relationship is consistently figured in hyperbolic romantic terms, as when Buffy tells Angel, "When you kiss me, I want to die" ("Reptile Boy" 2005). That Buffy has to kill Angel to save the world is the high (or low) point of this romance ("Becoming Part 2" 2022), and his return from hell is a typically excessive way of continuing it. The very familiarity of this metanarrative offers pleasure to viewers, even those who may question the nature of this romance (arguably another kind of pleasure).

Although Angel's vampire nature (exceptional strength) and his soul (goodness) seem to put him on a par with Buffy, the relationship can be read very differently. Angel is older and more experienced, and allegorically he is the dangerous older boyfriend, Buffy the young girl led astray. Furthermore, because Buffy sees the relationship as "fated," this leaves her powerless: "Don't love you? I'm sorry. You know what, I didn't know I got a choice in that" ("The Prom"). Buffy's emotional engagement with Angel leads her to neglect her responsibilities as the Slayer at several points (as with Kendra's threat to Angel). Thus Buffy's feelings for Angel make her, as her mother points out, "*just like any other young woman in love*" ("The Prom," my emphasis). Buffy's lack of agency is highlighted when Angel decides that it would be best for Buffy if he left Sunnydale and, despite her protests, does just that. Ang's reading of tragic soap characters such as Sue Ellen in *Dallas* can be applied in a modified way here.

> Whereas in other narratives pleasure comes from the assurance and confirmation of a happy end—as with the romantic union . . . involvement with a character like Sue Ellen is conditioned by the prior knowledge that no such happy ending will ever occur. Instead, pleasure must come from living through and negotiating with the crisis itself. (1997: 161)

Although Buffy is not as passive as Sue Ellen, viewers who are able to identify the conflicting metanarratives of horror (good is rewarded and evil is defeated) and serial drama (no one can be happy for long) recognize and experience pleasure in a similar way. Despite Buffy and

Angel's wish to love "forever," serial narrative ensures otherwise (Saxey 2001: 196).

This romance sets a pattern for Buffy's subsequent relationships, mainly short-lived until she meets Riley Finn in season 4. Buffy states that dating Riley was an attempt to be normal, but to long-term viewers this relationship has much in common with Buffy's first love. Riley is also older than Buffy, and as Agent Finn, rising star in the Initiative, he is a superhero too. Yet Buffy is able to have a "healthy" (normal, "good") sex life with Riley, with the implication that sex is no longer "bad" for young women. This is presented as tied strongly to the need for action: the relationship is all about physicality (see Simkin 2004b). Buffy's size becomes a visible issue with Riley as it was not with Angel: the camera shows full body shots of Buffy and Riley walking side by side in seasons 4 and 5, and Riley has to bend down to kiss the top of Buffy's head in "No Place Like Home." This highlights Riley's anxieties about Buffy's power (see chapter 4), and eventually Buffy's agency is denied when Riley also decides to leave. Buffy was able to "tame" Angel's vampire nature and helping her serves as his redemption; likewise she saves Riley from the clutches of the Initiative, functioning both times as good girl and moral guardian.

Buffy's death and resurrection leads to a period of alienation and "bad" behavior in season 6, as she rebels against her responsibilities and even her place in the Scooby family. This is figured through her relationship with apparently the most inappropriate male partner possible—Spike, the vampire neutered by the Initiative in season 4 (though the liaison accommodates many viewers' desire to see Buffy and Spike get together). Spike developed a crush on Buffy in season 5 (a factor in Riley's departure), but although she accepted his contribution to the group, she rejected his advances. The whole relationship is "bad," and that its violence is explained by Buffy having come back "wrong" seems to reinforce this. Spike was originally a villain; he has no soul to make him "good" even though he can no longer live out his vampire nature. The relationship is founded on sex and violence (more overtly than with Riley), and indeed the two engage in the kind of S/M sex that previously identified bad characters, as in season 2. Buffy is shown as engaging in the relationship physically but not emotionally, something generally ascribed to the male partner.

The show is careful to point out that Buffy "uses" Spike as well as the reverse, and Buffy is often shown as physically on top in their sex scenes (often a way of coding women as active and independent). The standard language of passive females is invoked when Buffy admits to Tara that she "lets Spike do those things to" her, though this is also a way for Buffy to dissociate her good-girl self from such "bad" behavior ("Dead Things"). That Buffy claims (and the show seems to agree) that she is "not herself" when she does "those things" allows the show to present her having violent loveless sex (that Spike at least enjoys) but at the same time not to endorse it as acceptable.

This is the first relationship that does not follow the pattern set by her romance with Angel in that Buffy faces the realities (problems) of a relationship and retains agency. Spike sees himself as at a disadvantage, since he is "in love" with Buffy. This overturns Buffy's previous romantic instincts: she rejects Spike's declarations of love, any notion of romantic idealism is removed from their liaison by its basis in sex and violence and by Buffy's admission that she is simply "using" him. A brief return from Riley and the revelation that Spike is still morally "bad" lead Buffy to reject him and return to her "good" self ("As You Were" 6015).

This rejection sparks an excessive "bad" reaction from Spike: he tries to rape Buffy in her own home ("Seeing Red" 6019). The attempted rape ties in with the parallel narrative strand of Warren (who is accused of rape by Katrina) and Dark Willow (who "rapes" Warren). I discuss this in relation to Spike in chapter 6, but its effect on Buffy is multi-layered. First, it reverses the power dynamic: Buffy is used to having the upper hand, since she "uses" Spike, but more important, the physically powerful Slayer is frozen and initially does not fight back, appearing briefly as the powerless, fearful female victim (figure 4). Although she does manage to stop Spike, her vulnerability normalizes Buffy (demonstrating a recognizably "real" reaction); and by becoming the "victim" she also retains (regains) her innocence. Spike tries to persuade Buffy that this is a grand passion, invoking the kind of romance Buffy once believed in, and the scene offers another "feminist" explanation—that the myth of romance can be used to justify sexual violence. That this is enough to send Spike on a quest to regain his soul[13] and be the man Buffy deserves is the most emphatic indication yet that she acts as a civilizing influence on males.

Angel and Spike are consistently presented as bad boys, and Buffy often refers to her "bad boy thing" as a problem for a good girl (Riley is an attempt to "solve" this). Furthermore, the two vampires can both be read as ambivalent in terms of gender (see chapter 6), thus potentially blurring Buffy's own gendering through heterosexuality. That is, gender is fixed through opposition: she must be feminine because her

FIGURE 4: *Spike's attempted rape briefly shows Buffy as the helpless victim ("Seeing Red").*

partners are masculine; if they are not clearly masculine, then she need not be feminine.

All Buffy's relationships are failures in that they do not last. Yet her "failure" to find romantic fulfillment follows the serial pattern of deferment: it presents Buffy as capable of looking after herself and also shows her negotiating the perils of postfeminist romance. Buffy rejects romance twice: once after Riley has left and she encounters April, and again at the end of the series when she tells Angel that she is not "ready" for a successful relationship because she has not yet discovered who she is ("Chosen"). This gives out typically conflicting messages. One implication is that heterosexual romance is still the ideal. Alternatively, Buffy is still working out how to balance her own independence with the conventional submission of the female partner to the male.

Buffy as the Slayer embodies the female as moral guardian. She retains sexual/moral purity (despite regular sexual activity) and avoids unjust killing. The Slayer has been interpreted simply as a killer ("Restless" 4022 and "Buffy vs. Dracula" 5001), but Helford notes that "[a]s long as [Buffy] does not seem to enjoy committing acts of violence overmuch, she is not condemned" (2002: 23), and during season 5 Buffy rejects the way characters like Faith and Riley posited action as a high. This is a typical superhero/cop tension: killing is not enjoyable; it is a necessity justified by the fight against evil. In later seasons Buffy sometimes resembles the ambivalent mavericks of action and cop films ("There's only me. I am the law," in "Selfless"). The show also presents Buffy as a just warrior by deflecting her kills onto nonhuman objects, and Whedon admits that vampires in Buffy are "dusted" largely "because he does not want Buffy to be killing things that look like humans every week" (in Early 2002: note 3).

Not killing humans is one of the show's fixed moral rules, and Buffy's role of just warrior is underlined. "Being a Slayer doesn't give me a license to kill," she says in "Villains." Buffy has twice been misled into thinking she has killed a human ("Ted" 2011 and "Dead Things"), yet the closest she comes is in season 3, when she almost kills Faith, the other Slayer. Faith is characterized as "bad" because she kills humans as well as demons, and Buffy is "good" because she resists this. Yet during the season finale Faith and Buffy fight, and Buffy is prepared to kill Faith. As Tjardes points out, "The poisoning of Angel legitimizes Buffy's transgression" (2003: 75): the reason Buffy is prepared to kill Faith is that she has poisoned Angel and the only cure is the blood of a Slayer. This may explain Buffy's action, but it contradicts the show's stance on individual vendettas. Two other things help "justify" what Buffy does: the fact that Faith does not actually die (which glosses over the intention to kill) and, more obscurely, the fact that Faith is a Slayer, not a normal human.

At different times other characters are prepared to kill so that Buffy will remain innocent. Giles kills Ben at the end of season 5 to prevent Glory's return (see chapter 5), and Dark Willow kills Warren. The fact that Buffy civilizes Spike gives her a killer on a leash, as obliquely addressed in season 7. Here the killer in Spike can be "triggered" by a kind of post-hypnotic suggestion from the First Evil, making him a tool to be used against the Scoobies (as Buffy and the Scoobies have been using him against "evil" since he got his chip). When Giles and Principal Wood conspire to kill Spike because he is dangerous, he turns the tables and almost kills Wood. Buffy tells Wood that she has no time for vendettas (despite her own previous behavior) and that if he tries again Spike will kill him. "And more importantly," she concludes, "I'll let him" ("Lies

My Parents Told Me"). Buffy is a Slayer but not a killer. Others kill for her so she can stay a good girl.[14]

Good Girls, Bad Girls

Buffy's good girls imply that adhering too strongly to ideal notions of femininity is a self-defeating strategy for postfeminist young women who aspire to autonomy. It has even been suggested that "the so-called 'women's virtues' are merely the traits women have developed to survive under patriarchy" (Miller 2003: 44). Kendra is too good because she is too passive and dependent (just as Faith is bad because she is too active and independent; see chapter 3). Tara is too good at being a nurturing "natural" female, and this positions her almost entirely in the personal or domestic sphere, a consequence of removing her from patriarchal structures. As a literal construction of femininity, April is too good to be true. Dawn is generally an object of protection rather than an active subject. The ability to construct more fluid good-girl identities is restricted to major characters like Buffy and Willow and, while apparently unaffected by sexuality and ethnicity, is still limited to particular race and class categories (white, middle class).

The really good girls all die: Buffy and Willow, in different ways, are also "bad." I demonstrate in the next chapter that good and bad girls share many characteristics, largely relating to power and its exercise. Buffy can be socially "bad" but always stays morally good, and she personifies the notion that a powerful girl cannot be a traditional good girl. "Plain old Willow" is good, while "Super Willow" turns bad before being redeemed. Willow remains more ambivalent (and more powerful) than Buffy. Because she is not "normal" (traditionally feminine) and not heterosexual, she blurs boundaries more effectively and manages to somehow exist outside patriarchal structures — she is the least contained by traditional categories.

Good partners offer the "reward" of romance, but these girls cannot have power *and* a successful relationship, partly because of the demands of serial narrative, but partly because they seek agency in their romance relationships. The subject positions offered by Buffy and Willow allow a recognition of the complex negotiation involved in romance by females trying to retain independence and agency. That Buffy is left without a partner at the end of the series has mixed implications for postfeminist protagonists and heterosexual romance. Of course, these ambivalences need not be taken up or recognized by any or all viewers. After researching male viewers of *Buffy*, Lee Parpart concludes that "for a certain type of 'cultured' heterosexual male reader there is nothing quite so titillating as a young woman with sound moral principles" (2003: 89). This is enhanced by Buffy's active sex life. Power, goodness, gender, and sexuality are inevitably linked in the representation of the good-girl characters, and in different ways than in the bad girls and the male characters discussed in later chapters.

3 Bad Girls

"IT'S NOTHING TO
BE ASHAMED OF,
IT'S WHO WE ARE"

Bad girls are often used on *Buffy* as dark shadows of good girls, so inevitably there are similarities between good girls and bad. While I have suggested that many female characters on the show are visibly negotiating viable postfeminist identities, the bad girls (with one exception) rarely seem to struggle to define themselves. Largely because they are not human (I discuss female vampires, Darla, Drusilla, Vamp Willow, and Vamp Harmony; the third Slayer, Faith; and the hell-god, Glory) and are not operating within "normal" human society, the bad girls do not need to adhere to socially produced gender roles. More complex is the interaction of "feminism" and "femininity" in these characters. Bad girls are often excessive, and their excess can reveal the ways in which femininity is constructed and policed. For example, bad girls are often sexualized. This makes them bad in the sense of "deviant" but also situates their power as sexual power, and therefore as operating within patriarchal structures. The show employs several strategies to contain the power and appeal of the bad girls so that they do not appear to be "better" than the good girls.

Bad girls and wicked women have always been popular with viewers, perhaps because the villainess was one of the few available examples of a strong female character. Hollows notes that Alexis from prime-time soap *Dynasty* attracted both female viewers and gay men, and studies have observed that the "villainess . . . was loved and admired for her transgressions and independence" (2000: 98). Just as some of the good girls in *Buffy* threaten to violate the conventions of patriarchy, so too and in far greater degree do the bad girls. It is part of what makes them bad. Like the villainess, the bad girls of *Buffy* allow the viewer to take up different subject positions that challenge those of focal characters. These subject positions allow the viewer to reject "good" appropriate behavior, to act out being bad, as I suggested in relation to Dark Willow. In this way, "the stock figure of the villainess on both prime-time and daytime soaps has not infrequently been given . . . a 'feminist' inflection" (Mayne 1997: 89). That the bad girls are not always punished for their behavior and that their stories often lack closure demonstrates how the show authorizes viewers' pleasure in these characters.

Female Vampires: Totally Buffy's Archnemeses

"Vampires are a paradox . . . demon in a human body [they] walk in both worlds and belong to neither" ("Who Are You?" 4016). As demonic monsters, vampires are opposed to humanity, but Joan Gordon and Veronica Hollinger point out that in postmodern vampire texts "boundaries between 'human' and 'monstrous' become increasingly problematized" (1997: 5). The struggle between humanity and monstrosity is played out literally and metaphorically in *Buffy*. Horror often presents monsters disrupting social stability (Tony Williams 1996: 18), but Whedon has argued that "twisted and scary" humans can replace actual monsters (in McDonald 2000: 64). *Buffy* unbalances binary oppositions in the way that Gordon and Hollinger suggest, and many of the show's human characters struggle with their own monstrosity or darkness. *Buffy*'s vampires can be both alien object (demon, monster) and sympathetic subject, souled or human (both Angel and Spike lose or regain their souls during the show). Arguably, male vampires are used to problematize boundaries between human and monster, while female vampires, though retaining the attraction of the villainess, remain monsters, objects of fear. Kathleen K. Rowe (in a discussion of *Roseanne*) explains that the "unruly woman" often "evokes not only delight but disgust and fear" (1997: 76), and many of the bad girls embody this contradiction.

Female vampires have been with us since stories were told about the "real-life" Countess Elizabeth Bathory (who reputedly bathed in blood to keep her looks) and Sheridan LeFanu wrote "Carmilla" (in 1872, before *Dracula* was published). A range of female vampire stories has since emerged in fiction and film. Like the horror and vampire genres, female vampires are about transgression, the disruption of stability and the boundaries between life and death, human and monster, old and young, and mother and child.[1] Hollinger sees vampires as deconstructive because of this boundary crossing (1997: 199), and the female vampire in particular undergoes many transformations (from good to bad, from weak to strong, from victim to predator, and from pure to sexual). Thus I agree with Barbara Creed that the female vampire is "monstrous

—and also attractive—precisely because she does threaten to undermine the formal and highly symbolic relations of men and women essential to the continuation of patriarchal society" (1993a: 61). Female vampires are almost always sexualized and, because of their aggressive predatory nature, masculinized (conversely, both male victims and the male vampire may be feminized). Female vampires have often been implicitly or explicitly lesbian (see "Carmilla," Jewelle Gomez's *Gilda Stories*, or movies like *The Hunger* [1983] and *Nadja* [1995]). Although horror usually works to disrupt institutions like the family (another vampire violation here is incest), I argue that female vampires on *Buffy* are initially defined through heterosexual relationships and "family," and these function both to gender and to limit them.

DARLA

The teaser for the very first episode of *Buffy* ("Welcome to the Hellmouth") shows a boy breaking into Sunnydale High with a cute blonde in tow. Described in the original script as "timid," she is apparently nervous, though identifiable even here as a bad girl (she is breaking and entering, and is implicitly sexually active). Once reassured that there are no witnesses, she transforms into a monster and feeds on the boy. This vampire, later named Darla, is the first on *Buffy*, the first to show the characteristic vamp face, and the first to attack and feed on a human. Her initial presentation adds another spin to Whedon's oft-quoted comment: "I would love to see a movie in which a blond wanders into a dark alley, takes care of herself and deploys her powers" (in Bellafante 1997: 82). Like the vampire slayer, the show's vampires reverse traditional generic roles: *Buffy*'s first vampire is not a tall dark stranger wearing an opera cloak; she is a petite blonde with a "catholic schoolgirl look" ("Angel" 1007). Darla was featured in *Buffy* season 1 until she was staked by Angel. She later appears in flashbacks and becomes an important character in *Angel* the series.

Darla is not a postmodern teen like Buffy and the Scoobies; she is hundreds of years old (though still presented as a "girl"). In flashbacks Darla wears period clothes, generally sumptuous dresses or ensembles finished by elaborate hairdressing or hats, and in addition to demonstrating her age, such costuming underlines traditional "femininity." Darla is often seen on *Buffy* in vamp face, making her more obviously a monster, while Angel and Spike are seen less frequently in vamp face as their popularity and roles increase. Although Zoe Williams states that "the vampiric lifestyle in *Buffy* is characterized by alienation, loneliness, guilt and self-loathing" (2001: 34), this is patently not true for the female vampires. Darla accepts her nature and tells Angel, "It's nothing to be ashamed of, it's who we are, it's what makes eternal life worth living" ("Angel"), words I have taken as characteristic of the bad-girl attitude, indicated by their inclusion in the chapter title.

At first glance it seems that Darla can "take care of herself and deploy her powers" as a vampire, but this power is presented in a contradictory fashion. Darla is more than 400 years old ("Angel"), and her physical power is clear: she kills henchvamps when they fail the Master, and she attacks Buffy's mother, Joyce. In the showdown at The Bronze in "Angel," Darla shoots Angel with two handguns. (Guns cannot harm vampires, as she points out, but they could easily kill Buffy; see season 6.) Yet Darla does not last long in *Buffy*. She is the first vampire to really fight Buffy (in "Welcome to the Hellmouth"), and this effort is less than impressive. She is saved by Luke, the Master's second in command; tells him that Buffy is "strong"; and then leaves him to deal with the Slayer.

Darla is largely identified by her relationships with significant male characters, and this is one way to limit her impact as a powerful female. In conversation about Sunnydale Darla says, "I have family here" ("Welcome to the Hellmouth"). The important members of this "family" in season 1 are the Master, an ancient vampire and the season villain, and Angel (Drusilla and Spike are added later). *Angel* reveals that Darla was sired by the Master; here in *Buffy* he laments her death, saying, "She was my favorite. For four hundred years" ("Angel"). This was implied in previous episodes as Darla escaped punishment for infringements of the Master's position (for instance, in "The Harvest" 1002). After Luke is killed, Darla becomes second in command, and even before this we see her leading the vampires to The Bronze for the Harvest (although the original script stipulates Luke in the center). But it is clear that Darla remains subordinate to the patriarch of the family and enjoys power only at his sufferance. She is his daughter, but it is Angel, her prodigal son, of whom the Master says, "He was to sit at my right hand come the day" ("Angel").

We see Darla sire Angel in flashback during "Becoming Part 1" (2021). It has been pointed out that "Darla turns Angel by slicing open her chest and forcing his mouth toward the open wound . . . , a gesture that Drusilla repeats when returning her former 'grandmother' Darla ["The Trial" *Angel* 2009]" (Busse 2002: 214). This is a powerful image of the female vampire as monstrous mother (though *Dracula* is another obvious intertext). Darla remains very aware that she is Angel's "sire" and that she has power over him. From her first appearance she plays the traditional vampire role of sexual predator, and subsequent episodes of *Angel* reveal that the human Darla was "a whore" dying of syphilis ("Darla" 2007, "The Trial")—her sexuality is labeled as socially "bad." When she turns Angel, he is easy prey because he sees in her the promise both of power (she is "a lady") and of sexual pleasure. Her taunt, "Are you certain you're up to the challenge?" further emphasizes her greater age and experience. Darla creates both Angelus and Angel, as she tells Buffy: "I made him. And I brought him that Gypsy girl" ("Angel"). Tania Modleski suggests that with a typical villainess, "the spectator has the satisfaction of seeing men suffer the same anxieties and guilt that women usually experience and seeing them receive similar kinds of punishment for their transgressions" (1997: 42): parts of Darla's relationship with Angel can be read in a similar fashion.

Yet in season 1 of *Buffy* Angel does not act like a child.[2] He and Darla are ex-lovers, and after deliberately making him angry, she says with satisfaction, "You're hurting me. That's good" ("Angel"), implying that (as with other vampire couples on *Buffy*) their sexual relationship is violently physical. Despite Darla's apparent control, the implication is that she still loves Angel (betraying "feminine" emotional weakness). She is unwilling to let him go, to the extent that the relationship rules and defines her. This is clear from the way she was a relatively minor character in *Buffy* but is key to revelations about Angel in his own series. In *Buffy* Darla functions as the rejected female, jealous and seeking revenge on the lover who cast her off and on his new romantic interest. Darla plans to bring Angel "back to the fold" ("Angel") and cannot understand why he rejects this "chance to come home" and to "rule with [her] in the Master's court for a thousand years."

Darla threatens Buffy through her identity as vampire and her relationship with Angel/us. She displays many disruptive aspects of the female vampire, yet she is kept in check by her positioning as subordinate to two males: she is the Master's daughter and Angel's lover (not primarily his "sire"—a refusal of the more common generic masculinization of the female vampire). This also serves to make her a bad *girl*, feminizing as well as domesticating her. The first bad girl on *Buffy* is punished with death by Angel, the ex-lover whose rejection colored her identity. Yet Darla doesn't stay dead. Dusted by a stake in *Buffy*, she returns, more powerful than ever, in *Angel*, but with her "feminine" weaknesses still intact.[3]

Drusilla, the second major female vampire, enters *Buffy* in season 2, when she arrives in Sunnydale with Spike and they take over the Master's power base. In recent scholarship, Drusilla is almost exclusively mentioned in connection with Spike (notably, he appears on screen first), Angel/us, Kendra (the Slayer she killed), or Darla. Although it might seem that Spike and Dru sweep away the Master's old order, Drusilla continues some of the Master's themes: she consistently refers to a particular group of vampires as a family, and she tries to reunite them. In *Angel* Dru refers to Darla as "grandmother"; in *Buffy* she refers to Angel as "daddy," and she makes a singular speech when Angel loses his soul and reverts to Angelus. "You've come home. . . . We're family again. We'll feed and we'll play" ("Innocence"). Kristina Busse comments, "What makes this scene so startling is the concurrency of sexuality, killing, and familial affection, pointedly exemplified in Drusilla's characterization of family as feeding and playing together" (2002: 210). As I have already mentioned in chapters 1 and 2, the Scooby family also mix sex, violence, and affection, and Buffy and Spike's season 6 liaison underlines this. Even at this early stage, then, the show demonstrates similarities between "good" and "bad" characters, and especially between "good" and "bad" girls.

Drusilla is Spike's sire, and at times she plays the nurturing mother, a "natural" female role. Initially she is weak and Spike acts as her protector and carer, but after a restorative ritual (involving a transfusion of blood from her sire), these roles are reversed. During "Passion" (2017) she brings Spike a puppy, going on to coax him to eat as a mother does a fractious toddler, even doing the airplane routine—"Now open up for mummy." In "Fool for Love" viewers see Dru turn William (the human who becomes Spike) in a scene reminiscent of that between Darla and Angel, and although we do not see Dru offer her blood (as she does to Darla in *Angel*), Kaveney points out the reference to mothers in this scene (2001: 36, note 15). The same episode demonstrates Dru's maternal pride as she tells Darla and Angel, "My little Spike just killed a Slayer." These later appearances emphasize Drusilla's family orientation and her mothering of Spike. Like Darla with Angel, Dru tries to persuade Spike "to be family again," calling him her "darling deadly boy" and nurturing him physically and emotionally ("Crush" 5014). Arguably Drusilla's role here is tailored to demonstrate Spike's transformation, and Dru's attempt fails as Darla's did because Angel and Spike are in love with their antithesis, the Slayer—bad-girl vampires can never be better than good-girl Buffy.

Again this female vampire is lover as well as parent. It has been pointed out that season 2 was "the first time romantic love between two vampires has been shown in the Buffy-verse" (Larbalestier 2002: 232), and Kaveney further suggests that "[Spike's] tragedy, and that of Darla and Drusilla, is that they are capable of passionate love, but not of the broader emotional register that goes with it" (2001: 9). Dru confirms this in "Crush" when she says, "We can love quite well, if not wisely." While the ability to "love" can be read as a positive development within the horror genre, in that it strengthens Dru's "humanity," from a feminist point of view heterosexual romance subordinates a powerful female character by situating her within patriarchal structures. This is exaggerated in Drusilla, since she appears as one-half of a traditional gender binary—she is passive, weak, and emotional, while Spike is active and strong. To Spike, Dru is a romantic ideal of femininity, she is his princess, pet, baby, "black goddess" ("What's My Line? Part 2"), his "salvation" ("Crush"). But no one can live up to an ideal, and Dru is presented as not above taking advantage Spike's love for her, manipulating him in a typically "feminine" way by playing up her weakness. Romantic love is further complicated by the family Drusilla values. When Angelus returns, a triangle is reestablished, and the two males vie for her attention.

This triangle is based on sex (and for the first time introduces overtly sexual vampires into *Buffy*).[4] Darla and Dru embody diametric representations of femininity: whore and nun. Angel describes his turning of Dru as one of the worst things he has done, because she "was pure and sweet and chaste." Angelus tortured her and killed her family until she "eventually fled to a convent, and the day she took her Holy Orders, I turned her into a demon" ("Lie to Me" 2007). Thus Drusilla also violates boundaries between good and evil, Christian and pagan, pure and sexual. While Darla is presented more traditionally as a sexual predator, Drusilla is initially a sexual victim (of Angelus), and she is removed as a sexual threat to other characters because she is always presented as partner to Spike or Angelus.

Dru's sexual relationships are cast as "deviant," involving S/M and incest (violating family boundaries), and this identifies her as a bad girl in both senses (in terms of morality and traditional gendering). The links between sex and violence can be seen in her relationships with both Spike and Angelus and, like Darla, Dru taunts Angel, reminding him of how he used to "hurt" her ("Lie to Me"). Although the sexual aspect of the scene where she turns Spike may be less overt than in the Darla/Angel scene, it is still present ("I see what you want. . . . Do you want it?"). Diane DeKelb-Rittenhouse notes that "blood drinking as the primary erotic act" in *Buffy* is illustrated by Dru's first appearance: "Drusilla cuts open Spike's cheek and licks off the resulting blood in a highly sensual exchange between the two" (2002: 149–150). In "Crush" these connections are made explicit when Dru offers Spike a female victim at The Bronze and feeds on a male, moving to the music with pelvic thrusts.

These relationships work to present Drusilla as unfaithful, promiscuous. As Zoe Williams points out, "Throughout vampire literature, the undead have turned ordinary, chaste women into crazy slappers (compare Lucy in *Dracula*, turned to 'voluptuous wantonness')" (2001: 34). During Buffy and Spike's temporary truce at the end of season 2, Buffy exclaims, "The whole earth may be sucked into hell and you want my help because your girlfriend's *a big ho*?" ("Becoming Part 2," my emphasis). *The Watcher's Guide* blames Dru, rather than Angelus or Spike, for the tense sexual triangle (Golden and Holder 1998: 115). Michael P. Levine and Steven Jay Schneider suggest that Dru in particular is "debased" because of her promiscuity, concluding, "These are the girls that one has sex with according the rules of the diegesis, not the ones who are love objects" (2003: 307). This discounts Spike's "love" for her, and in any case reading Drusilla as either a sex object or a love object reduces her to a passive female. "Lover's Walk" reveals that Dru has been unfaithful to Spike with a chaos demon.[5] This is subsequently reversed, so that Dru explains her behavior as a result of Spike's developing crush on Buffy: "You can't blame a girl, Spike, you're all covered with her. I look at you, all I see is the Slayer" ("Fool for Love"). Added to her victim status with Angelus, this reinforces Dru not as a sexually active and independent female (like the postfeminist good girls) but as a victim who cannot keep her man.

Yet Drusilla remains powerful and threatening. Initially she is physically weak: she was almost killed by a mob in Prague, and at her first appearance Spike tells her, "You shouldn't be walking around, you're weak" ("School Hard" 2003). In "Lie to Me" she is taken hostage by Buffy, who uses her to escape from Spike and his henchvamps. Dru is thus seen to be both human (weak) and monstrous (strong), though alternatively her strength could be "feminist" and her weakness "feminine." She is not only Angelus' child, she also has a childlike manner, and her collection of dolls underlines both this and a conventional "femininity." Most often this is displayed through desires that must be instantly gratified, as when her insistence, "I want a treat. I *need* a treat," persuades Spike to include her in the ill-fated outing in "Lie to Me." After the ritual Drusilla undergoes a transformation from weak and passive to strong and dominant, an almost direct role reversal in terms of gendered characteristics. "I'll see that you get strong again," she tells the unconscious Spike, "like me" ("What's My Line? Part 2").[6] This transformation is coded clearly through clothing, so that Dru wears white nightgowns when sickly and languishing, but red and black when restored to health and power, and Arwen Spicer notes that Dru even adopts Spike's "signature colors" in a visualization of their reversal (2002: 8).[7] Like Darla, Dru is at once a girl in appearance and often in behavior but also a powerful and experienced woman.

Transformed, Dru is more obviously hedonistically evil. In "Surprise" (2013) she threatens another vampire with blinding, delights in Spike's present of the apocalyptic Judge, and squeals, "Do it again! Do it again!" after the Judge kills for the first time. Later she suggests to Angelus that he should kill a toddler ("I Only Have Eyes for You" 2019), subverting "natural" female mothering. Dru also becomes the leader of the vampire group, though even before this Angel offers her the chance to take Spike and leave Sunnydale, as if she were in charge ("Lie to Me"). Drusilla rarely engages in prolonged physical fights, but both she and the Master are more powerful as vampires because of their ability to hypnotize their prey.

The real proof of Dru's power comes at the end of season 2 when she kills Kendra ("Becoming Part 1") — becoming the only vampire except Spike known to have killed a Slayer.[8] After Dru makes a confident "come on" gesture to Kendra there is a brief fight, and Dru takes Kendra by the throat. With a few words — "Look at me, deary, be in my eyes, be in me" — Drusilla hypnotizes Kendra; they sway together until Dru slashes Kendra's throat with her nails. The dialogue here places Drusilla in the dominant position, relegating Kendra to that of a subordinate, or a child. As Kendra's body falls, Dru the monstrous mother says, "Night night," and blows her a kiss. The shock value is heightened because Dru neither shows her vamp face, nor feeds on her kill. Reading the scene is further complicated since Kendra is a less developed character; the viewer may be less likely to take her position (as mentioned in the previous chapter). Indeed, viewers may find themselves taking up contradictory positions here: that Dru's power is finally demonstrated is an attraction; that she kills Kendra makes her morally bad.

Chin describes the hypnosis as "an almost sexualized dance" and calls the clash "a G-rated lesbian interlude" (2003: 98). With this in mind and given what is shown in flashbacks, it is interesting to speculate on how Darla and Dru interacted. I have often wondered if they and Angelus formed a triangle similar to that in season 2 with Angelus, Drusilla, and Spike (Angel calls Dru and Darla "my women" in "Fool for Love"). Alternative readings like this can enhance Dru's "feminist" potential; if she is no longer strictly heterosexual then, like Willow and Tara, she escapes at least some of the patriarchal social structures designed to keep women subordinate to men.

Part of Drusilla's menace comes from her mystical power (hypnosis but also visions) and her madness (both signs of her mysterious female nature). Spicer observes that Dru is "so much the 'irrational woman' that she is literally insane" (2002: 7), and Rowe notes that "[l]ike other labels of deviancy, madness is often attached to the unruly woman" (1997: 78, note 8). Dru's mystical power is emphasized from her first appearance, when she identifies the Anointed One and has a vision of the Slayer ("School Hard"). Drusilla's visions simultaneously give her power and code her as a disruptive female. In "Becoming Part 1" a flashback to "London 1860" shows Angelus playing with the human Drusilla in a fascinating scene which highlights this tension. Throughout Drusilla calls Angelus "Father," thinking that he is a priest: later he becomes her "daddy" and vampiric sire. Dru is in church to confess and receive absolution, and she insists, "I want to be good, I want to be pure." But her ability to "see" things is clearly marked as a transgression of the patriarchal order connoted by the church in which she confesses, an order policed not only by men of authority but by women who know their place: "Me mum says I'm cursed. My seeing things is an affront to the Lord. That only He's supposed to see anything before it happens." Thus even as a pure and devout human, Drusilla is already "an evil thing." A comparison could be drawn here with Tara's situation in "Family," discussed in the previous chapter. Both Tara and Dru have a mystical power that is limited by the structures and language of patriarchy. In Dru's case, however, the show does not insert a sympathetic "feminist" explanation; rather, such explanations are up to individual viewers to construct.

Wall and Zryd state that Drusilla is "the most chaotic character, figured as both insane and guided by her 'gift' of prophesy [*sic*] and premonition" (2001: 57). Dru's prophetic pronouncements combine (using Julia Kristeva's terms) both the pre-oedipal semiotic of the female (she often seems to talk nonsense) and the symbolic law of the father (her words come true). Drusilla demonstrates "instinctive" knowledge, which can be characterized as "naturally" female. Busse notes that *Buffy* implies "the deep connection between those who have shared blood" because "Drusilla knows instinctively when Angel has lost his soul" (2002: 213). This is not true for all vampires, since Angel insists that Drusilla must be dead in "Surprise." Dru later tells Spike, "I don't believe in science. All those bits and molecules no one's ever seen. I trust eyes and heart alone," articulating a clear opposition between masculinized science and feminized "nature" or instinct ("Crush").[9]

Drusilla's psychic abilities link her with Buffy. Buffy dreams that Dru kills Angel in "Surprise"; later she dreams herself at Dru's party, wearing Dru's own nightgown, and when she really appears at the party Dru tells her, "I only dreamed you'd come." Following Nina Auerbach (1995), all vampires could be seen as reflections of ourselves, dissolving the boundaries between self and enemy, and this fits into the show's postmodern presentation of identity as inherently unstable. Buffy and Dru are further paralleled through their complex and tainted relationships to Angel/us (as are Darla and Buffy in season 1). Drusilla's transformation in season 2 mirrors Buffy's own developing sexuality, also figured through a relationship with Angel/us, though Buffy's is (perhaps superficially) more equal and postfeminist, while Dru is presented as a passive victim.

Like almost all the bad girls, Drusilla escapes several times, the serial nature of *Buffy* allowing her to reappear at intervals. These recurrent appearances underline not only Dru's power but also her insistence on identifying herself as part of a vampire family, accepting her role as subordinate. Dru's disruptive potential is always contained by her relationship to Angel or Spike: she never appears independently of them. I see Drusilla as one of the most conservatively presented female characters: she has little of the good girls' postfeminist agency, and she displays many negative "feminine" characteristics: weakness, passivity, manipulation, childishness, infidelity, and madness. Drusilla's madness can "excuse" her inappropriate behavior (the same strategy is adopted with Faith and Glory). That she is labeled "mad," "bad," and sexually "deviant" is itself an indication of how gender roles are policed.

VAMP WILLOW

"The Wish" introduced a parallel version of Willow as a vampire, reprised in "Doppelgangland." Playden has noted Willow's " 'nomadism,' her crossing of social and moral boundaries" (2001: 140), and I have already mentioned that Willow's identity is presented as particularly unstable. Vamp Willow at first seems to be Willow's dark shadow but with hindsight acts more as a *fore*shadowing of her internal contradictions, brought out subsequently in Dark Willow. Thus Vamp Willow in dress, speech, and action appears to be everything Willow is not and offers similar viewing pleasure to Dark Willow. Where Willow is at this stage still timid and retiring, Vamp Willow is confident, powerful, and successful in establishing what she wants and getting it—characteristics that might be identified as "feminist." Although Vamp Willow appears in "The Wish" with Vamp Xander, she does not appear subordinate to him. Arguably in this alternative reality, Vamp Willow takes Darla's role as the Master's favorite,[10] holding a high position in the vampire hierarchy (she and Vamp Xander are described as the Master's "most vicious disciples"), but she is not explicitly positioned as the Master's child.

Vamp Willow is physically powerful (she beats up the Mayor's henchvamps in "Doppelgangland"), but her character is based on an overt sexuality that stands out against the innocence of good-girl Willow. Appearance is one aspect: Vamp Willow, like many other vampires, wears leather and similar colors but more modern styles than Dru.[11] She verges on a parody (or "masquerade") of "femininity": her cleavage is emphasized—in "Doppelgangland" Willow dressed as Vamp Willow exclaims, "Gosh, look at those!"—and she is heavily made up. Her relationship with Vamp Xander and her scenes with Angel in "The Wish" establish Vamp Willow as sexual; the latter highlight the kinky "bad" nature of this sexuality—"That's right, puppy, Willow's gonna make you bark." Like Drusilla, Vamp Willow derives sexual pleasure from pain, and while Willow calls Angel "puppy," Dru referred to Angelus as "bad dog" ("What's My Line? Part 2"). Vamp Willow also talks a lot about "play." These torture scenes (and the fact that she appears often in vamp face) clearly establish Vamp Willow's badness: like Dru, she is both morally bad and not a traditional good girl. Pleasure can certainly be gained from her alternate version of Willow, her acting out as "bad" and as more sexy or sexual than regular Willow. Sexuality is further explored in "Doppelgangland," where Willow comments that her double seems to be "kinda gay," foreshadowing her relationship with Tara. This fits previous representations of female vampires as lesbian, and it further collapses boundaries: a "same-sex" pairing here is also "a same-person pairing," as Justine Larbalestier points out (2002: 231). Vamp Willow's "badness" is so exaggerated that she seems unlikely to instill conscious fear in the viewer, but her appearance questions the good-girl persona of regular Willow.

The use of Vamp Willow demonstrates *Buffy*'s tendency to blur boundaries, particularly those between self and other. She is another example of the transformation that affects every regular character on the show. Her disruptive potential is contained largely by her positioning in an alternative reality rather than by making her subordinate to males (just as Willow resists the limitations of patriarchy and heterosexual romance). While she enters the regular Sunnydale, Vamp Willow is hugely entertaining because of the trouble she causes and her contrast with Willow, creating viewing pleasure and a new subject position safely relegated to fantasy (unlike the later Dark Willow). But like Darla she is staked, punished for her transgressive behavior by her ex-lover, in this case Oz. In fact her death is shown twice, at the end of each episode; but, as mentioned in chapter 2, she returns more subtly at the end of season 6, when her words are repeated by Dark Willow.

VAMP HARMONY

Vamp Harmony offers another vampire version of a character viewers knew first as a human. As the show intimated through Vamp Willow, a vampire's nature is not entirely removed from that of the human it was. The human Harmony was one of the Cordettes and took over that group when Cordelia lost her cool by dating Xander. Vamp Harmony first appeared in season 4 (having been bitten during the graduation day battle at the end of season 3) and recurs subsequently as a sometime girlfriend of Spike. This pairing constructs Vamp Harmony in particular ways. First, it positions her as an adjunct to a more popular and focal male character, again gendering through heterosexuality. Second, Spike's role as a comic character here means that Vamp Harmony's function is also largely comic. This works because Vamp Harmony, unlike most other female vampires on *Buffy*, is *not* a threatening and powerful figure. In general she is ineffective and a failure at whatever she tries to do, whether it is becoming "totally [Buffy's] archnemesis" ("Out of My Mind" 5004), getting her own gang together, or maintaining a relationship with Spike.

Harmony is not substantially transformed by her vampirism; she is a parody of a vampire villainess. She has enhanced strength, but the slow-motion slapping and hair-pulling fight scene with Xander in "The Initiative" (4007) shows that she does not always use it. Vamp Harmony also displays an enhanced sexuality,[12] but this does not empower her—her relationship with Spike is highly sexualized and unequal. Though at one stage Vamp Harmony tells him that she won't take him back (using

"feminist" rhetoric reminiscent of Anyanka)—"I've been doing a lot of reading and I'm in control of my own power" ("Pangs" 4008)—she capitulates. That she puts up with Spike staking her in "The Harsh Light of Day," with his rebound from Drusilla, and with his developing crush on Buffy (to the extent of being persuaded to "play" Buffy in sex games) only demonstrates Vamp Harmony's weakness. Thus, although she tells Spike, "I'm powerful and I'm beautiful and I don't need you to complete me" ("Pangs"), like Darla and Dru, Vamp Harmony is victim to "feminine" emotions and *is* defined primarily by her relationship with a more significant male.

She is also the epitome of the dizzy blonde. In this way Vamp Harmony takes on a contemporary female comic role, as Zoe Williams describes it: "Ladies still get the laughs, but usually on account of that hilariously dozy/self-deluding/imbecilic thing they've just done" (2001: 33) and she functions as Buffy's antithesis (as with Anya, viewers laugh *with* Buffy but *at* Harmony). Harmony therefore serves to contrast Buffy and Willow's postfeminist strength and independence. Yet Vamp Harmony's very position as a comic character offers various subversive pleasures, disrupting what viewers thought they knew about vampires and confirming the transformation of Spike. And at times Vamp Harmony's comedy value lies not simply in what she is (butt of the audience's laughs) but in what she dares to say. Like Anya, she acts as a wise fool, a truth teller. In one thing Vamp Harmony *is* successful: she escapes punishment and death in both *Buffy* and *Angel*. Perhaps this confirms her weakness (she is not worth the effort), but it means her story need not be over yet, and I was delighted to discover while writing that Vamp Harmony is to return in season 5 of *Angel*.

The Human Monster

One of the most interesting bad girls in *Buffy* is the third Slayer, Faith (the episode where she bonds with Buffy is called "Bad Girls"; see figure 5). Kendra's death at the end of season 2 activates Faith, who arrives in Sunnydale during season 3. Faith shares characteristics with the other bad girls, yet she is human, and arguably she is meant to be a good girl, a hero, another Buffy. Of all the bad girls I identify here she is the only one allowed redemption, and she is the most discussed in *Buffy*

FIGURE 5: *Faith shows Buffy how to have a good time,*
bad girl style ("Bad Girls").

studies (because of this, I mention only key factors). Like Drusilla and to
some extent Darla, Faith helped illuminate Buffy as a dark shadow of the
Slayer. Marti Noxon, writer and producer, has described Faith as "the
expression of the darker side of what it might mean to be empowered as
a slayer" (in Tjardes 2003: 70). Buttsworth notes that "women have been
constructed as more dangerous than men because they are supposedly
uncontrollable when violent" (2002: 192), and Faith, like Dark Willow,
exemplifies the uncontrollable nature of female power on *Buffy*.

Because Buffy and Faith are both Slayers there is inevitably competition between them, but Buffy always emerges as the "good" girl and
responsible Slayer. Like other young female characters in *Buffy*, Faith
is shown negotiating an identity that combines "feminism" and "femininity." The show's writers remove her as a threat to "good girls" Buffy
and Willow (in terms of succeeding in her negotiation better than they
do) by making her morally bad and by suggesting that Faith's difference arose because she has not had Buffy's advantages. "Different cir-
cumstances, that could be me," Buffy observes in "Doppelgangland," a
rare acknowledgement that her privileged position enables her to make

"choices" for her postfeminist identity that are not available to all young women. Like Kendra, Faith is Other than Buffy, if in more ambivalent terms.

In her discussion of all three slayers, Helford suggests that, "because [Faith] never repents her thievery, never attends school or displays any other evidence of seeking education, and never dresses in the kind of attire Buffy wears as part of 'proper' Sunnydale teen girlhood, the series casts her as lower in class than Buffy and her friends" (2002: 31). Faith therefore offers an interesting new subject position. She cannot fit in with the Scoobies because she does not share their middle-class background and her upbringing produces a different version of femininity. Helford points to various indicators of Faith's class, and the show hints at an abusive family background with an alcoholic mother. These factors are not restricted to working-class families, but they do not appear in the lives of the predominantly middle-class characters on the show. Family violence and drinking are only ever mentioned in Xander's home environment, and in chapter 5 I identify him as another character with ambivalent class origins.

The point is that Faith, being Other, can never be like Buffy. She herself notes: "Everybody asks, 'Why can't you be more like Buffy?' but did anyone ever ask if you could be more like me?" ("Enemies" 3017). This is brought to a climax in season 4 when Faith swaps bodies with Buffy, enabling Faith to finally experience Buffy's middle-class suburban life. In the showdown fight Faith-as-Buffy, having violated the boundaries between them, desperately tries to destroy herself and retain the Buffy-body that represents approval and respect. Hollows observes that "white middle-class femininity has not only been privileged over other forms of feminine identities, but only gets its meaning through its difference to forms of feminine identity which have been labeled as 'deviant' or 'dangerous,' identities which have usually been identified with black and white working-class women" (2000: 31). Faith is a prime example of this strategy.

The first indication that Faith is a bad girl is her unbridled sexuality (perhaps again related to class). Faith's femininity is sexualized, focused on her cleavage and glossy pout, and she is described by Willow as a "cleavagy slut-bomb" ("This Year's Girl" 4015). Her negotiation of a gendered identity contrasts sharply with Buffy's more demure version of femininity. *The Watcher's Guide Volume 2* describes Faith as "outrageous and visceral enough to make Buffy seem conservative by comparison" (Holder, Mariotte, and Hart 2000: 365), and this is underlined visually through coloring, hair, and clothing. Unlike Buffy and the other good girls, Faith does not restrict her sexual activity to long-term romance relationships. Instead she adopts a much more "masculine" independence, using sexual partners to satisfy her needs and then rejecting them and any emotional ties, as when she seduces and dismisses Xander in "Consequences" (3015). Like Anya's, Faith's sexual independence is not coded as a progressive "good" sign of postfeminism. Her teasing of Spike in "Who Are You?" and her familiarity with kinky S/M sex define her sexuality as transgressive, and when Faith has sex with Riley in Buffy's body ("Who Are You?"), she teases him, asking, "Am I a bad girl? Do you want to hurt me?"

Mendlesohn has argued that it is possible to read the connection between Faith and Buffy as a typical "antagonistic romance" (2002: 59–60), and Kaveney notes that when Faith is first in Buffy's body, she takes a bath that can be seen as "a form of perverse love-making" (2001: 22). Tjardes calls such readings "a resistant construction" (2003: 71), but if one pursues their line of reasoning, Faith's sexuality is not only transgressive in its predatory and promiscuous nature but in its very desire. Certainly this adds another dimension to Faith-as-Buffy's sexual teasing of Riley and Spike: she is not only trying to arouse them, she is also using her own sexuality to arouse Buffy's body. As with Drusilla, such resistant readings enhance Faith's "feminist" potential by removing her from the compulsory heterosexuality of patriarchy.

Faith brings a similar appetite to the violent activity of Slaying, and she connects sex and Slaying: "Isn't it funny how slaying just makes you hungry and horny?" Tjardes notes that "this line is one of the most quoted in viewer sites; it is often used as symbolic of Faith's attitudes" (2003: 69). In contrast with Buffy, Faith is "bad" not because she participates in sex and violence but because she enjoys them. Whedon reported, "We wanted to explore being a slayer—the power of it, the fun it could be, how intoxicating it could be. We used Faith" (in Tjardes 2003: 70), and arguably Faith verbalises the viewer's enjoyment of both sex and violence in the show.

Faith is presented as lacking the sense of responsibility and morality that Buffy and the other good girls display. While Buffy sees Slayer power as a responsibility, Faith sees it as evidence of superiority: "We are better. That's right. Better. People need us to survive" ("Consequences"). Faith lies, manipulates others (another "bad" and "feminine" trait that Darla and Dru share), commits crimes, and, when in Buffy's body, mocks Buffy's policing with her repetition of the phrase, "Because it's *wrong*." As Karl Schudt notes, Faith's play with these words demonstrates her understanding that "the word 'wrong' is an empty, emotivistic claim, which only has meaning because of the force behind it" (2003: 30). Faith even parodies Buffy's attitude: "I [Buffy] could be anything I want but instead I choose to pout and whine and feel the burden of Slayerness." It is the combination of Faith's exceptional power as a Slayer (force) and her desire to control her own destiny (be anything she wants) that makes Faith so menacing. Her excess and parody also help make visible the policing of gender roles.

Buffy is backed up physically and emotionally by the Scoobies, but Faith claims to neither want nor need help from anyone: "*I'm* on my side. And that's enough" ("Revelations" 3007). This masculinizes Faith further. Even before she turns "rogue," she rejects the control of the Council when they try to appoint her a Watcher: "I just have this problem with authority figures" ("Revelations"). Of course, Buffy's rejection of the Council has been presented and read as a "feminist" choice of independence. With Faith, however, the Council members attempt to enforce "the judgment of the disciplinary committee" ("Consequences"), and although I might read her disruptive female behavior here as being ordered by a patriarchal institution, the show's presentation avoids this interpretation by focusing on morality rather than gender. Buffy's resistance to authority is presented as a good postfeminist strategy, but Faith is shown to be increasingly uncontrollable. When she accidentally kills a man in the heat of a fight, she tells Buffy, "*You* don't get it. I. Don't. Care" ("Bad Girls"). Despite indications that she does feel the remorse she verbally denies to Buffy, as Tjardes points out, *Buffy* emphasizes Faith's remorselessness rather than her half-glimpsed confusion by repeating the above line in the "previously on *Buffy*" openings (2003: 71). Faith's rejection of emotion for action is another "masculine" trait, and Tjardes notes that she is "unwilling or unable to respond 'appropriately' [to the accidental death] through feminized dialogue and emotional processing" (72). That is, she denies emotion and lacks "natural" female skills in dealing with it.

Faith signs on with the Mayor, season 3's "big bad," after this crisis, a clear indication that she is now a bad girl in moral terms. Her work for the Mayor undercuts her independence by presenting her as the perfect subordinate and compliant daughter to the Mayor's boss and father figure (see chapter 7 for more on the Mayor). It has been suggested that "Faith's emotional insecurity—a consequence of childhood neglect and institutional abuse at the hand of her Watchers—leads her" to the

Mayor (Wall and Zryd 2001: 58). Certainly this relationship parallels and shadows that between Buffy and Giles and does offer security. As part of her larger argument concerning Buffy's relationships with men, Mendlesohn suggests that Faith fits a "girl-hater/girl-fearer paradigm, something that helps explain why Faith is incapable of trusting Buffy but creates her own 'Watcher' father figure in the person of the Mayor and was later willing to turn to Angel for help" (2002: 55). But this relationship is problematic for Faith's representation as an independent female agent. Faith's redemption begins with her betrayal of the Mayor—lying in a coma, she helps Buffy in a vision, giving her strength and knowledge for the finale fight.

Several commentators note that the show's treatment of Faith emphasizes the consequences of killing humans, but they do not directly connect this to Buffy's attempt to kill Faith, as discussed in the previous chapter. Similarly, *The Monster Book* positions Faith under the heading "The Human Monster," where she is described as "a supernatural being and, thus by our definition, a 'monster'" (Golden, Bissette, and Sniegoski 2000: 363), but Buffy is never defined in this way. Donald Keller observes that the show presents "Faith's feeling, throughout *her* dreams, that Buffy is a cold and methodical killer and that Faith is helpless to oppose her (the reverse of our usual assessment of the two)" (2002: 173), highlighting a rare authorization of Faith's subject position. That Faith is powerless to resist internalizing the conventional judgments of society is expressed by her gendered language in "Who Are You?" when she takes over Buffy's body. Here she tells Buffy-as-Faith, "You're nothing! You're disgusting! A useless, murdering bitch! You're *nothing*," and Greg Forster equates Faith's self-disgust and her moral awakening (2003: 18). Faith escapes and reemerges in *Angel* ("Five by Five" 1008 and "Sanctuary" 1009), where she begins her redemption. Unlike the female vampires, Faith cannot accept her "bad" nature. Instead she chooses to accept the law and take her place within ordered (patriarchal) society. Arguably Faith is allowed this chance at redemption because she proves she really *wants* to be a good girl, with all that implies for gendering as well as morality.

When Faith returns to *Buffy* toward the end of season 7 she is changed. She takes over leadership of the Scoobies and the Potentials from Buffy ("Empty Places"), but she seems reluctant to do this, takes the responsibility seriously, and never forgets who she is (in "Chosen" she says, "I'm an ex-con who didn't even finish high school"—class difference is again a subtext). When Faith is wounded in her one major engagement with Caleb and the First, Buffy takes over again. Although Buffy tells Amanda and Kennedy that what happened to Faith could have happened to her, it *does* happen to Faith and proves that Faith is always second best.

Faith's sexuality remains one of her defining characteristics, and the sexual tension between her and Spike threatens Buffy as much as her Slayer identity ("Dirty Girls" 7018). When Faith and Principal Wood have sex ("Touched" 7020), Faith both usurps Buffy's position (Buffy went on a date with Wood in "First Date" 7014) and accepts what Buffy has rejected ("We're just good friends," she tells Faith in "End of Days" 7021). In my reading, Wood functions as a domesticator. His relationship with Faith begins as a sexual one, and he matches her in boasting of sexual prowess, but he has more to offer. That he survives to "surprise" Faith with the realization that some men are "pretty decent guys" is a clear indication that Faith's redemption is complete—she wins the reward of romance ("Chosen"). Implicitly this also includes "proper" gendering through heterosexual romance: Forster has suggested that while in Buffy's body, Faith realized Buffy has a better sex life than her own because Riley loved her (2003: 17). Schudt's reading that to Faith a "man is not to be valued as a person in his own right worthy of respect, but simply as a means to satisfying a physical desire" (2003: 27) positions Buffy's own search for a relationship based on equality as the ideal. This is why Faith's relationship with Wood is so important: it promises to be a "good" relationship, and rather than simply allowing her to exercise her sexual and physical power, it encourages Faith to articulate emotion (in "Touched" she tells Wood that the Mayor was "like a dad" to her). Wood's comment that Faith's sexual performance was very "enthused" and that she needs "a little more experience" even implies that she retains a level of innocence (as I suggest Buffy does).

Faith's badness is punished and then redeemed because "the power of a slayer must be positioned within not just a code of warrior justice, but one of feminized responsibilities and restraint" (Tjardes 2003: 74). Her admission that she no longer wants to "be" Buffy indicates that Faith has moved on from ("masculine") competition. Her "uncontrollable" appetite for sex and violence is tamed by her acceptance of the responsibilities that come with being a powerful good girl and by making wider relational connections (she, rather than Buffy, spends time with the Potentials and knows their names). That Faith's negotiation of gender is more "real" that that of the female vampires (because she is human) makes her a more sympathetic character and a more attractive subject position for viewers than other bad girls. Yet despite the freedom and ability to cross borders that Tjardes notes in Faith (69), she is finally and willingly identified as a good girl.

Something Old

Season 5 presents apparently the most powerful bad girl ever to appear on *Buffy*: a female hell-god called Glory (the term *goddess* is avoided, perhaps because of its association with "good" Wicca power). Glory is searching for a Key to her own dimension, hidden by monks who want to prevent her departure because it will collapse the boundaries between our world and the hell dimensions. In "Blood Ties" Giles says that Glory is from "one of the more seriously unpleasant demon dimensions" which are "pushing on the edges of our reality trying to find a way in." Already Glory has great disruptive potential. Yet she is presented in such a way as to heighten her power as a villain (the bad aspect) but diminish it as "feminine" (the girl aspect).

The two most obvious things that characterize Glory are her power and her appearance. Glory's femininity is coded not sexually (at least overtly) but materially. She tends to wear red and gold and has a different outfit for every episode. These "feminine" ensembles are almost always dresses or skirts, completed with high heels, gold jewelry, and red lips and nails. At one stage Glory does not pursue Buffy because she breaks the heel of her shoe and then destroys a warehouse by stamping her foot in annoyance ("No Place Like Home"). Her hyperfeminine appearance is highlighted when Dawn teases Buffy, "I just think you're freaking out because you have to fight someone prettier than you" ("Blood Ties"). Note the similarity of these two exaggerated versions of femininity: Wilcox has described Glory as "a parodic version of the overdressed blonde bimbo some have considered Buffy" (2002a: 17). Parody and excess work to ironize or destabilize traditional gendering, as Buffy and Faith also demonstrate. That Glory herself disputes her identification as materially "feminine" (asking Willow, "You think I care about all this, the apartment, the clothes?" in "Tough Love") points to her hyperfemininity as a "masquerade" of gender.

Viewers are constantly reminded that Glory is a god and therefore almost omnipotent. Physically she is the most powerful foe Buffy has ever faced. Xander tells the Slayer, "Buffy, this chick creamed you last time" ("Shadow" 5008; note the pejorative terms used), and Glory taunts

Buffy with her power in "Checkpoint" (5012). This power comes from Glory's origin.

> Tara: What if she's something else altogether?
> Giles: Something new, you mean?
> Tara: Something old. So old it predates the written word.
> Willow: Giles, the Dagon sphere, you said that was created to repel . . .
> Giles: . . . that which cannot be named.
> Willow: So I'm thinking maybe she . . .
> Giles: . . . predates language itself? ("Shadow")

The above exchange presents Glory as prelanguage, pre–patriarchal order. Yet she is not as disruptive as might be expected. She directs a group of demons as her minions like a typical supervillain, yet more often than not she uses her power capriciously, in a way that is coded as "feminine." A typical villainess, Glory is surrounded by men willing to do whatever she says, and, like Drusilla, Glory has desires that must be instantly gratified. "I'm the victim here," she tells the monk in "No Place Like Home," going on to demand the location of the Key: "I want it, I need it and I've gotta have it." Anne Millard Daugherty suggests that Glory "represents the legendary great Hollywood divas who cared only about their appearance and desires" (2001: 161). Thus on the one hand, Glory is an obsessive female who expects everyone to attend her slightest whim.

Yet on the other she is a monstrous killer, sucking the minds of various humans (and eventually Tara), torturing or killing, and threatening Buffy's family and friends. Glory's scene with Tara is integral to my reading of her character. Sitting on a bench in the middle of a fair, Glory holds Tara's hand (figure 6). She discovers that Tara is not the Key and tortures her to find out who is, squeezing until blood trickles between their joined hands, and then licking it off (as part of her monstrous femininity Glory is connected to blood consistently: she wants to "bleed" Dawn; viewers are told in "Spiral" 5020 that the dimensions will "bleed into each other"). Glory then explains the sensation of her brain-suck, echoing Faith's speech to Riley by saying it makes "you feel like you're in a noisy little dark room, naked and ashamed and there are things in the dark *that need to hurt you because you're bad*" ("Tough Love," my emphasis). Here Glory seems to identify Tara as the bad girl, but the delivery of the line and Glory's unstable identity mean that it could also refer to her-

FIGURE 6: *Glory and Tara spend "girl time" together ("Tough Love").*

self. Although Glory appears asexual, she spends "girl time" with both Tara and Dawn, and at one point she tells her prisoner Dawn, "Let's have big girl fun" ("The Weight of the World" 5021). Her interaction with Tara, a character identified early on as lesbian, gains significance in this context, especially if we recall the erotic blood-licking scene between Dru and Spike. As with Dru and Faith, a lesbian reading of Glory awards her more feminist potential by positioning her outside patriarchal heterosexuality.

But Glory is literally contained by male presence: the female god is housed in a male human body. In "Blood Ties" Dawn eventually discovers that Glory is Ben, the friendly hospital intern. "It's an eensy [bit] more complicated than that. Family always is, isn't it?" responds Glory, placing herself within a similar familial structure to other bad girls. The Glory/Ben split relates to another aspect of Glory's female power: like Faith and Drusilla, she is labeled mad. Giles explains in "Blood Ties" that being out of her own dimension is "seriously affecting her mental state," and as Sayer points out, this is visualized by "the use of dislocating cuts to represent Glory's wobbly sanity, inter-dimensional instability and fluid identity" (2001: 104). This is part of Glory's boundary-crossing nature. Yet it also implies that her madness is directly related to her power: when she is out of her place (a female god in a patriarchal society), she cannot contain the power—it drives her mad (just as Willow could not control her power and Faith's appetites were presented as uncontrollable). Glory talks a lot about blood,[13] cannot control her unstable body, and is repulsed by its physicality (female viewers in particular may experience some recognition here). She also has a controlling ego that motivates most of her behavior (at the same time hyperfeminine and unacceptably masculine), while her "madness" is seen as a weakness. Glory's power is inevitably limited by her relationship to Ben, and Ben is one cause of her instability.

The Key is protected by an order of monks, and Glory is pursued by another patriarchal and all-male organization, the Knights of Byzantium. These two patriarchal forces refer to Glory as the "beast," or the "abomination," suitably apocalyptic terms that define her as Other and evil, and another example of labeling as a form of patriarchal control. (Although again reminiscent of Tara being condemned as a "demon," the show deflects a sympathetic feminist explanation here by underlining that Glory *is* a hell-god.) Arguably without Buffy, the female Slayer, Glory would easily rout the forces of patriarchy, yet the monks succeed by giving Buffy the Key. Although the group works together and Buffy, the female Slayer, and Willow and Tara, the female witches, weaken Glory in the final conflict, it is Giles who kills Ben to prevent Glory's return ("The Gift" 5022) and a male demon, Doc (another patriarchal learned authority), who opens the interdimensional portal. Thus the most powerful female ever on *Buffy* is also the most parodically feminine, the least stable, and the most clearly contained within her relationship to a male character. Yet Glory's plan succeeds in killing Buffy, making her the only season villain since the Master to slay the Slayer.

Night Night, Bad Girls

Tjardes notes that "the complexity and attendant openness of [Faith's] character arise from the lack of information directly from her" (2003: 73). The openness of all the bad girls allows them to retain their power within and without the text, but this lack of development simultaneously marginalizes and demonizes them. Although viewers may find these bad girls attractive, they do not match the popularity of bad boys like Angel and Spike. Whereas in male vampires love enables development and redemption, for bad girls it merely undercuts their

strength and independence, rendering them submissive to male partners. Heterosexual romance presents problems for any strong, independent female, yet good girls like Willow and Buffy have more success in
negotiating it than the bad girls.

The lack of closure in the bad girls' stories (even when they are dead)
means that their disruptive potential survives but they are not generally
allowed the reversal of character that serial narrative can offer, and that *is*
demonstrated by others. I suggest that across the seasons of *Buffy* there
has been an increasing exaggeration of bad girls, from traditional female
vampires like Darla and Dru to a Vamp airhead like Harmony to a parodic diva like Glory. In some ways, instead of challenging stereotypes
of bad girls, the show has emphasized them. This matches the development of the show's good girls. If good girls can be "bad" and morality is
blurred, then bad girls become redundant (the same ambivalence leads
to the erasure of the "big bad" role in season 6). Disturbing similarities to
the good girls are part of the bad girls' function and are acknowledged,
but their representations fall back on conventional moral and gendered
"badness."

Like the female villains of soaps or serials, the bad girls demonstrate
strength and power, and their transgressions can be read as "feminist."
Their enjoyment of that power and transgression offers pleasure to many
viewers. Yet their very acceptance of who they are defuses some of the
bad girls' potential. Good girls like Buffy and Willow are constantly en-
gaged in constructing their postfeminist identities, incorporating both
"feminist" and "feminine" aspects. The more static nature and restricted
development of the bad girls trap them in their role as villains, and they
are (at least superficially) complicit with heterosexual, patriarchal structures. As a villain, a bad girl must be bad; only Faith attempts to construct the valorized postfeminist identity that in Buffy and Willow enables power, strength, and independence to be good.

4 Tough Guys "I'm a Man"

Discussion of *Buffy* has tended to make much of its representation of female characters but if *Buffy* is a negotiation of gendered identity, then this must affect men as well as women. The changing context of recent decades referred to in the introduction has led to what has often been called a "crisis of masculinity." The causes for this "crisis" are numerous: Jim McGuigan cites "the undermining of the father's authority in the home, changes in working patterns that favor female labour and girls' greater educational success than boys" (1999: 85). Social changes and the challenge of second-wave feminism have prompted discussions of masculinity—until recently the invisible gender, the universal, the norm. In revisioning masculinity *Buffy* is following a trend in popular culture: even action movies have changed their representation to question "whether and how masculinity can be reproduced successfully in a post-Vietnam, post-Civil Rights and post-women's movement era" (Jeffords 1993: 247). Jeffords' comment reminds us that postmodern society's renegotiation of gender is in part a challenge to white male supremacy.

The next three chapters suggest that masculinity in *Buffy* struggles with a binary construction: it is either old or new. In simple terms old masculinity is macho, violent, strong, and monstrous, while new masculinity is "feminized," passive, emotional, weak, and human. Many male characters on *Buffy* display both at once, a kind of split personality. In chapter 1 I cited the increase in female action heroes or tough women, but tough guys abound in film and television. *Buffy*'s tough guys are not modeled on action *heroes*—they relate more to action genre villains; and I argue that their villainy and their excessive masculinity are intertwined. "Real men" in *Buffy* may not even be *men*; they are often monsters. Traube has noted of more recent representations of masculinity that "the antagonism implicit in gender opposition predominates over complementarity. From the masculine perspective, women appear to exercise a power that robs men of their essential selves, and real men are those who refuse to submit" (1992: 132). Similarly, the tough guys in *Buffy* are used to allegorize violence against women or to contrast alternative versions of masculinity (such as the new men), and their function as knockdown villains contributes to the viewer's pleasure in Buffy (or the others) defeating them. Since the tough guys I discuss here have clearly not negotiated new gender roles for themselves, they are static "old" versions of masculinity, adapted neither to contemporary gender roles nor to the ever-changing serial world of *Buffy*.

Tough guys are homosocial and often defined in relation to patriarchal groups or institutions. Tough-guy masculinity in the show is based on physical and/or institutional power, the repression of (human/ "feminine") emotions, and is increasingly aligned with technology. Simkin has noted, and I agree, that most of these tough guys see Buffy herself "as a site for erotic desire, competition and control" (2004b: 1) and thus are often presented as problems that she must re/solve, season villains who must be defeated, or even lovers. In this way they demonstrate the need for change, the need to negotiate gender in a postfeminist era. *Buffy*'s representations of constructed masculinity imply that power and strength may be seen as "natural" masculine characteristics but that tough-guy masculinity is an unnatural construction. The excess of gendering also results, as with some of the bad girls, in showing up the ways in which traditional masculinity is constructed and policed. Riley will be discussed in detail here, and I also examine Daryl, Pete, Jack O'Toole, Forrest, Adam, Warren, and Caleb.

Alienation and the Traditional Monster

In "Some Assembly Required" (2002) *Buffy* presents a tough guy and its (first) version of the Frankenstein story. Sunnydale High student Daryl Epps was killed in an accident but has been reanimated by his younger brother, Chris, who along with his friend Eric is robbing graves and assembling parts to make a "girl" for Daryl. Human Daryl was a model of traditional masculinity: all-star football player, rock climber, attractive and popular. The episode includes a school football game that Ms. Calendar describes to Giles as "unadorned aggression." What Daryl was best at, in other words, was being aggressive, and he was encouraged to act that out in an acceptable arena. "Football star" became Daryl's identity, and he, Chris, and the family are shown as still affected by this— Chris is ignored; his mother is living in the past, smoking and watching reruns of Daryl's glories on video (no father is present). Daryl himself is still invested in his achievements; he repeats a football chant to Chris as a way of affirming their bond, and toward the end of the episode Daryl waits underneath the bleachers as the game plays out. The sounds fade away into a melancholy piano tune, indicating Daryl's nostalgia and his recognition of his changed state.

Monster Daryl exhibits rage and violence, but in context his anger is associated with the alienating experience of returning as a monster. Instead of being loved and adored by all, Daryl now refuses to go out and is dependent on "the brains" of his little brother rather than his own physical strength (which in itself might be read as a comment on changing masculinity). Daryl dominates Chris with emotional appeals ("You promised me, little brother, that I wouldn't be alone") as well as with physical displays of temper. Heterosexuality and hierarchy are integral to the structures of traditional patriarchy. Outside the acceptable arena of the football field, Daryl's toughness is more clearly directed toward what Simkin calls the "objectification of the female body . . . through a narrative in which women are reduced to spare parts" (2004b: 10) and the domination of weaker males like Chris and Eric. Thus Daryl condones and even encourages Chris and Eric to make a companion like the later April for him ("You won't go out, you won't run away, but we can hide together"); he is willing for them to kill (Cordelia) to complete "her."

That Daryl retains some emotional connections to his brother Chris shows that he is not just a tough guy. In the monster narrative this demonstrates his humanity, but in terms of gender his emotional ties present a more "feminine" aspect. Even as a popular football star Daryl supported and protected Chris, though only the brothers remember this. Chris tells Buffy, "I was just trying to look out for him, like he would have done for me." The episode is framed by romantic interludes between Buffy and Angel, and Willow sets the tone when she tells Buffy, "Love makes you do the wacky." The show demonstrates that it is not just romantic love that makes you do the wacky, but family love: Daryl is brought back to life because of Chris Epps' love for his older brother. In the showdown, Daryl has a chance to kill Buffy but pauses when his brother calls his name, then he chooses to die in the burning "lab." Daryl's existence as a monster is presented as a mistake, resulting in alienation and confusion because he cannot fit into the human world. Chris is seen to be acting through misguided affection (as Buffy and other characters later do): he is far from the conventional mad scientist.

I would suggest that the episode allocates the strongest will to objectify to Chris' accomplice, Eric, rather than Chris or Daryl. Eric is a voyeur, snapping female students with his camera, and is eager to "harvest" a head for the "girl" (his objectification of women is underlined by mention of his prodigious pornography collection). Xander's question here, "Why would anyone make a girl?" is echoed later in the series about Warren and April, and Eric could be regarded as a forerunner of Warren.

The Beast Within

"Beauty and the Beasts" (3004) focuses on high school student Pete, who abuses his girlfriend Debbie. A body is found savaged in the woods during a full moon, and both Oz (werewolf) and Angel (newly returned from hell) are possible suspects—they too struggle to contain the beast within and threaten their girlfriends with violence. Thus *Buffy* suggests that all males have to deal with aggression. Readings from Jack London's *The Call of the Wild* frame the episode, underlining how close to the surface these primal instincts are. Classic American novels like this reinforce gender binaries: nature is "not what men represent but what they conquer, inside themselves and outside in the world," while "the same matrix of oppositions generated a romantic narrative that presents nature in a different light as the refuge to which men return in search of their true masculine selves" (Traube 1992: 132). These oppositions inspired the 1990s men's movement to go on wilderness retreats to rediscover their "inner warrior" or "wild man" (Robert Bly's *Iron John* is a key text here).

Thus in the teaser Faith claims, "All men are beasts, Buffy. Every guy, from 'Manimal' right down to 'Mr.-I-Loved-*The-English-Patient*.'" Buffy is uncomfortable with Faith's cynicism partly because, as I have argued, Buffy clings to romantic ideals but also because she, like the show itself, valorizes more postfeminist versions of male and female. Violence is sexualized here, and the episode makes a direct correlation between primal or bestial aggression and masculinity: all the possible monsters are male. Despite his apparent sensitivity (see the next chapter), Oz avoids "an upsetting conversation" with Willow by saying, "Sometimes it's a necessary guy thing," underlining the connection between his masculinity and his primal nature. The chains that Buffy restrains Angel with remind viewers of the pleasure/pain games that Dru and Angelus used to play as well as his nature as a brutal demonic killer. The love of a good woman may "soothe the savage breast," but romantic love is used here as an excuse for violence, and the story demonstrates how women can be blamed for male aggression. This exemplifies both the female civilizing influence and the undercutting of romance in *Buffy*.

When Buffy questions Giles on the possibility of Angel returning intact from hell, he says, "Most likely he'd be a monster," and then delivers a short speech: "In my experience there are two types of monster, the first can be redeemed, or more importantly wants to be redeemed. . . . the second is void of humanity, cannot respond to reason or love." This sets out the morality of the episode (and the show's valorization of emotion). Naturally, neither Oz nor Angel is responsible for the violent killing in the wood, and later of Mr. Platt, the school counselor; Pete is. In line with Faith's remarks about aggressive masculine sexuality, Pete's violence is directly linked to his relationship with Debbie, and initially to sexuality (he persuades Debbie to go into the school basement to make out but then gets violent). Pete is *Buffy*'s take on *Dr Jekyll and Mr Hyde*: he is a split personality, using "formulas" to become stronger and more violent. When he discovers that Debbie has tried to get rid of these, Pete explains: "You're the reason I started the formulas in the first place. *To be the man you wanted* [my emphasis]." Pete no longer needs the formula, telling Debbie that her behavior is enough to make him change. He accuses Debbie of infidelity (he later calls her a whore); he hits her, abuses her verbally, and concludes, "I'm all you've got." Apparently repentant minutes later, he still manages to blame her: "you know you shouldn't make me mad, you know what happens."

This pattern of abuse fits the teen allegory element of *Buffy*'s early seasons and the viewer can recognize it as a classic pattern of abuse, just as most of the school students don't realize "the Pete-was-a-monster part." Furthermore, it draws attention to the links between heterosexual romance and male dominance. As Jackson notes, "The passionate compulsiveness of love raises the issue of eroticized power and violence. . . . It can also be read as a pretext for violence which, if provoked by a jealous rage, can be read as proof of love—as can rape" (1999: 117): such a reading underlies both Pete's behavior here and Spike's attempted rape of Buffy in season 6. *The Monster Book* notes that writer Marti Noxon "has made clear that the episode's most powerful metaphor has to do not merely with abuse, but with the way in which some women are attracted to the 'Alpha dog,' the bad boy" (Golden, Bissette, and Sniegoski 2000: 227). Thus the episode also highlights female behavior and gendered relationships. Willow and Buffy's exchange, "I think we broke her [Debbie]," and "I think she was broken before this," also foreshadows the presentation of both April and Katrina, who are "broken" by Warren, another abusive male. Buffy cannot understand Debbie's defense of Pete, and the fact that Debbie is eventually killed by Pete because she believes he loves her validates Buffy's apparently empowered viewpoint. Yet at the same time, Buffy believes in romance and is therefore complicit in patriarchal subjection of women, and in her later liaison with Spike she is at a loss to explain why she "let[s] him do those things to" her ("Dead Things").

In the final showdown, it is not Buffy the female hero who defeats Pete: he beats on her fairly successfully, classing her with other women: "You're all the same." More extensive coverage is devoted to Pete's fights with first Oz (a target for jealousy because he offers to help Debbie with schoolwork), who wolfs out shortly after the fight begins, and finally with the wild Angel, who kills Pete with his chain. Having killed Pete-the-monster, Angel devamps as he looks at Buffy, then falls to his knees and clasps her round the waist (as he saves her, she also saves him by evoking emotion). Both Oz and Angel prove themselves the first type of monsters because they respond to love and want to be redeemed. Pete was the second kind—a tough guy who would not listen to reason and who shows clearly how heterosexual "love" can be domination. "The only thing was, after a while he didn't need the potion to turn *into a bad guy*—did it just fine on his own [my emphasis]," concludes Buffy. The equation is clear: Pete was "a bad guy" because he thought being a man was about being a tough guy. Like Daryl, he achieved this tough-guy state through science, inevitably coded masculine, while emotion and love (coded feminine) were repressed. All of Pete's toughness was about compensating for what he saw as weakness, and trying to be what he thought he *should* be.

The Least Fear

Though he first appears to be a loner like other tough guys, Jack O'Toole from "The Zeppo" (3013) is homosocial. Even at the beginning of the episode he talks about his "buddies," and later Xander witnesses the "raising" of Jack's dead friends. Simkin describes Jack's gang as "stereotypical jocks on a male bonding night of high jinks" (2004b: 14), and certainly "Big Bob" wears a football jacket and is somewhat reminiscent of Daryl Epps. However, Jack and friends are presented (largely through their speech) as "hillbillies" (they mention *Walker, Texas Ranger*, and Jack talks about his "grandpappy"). This kind of "simple," working-class masculinity has been valorized by authors like Jack London as more rugged, more physical, and more "authentic" than middle-class masculinity, seen to be feminized by changes in employment and increasing domesticity. Jack's friends act like boys, not men, and although they suggest finding some "girls," their largely homosocial behavior is underlined as they discuss a rival gang, the Jackals.[1] Of course, Xander is not "part of the group" because he is not like them: this difference of masculinity is articulated as a physical difference: Xander is not dead, while these tough guys are so tough they have all died proving it. The gang also map out a kind of working-class masculinity that Xander is anxious to escape (see chapter 5).

While Pete used his power as a tough guy to dominate and control women, Jack is a recognizable bully who preys on weaker males with threats and violence. The episode is set up to contrast Xander with Jack, and this interaction begins at school with a football-throwing scene, signifier of physical, homosocial masculinity. While Xander wants to be included, Jack does not: he sits in the shadows, coded as a marginal figure. When Xander misses the catch and the football drops in Jack's lunch, he offers typical tough-guy insults and challenges, "You want to be starting something?" Even at this stage, however, the way Jack talks about getting his "buddies" together may indicate that his power lies largely in his gang.

The second scene with Jack plays on similar elements: Xander runs into the back of a car Jack is sitting in outside The Bronze. While Xander is keen to "work this out," Jack pulls out a large Bowie knife (figure 7), and Xander's reference to "frontiersmen" brings another connotation of rugged masculinity into play. Jack's threats are here loaded with a sexual subtext ("Where do you want it?" and "I'm fairly certain I don't want it at all"), played into with the subsequent "rasslin', but not in a gay way" comment from Xander. The connection here is between homosexuality and a lack of real masculinity: real men are heterosexual. After taunting Xander about being "scared" and losing face in front of Lysette, the girl Xander has just picked up, Jack suggests that the difference between them is "who has the least fear." Jack's nature as a "psycho" tough guy is emphasized, but the situation is resolved because Xander covers for Jack, showing male solidarity when a police officer stops their scuffle. Thus although Xander is positively contrasted with Jack, he is still complicit in preserving both tough-guy masculinity and its structures of domination through violence.

Later Jack is stripped of his support as the gang is taken out (but not

FIGURE 7: *Jack O'Toole and Xander demonstrate different versions of masculinity ("The Zeppo").*

by Xander) during a chase around the school. When they face off man-to-man, Jack's bullying tough-guy talk is now countered by Xander and after Jack gives in and defuses the bomb the gang has planted in the school basement, Xander asserts *his* dominance, calling Jack a "Good boy" and ordering him not to come "on campus anymore." Xander does the "right" thing and achieves a "good" outcome; but if we adopt a slightly resistant reading, his masculinity is validated by having "the least fear." Status through dominance is reversed, but preserved: Xander wins on Jack's terms, not his own. Like Pete, Jack is attacked by Wolf-Oz (when he picks the wrong door to exit the basement) and eaten (consumed by a wilder masculinity than his own).

Xander recognizes that Jack is a "psycho"—that is, he doesn't appear to care what happens to him, or what people think of his behavior. Yet despite the fact that Jack is "a sub-literate who's repeated twelfth grade three times," he is still "cooler" than Xander because of this psycho factor (in this case, cool seems to imply masculine). This episode suggests that Jack's tough-guy nature is not a consequence of him being a monster (living dead), as Daryl's aggression stemmed from alienation. Jack was already a bully, just as Pete seemed potentially abusive. One possible inference from this is that violence and domination are inherently masculine, or at least are part of social conditioning for boys. Jack's tough-guy identity is constructed through his reputation as a psycho, built up through confrontations he knows he can win. Perhaps to emphasize this, Jack never goes up against Buffy, the female action hero; his toughness is played out exclusively among men. Many tough guys appear to be static, unlike regular characters on *Buffy* whose identities are unstable and under constant reconstruction. Jack does not exhibit a split personality, but like Warren later, he is always *trying* to be tough and to prove this toughness (underlining that he is part of the "real" world). This can be read as a kind of reconstruction. It is not the renegotiation of a different gendered identity, but an indication of the work required to shore up a tough-guy image. The final analysis demonstrates, as with Daryl, that any attempt to reanimate the tough guy is ultimately a failure. The additional significance here is that Jack is defeated by an apparently new and different type of masculinity.

I Am How They Trained Me

RILEY

Riley Finn seems at first to be a new man, and he apparently does not suffer from the split personality displayed by so many *Buffy* males. At face value Riley is a regular guy, consistently presented and viewed by other characters as the most normal of young men. That he is white, middle class, and heterosexual merely makes him even more "normal." Spike refers to Riley as "the enormous hall monitor" and "Captain Cardboard" ("Out of My Mind" and "No Place Like Home," respectively), and it is no coincidence that the show allows Spike, a more transgressive and popular male character, to articulate what many viewers felt about Riley. Though he is shown upholding liberal values (helping with a college Lesbian Alliance banner), Riley reacts badly to the news that Oz is a werewolf, to which Buffy replies, "God, I never knew you were such a bigot" ("New Moon Rising"). Riley is traditional and conservative and displays all the characteristics of a tough guy. His early interactions with Buffy demonstrate that he wants to protect her. Although Early suggests that in comparison with the other Initiative soldiers, Riley is "a nurturing and caring New Age man" (2002: 25), I would argue that rather than sensitivity, Riley displays paternalistic chivalry. Buffy is shown to resist this, and indeed writer Doug Petrie has described Riley as a "sexist doof" (in Simkin 2004b: 24). Riley pays lip service to political correctness—he recognizes the need for change and manages to present an appearance of political correctness without actually changing.

His involvement with the Initiative means that Riley is primarily homosocial, and he lives in a fraternity house on the campus of U. C. Sunnydale. Although season 4 has been called the "James Bond" season (Petrie in Simkin 2004a: 2), it is notable that the tough guys of the Initiative are not individualist heroes like Bond but members of a homosocial "family." The Initiative family is not like the Scooby family, however. It is based on hierarchy rather than communal effort, encourages competition rather than cooperation, and, ironically, requires passivity (following orders) rather than initiative. Madeline M. Muntersbjorn suggests that "[t]here is no such thing as informed consent inside the Initiative for men or monsters," implying a lack of agency in these supposedly active males (2003: 99). The post-Initiative Riley does become individualist: on patrol with the Scoobies he is unreliable, taking on situations alone or not showing up at all. Riley's instinct when faced with various crises is to call on military expertise, and eventually ex-comrade-in-arms Graham offers him a place on a military demon-fighting mission to Belize. Thus Riley returns to the familiar, regulated, yet physically challenging life of the military, detached from "contact with civilians" ("Into the Woods" 5010). As with Daryl's football prowess, this affords an acceptable arena for certain types of "bad" behavior and "real" masculinity. Like Daryl and in contrast to many characters in *Buffy*, Riley believes his identity is fixed and known: he is a soldier and a man.

Riley also demonstrates the artificial, constructed nature of tough-guy masculinity. The Initiative modified Riley with drugs, so that he is faster and stronger: in short, Riley has been *made* a better soldier. He admits, "I am how they trained me" ("The I in Team"); arguably, patriarchal society and the homosocial institution of the military also *make* Riley a man through gender norms and policing. Despite this, he asserts independence, humanity, and masculinity: he says to Adam, "I cannot be programmed. *I'm a man*" ("Goodbye Iowa" 4014, my emphasis). Although Riley conflates humanity and masculinity ("I'm a man") and is presented as heroic and human, he has his monstrous side, in Adam and in himself. The power of the Initiative, based on masculinized science and technology, clearly contrasts with the feminized, mystical power of the Slayer and the Scoobies. Riley's valorization of "masculine" strength leads to problems: he enjoys his power and is anxious about losing it.

When Buffy wants to take him to hospital to be treated he responds, "Best case scenario they turn me into Joe Normal. Just another guy" ("Out of My Mind"). Angel and Oz reject their monstrosity (want to be redeemed); Riley's monstrous side is unnaturally induced and therefore could be changed. Yet Riley embraces it and is reluctant to give it up because he thinks its loss will emasculate him.

This constructed power is used to dominate others, and the hierarchical framework of the Initiative means that competition is encouraged. Although by day Riley is "the goofy, lovable college boy" (script notes from "The Initiative" in Holder, Mariotte, and Hart 2000: 73), by night he is "Special Agent Finn," taking orders to track and kill or capture "hostile subterraneans" (Money notes his "Human Good, Demon Bad" mentality, 2002: 105). Buffy's dream in "Restless" is a striking view of Riley, here a gun-toting soldier concerned with "world domination," implicated in national patriarchal institutions and colluding with villain Adam. Whedon has even suggested that in this scene Buffy "was seeing that they [Riley and Adam] were two sides of the same coin" (in Topping 2002: 324). The show makes it clear that Buffy is physically stronger than Riley, and he continually tests this in training fights and on patrol. They are in competition from the moment she is introduced to the Initiative and Maggie Walsh encourages Agent Finn to tell Buffy how many "HSTs" he has taken. Buffy's response—"Huh. Wow. Well, that is . . . I mean . . . seventeen"—is understandable to the viewer, and her own tally is not revealed on-screen ("A New Man" 4012), so that she does not visibly engage in this kind of ("masculine") point scoring. Interactions with other males are also revealing: Xander may call Riley "big guy," but in the same episode Riley meets Angel, who tells him, "Don't push me, boy" ("The Yoko Factor" 4020).

Tough-guy masculinity requires the repression of "feminine" emotions (though not "masculine" aggression and rage), often demonstrated through Riley's relationship with Buffy and with his "brother" Adam. Part of Riley's identity as a man is founded on his "superpowers," and this reaches a crisis point in "Out of My Mind." While Riley admires Buffy's strength, he believes that she would reject him if he became normal. Graham also points out Riley's potentially passive role: "You used to have a mission and now you're what? The mission's boyfriend, the mission's true love?" (Graham is not the only one who sees Buffy as a bad influence; see my discussion of Forrest, below). Because of their homosociality, tough guys often have difficulty relating to women, but Riley does not seem to suffer from this. However, his physicality is expressed in his relationship with Buffy, which quickly takes on a physical/sexual aspect that is emphasized again and again (as mentioned in chapter 2), to the point that it traps them in one episode ("Where the Wild Things Are" 4018). Simkin points out the explicit connections made between fighting and sex in the relationship (2004b: 25), clearly seen when Buffy and Riley take down a Polgara demon: the fight scene is intercut with a "later" scene of them having sex for the first time ("The I in Team"). Commentators have also noted that despite his physicality, Riley cannot satisfy Buffy; she has to seek further action in Slaying (see "Buffy vs. Dracula"; Simkin 2004b and Daugherty 2001: 161). Riley's first "crisis of masculinity" is centered on a physical disintegration, and Buttsworth notes the importance of the " 'integrity' of the masculine body" (2002: 188).

Melissa M. Milavec and Sharon M. Kaye observe that as "Buffy and Riley grow closer physically, they also become emotionally distant and detached" (2003: 175). Riley's inexperience in dealing with emotion or relationships (typically "masculine") is demonstrated when he tells Buffy, "Loving you's the scariest thing I've ever done." Like other tough guys, Riley constantly feels that his masculinity is threatened, especially by Buffy. While he first wanted to protect Buffy, Buffy often protects him, and she also advises him when he is confused about leaving the Initiative. Feeling distanced from Buffy as she copes with her mother's medical tests and operation, Riley gets his kicks elsewhere, ending up as a regular in a vamp nest where, as Spike puts it, he pays for "suck-jobs from two-bit vampire trulls" ("Into the Woods"). The implications here are of both addiction and prostitution: Anya and Giles explain that humans have been doing this for centuries, attracted both by the danger and the (presumably sexual) "rush" of being fed on. Buffy tells Riley, "You just can't handle the fact that I'm stronger than you," pointing out that he is threatened not just by her physical strength as the Slayer but also by her ability to support her family in a crisis (a "feminine" quality). Riley also confesses that part of his motivation in visiting the vamp nest was "to even the score" after Dracula and Angel fed on Buffy, but he insists to the point of cliché, "It was just physical." Riley continues to suppress his emotions while craving physical feelings. When Buffy claims that she has given him her heart, body, and soul, he replies, "You say that, but I don't feel it," yet he tells her that the vampires that fed on him "made me feel something . . . something I didn't even know I was missing" (just as Buffy claims Spike makes her "feel" in season 6). Money

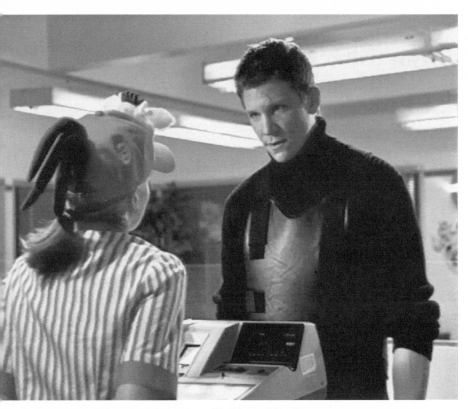

FIGURE 8: *Was Riley "always this tall" ("As You Were")?*

even implies that Riley appears at some points less human than Adam (2002: 107).

When Riley returns in "As You Were," he seems to have reverted back to "normal." A clash with Spike contrasts Riley's uncomplicated persona with a far more complex version of masculinity *and* morality, and with a more popular character. Riley's hypermasculine appearance is now ridiculed: he has an obvious scar,[2] and Buffy dazedly asks, "Were you always this tall?" (figure 8). His association with the military and technology is also ridiculed when Buffy notes that all his "James Bond stuff" is "so cute" and Riley admits, "Boys like toys." Riley is now literally married to the job. His wife and coworker, Sam, is as wholesome and gung-ho as he is (Topping [2003: 130] suggests that she is "a female clone" of Riley, and notably she is in scale with him physically, being taller than the other women).[3] Even Sam joins in the gentle ridicule of Riley's attitude (she calls him "Captain Can Do"), and although she allows him to banter, she does not let him dominate her ("He's your boss too?" Buffy asks, "He wishes," Sam responds). But Riley's tendency to compete is raised in the following (albeit lighthearted) exchange.

Riley: . . . got some big stories to tell you too.
Buffy: Did you die?
Riley: No.
Buffy: I'm gonna win.

Now Buffy demonstrates more awareness about their relationship, warning Riley not to "patronize" her, and eventually he admits, "You're still the first woman I ever loved, and the strongest woman I've ever known." Thus his relationship with Sam is articulated as a shadow of his relationship with Buffy, and tough guy Riley is paradoxically attracted to strong, that is, independent postfeminist women who might be expected to challenge his version of masculinity. Riley's parting comment, "This isn't about who's on top," seems to dismiss the idea of competition, but he has achieved what Buffy always wanted, an extra/ordinary life with a partner who understands and shares his mission. Riley can afford to patronize Buffy now, because he feels that *he* is back on top.

Anita Rose sees Buffy as "saving" Riley from the Initiative (2002: 139), another example of the female civilizing influence. Taking on board Money's Huck Finn analogy (2002: 106), the reprise of Riley shows that he has enough awareness of social constraints and changing gender roles to make it appear that he is a civilized new man and he displays his toughness in an acceptable, military fashion. (This analogy also ties into notions about masculinity, civilization, and nature, cited in my discussion of Pete.) This does nothing to dispel his anxiety about his masculinity, and he is shown going backwards to keep up its appearance. The fact that his static nature leads to ridicule (however affectionate) shows that he no longer fits into the world of *Buffy*, and his unchanging nature only emphasizes how Buffy and the others have developed.

FORREST

Forrest acts as a foil for Riley: he is at once a token black character and a subordinate to the male "hero" (Edwards [2002: 96] describes him as Riley's "sidekick"), but this function exaggerates his tough-guy characteristics. His homosocial nature is underlined by his references to the Initiative family, and he sees Buffy as an intrusion. Forrest is keen to deal with "problems" internally, "in the family" ("This Year's Girl"). As Riley is shipped off to military hospital for withdrawal recovery in

"Goodbye, Iowa," Forrest tells Buffy, "We take care of our own around here." In "Who Are You?"[4] he again acts to protect his "brother," telling Buffy (Faith-as-Buffy) when he sees her leaving Riley's room, "Hope you left him alive," playing on her abilities, her role as the Slayer, and his interpretation of her as a disruptive femme fatale when he continues, "Yeah, you're a killer." Buffy even makes a "feminist" allusion to the exclusive nature of their group when she asks, "What, no girls in the club?" and Forrest is left to imply that she and, one assumes, other women are "bad" elements and bad influences: "Riley had a career, a future, till he met you" ("The Yoko Factor"). In a subsequent argument with Riley ("Goodbye, Iowa"), Forrest attributes "typical" female behavior to Buffy; "she tends to put her nose where it doesn't belong" (she disrupts the homosocial status quo). Thus Forrest articulates what Buttsworth characterizes as a prevalent cultural attitude to women in the military, that they are "'unpredictable,' dangerous to unit cohesion, sexual distractions and weaker links in the team structure" (2002: 194–195).

Perhaps because of his racial difference, Forrest is even more competitive than Riley. He expresses anxiety about Buffy's intrusion into the homosocial group, complaining to Graham, "I've always been Riley's second in command; instead he picks a girl" ("The I in Team"). When Graham points out that it is *his* girl," Forrest retorts, "Three guesses on what that boy's thinking with," reducing Buffy's importance simply to sex.[5] The relationship between Riley and Forrest is clearly complicated, and Graham's suggestion, "Maybe he just wanted to give you a chance to get out from under his shadow," elicits an angry reaction. This response (a veiled allusion to race?) is deflected with a reference to gender: "It was just a joke, man, don't get your panties in a bunch," and tough guys' language frequently works to uphold gender binaries and police their boundaries. Riley later counters Forrest's resistance to Buffy by asking, "Is it because she's a better soldier than you?" ("Goodbye, Iowa"). Ironically, Riley too both blames Buffy and competes with her.

Forrest's constructed nature is literalized when he is defeated by Adam and turned into a cyber-demon. That he welcomes rather than regrets this transformation is a sure sign of his investment in physical strength and hypermasculine aggression. Even more explicitly than Riley, Forrest embraces his constructed strength and rejects human emotion as a weakness. He tells Riley that he is "surging with life and strength. Adam made me to be nearly *as bad* as he is. . . . I'm free of all my weaknesses and my doubts" ("Primeval," my emphasis; note the conflation of badness and strength). Now Forrest threatens Buffy, believing he can win, and reaffirms his bond with Riley: "Back on the same side . . . brother." But he simultaneously enjoys the reversal of their previous roles when he says, "Watch me kill your girlfriend, Finn. That's an order."

As a black student and a black soldier Forrest is whitewashed — an instance of color-blindness in that his racial difference is never noted. Forrest's rank is never revealed (although black soldiers make up a large proportion of the U.S. military, there are few nonwhite commissioned officers; Gill 2003). That Forrest is a college student may imply a middle-class background, indicating an easy way for him to assimilate among his white friends (as with Kendra, adoption by the inside group tends to erase difference). It is worth asking why, if Forrest is so whitewashed, he is black at all. In a discussion of television soaps, Geraghty notes what she calls the "exotic strategy," explained as "the short-term use of a black character to make more dramatic their troublesome effect on the community" (1991: 141). I would suggest that Forrest's blackness (like Kendra's) is used in exactly this way.[6] He is primarily a foil for Riley, and his race adds further tension by offering a visible level of difference. It also adds intensity to the clash between Forrest and Buffy.[7]

ADAM

Adam is perhaps the mostly clearly constructed tough guy. He is a reprise of the Frankenstein's monster, aware of his monstrous status from the beginning: "What am I?" he asks a boy he meets in the woods, and when he receives the reply, "You're a monster," he merely says, "I thought so" ("Goodbye, Iowa"). Like the original monster, he experiments and reflects on human life and his own existence. Adam acts out what Isaac Asimov termed the "Frankenstein complex" (1993: 133), the fear that a technological creation will turn on its creator, though Adam goes on to become a creator and wielder of technology himself. In his relation to the military, science/technology, and monsters (he is partially constructed from demon parts), Adam is always coded specifically as masculine (but he also seems to be asexual). He embodies what Buttsworth calls the "hyper-muscularity of the Initiative commandos," which she argues is "an expression of their masculinity, but . . . *not* natural" (2002: 194).

Adam is homosocial and part of the same all-male family that Riley and Forrest belong to. His speech, "I saw the inside of that boy, and it was beautiful, but it didn't tell me about the world. It just made me feel. So now I want to know about me. Why I feel. What I am. So I came home," relates his anxiety about "feeling" ("feminine" emotion), identity, and the idea of "coming home" to the homosocial environment of the Initiative ("Goodbye, Iowa"). Social studies once saw violence or "delinquency" in young men as a reaction against domineering mothers and absent fathers (see Kimmel 1997: 244). Similarly, Attebery suggests that "the transition to manhood in most cultures has required a violent separation from a matrix (literally a womb) of femaleness" (2002: 7). That Adam's first word is "Mommy" and that he says it just after he has killed his creator, Professor Maggie Walsh, plays out such ideology. In this way, Adam's hypermasculinity could be said to be constructed by a woman, and in resistance to femininity. Walsh herself invests both Adam and Riley with the same parental ambition to "make [her] proud" ("The I in Team").

Because the "family" of the Initiative is a hierarchical institution, and because Adam is the ultimate constructed soldier, he is destined to be a leader and takes on typically male roles in doing so. Adam embraces his construction and his purpose with religious fervor. "I have been blessed. I have a gift that no man has, no demon has ever had. I know why I'm here. I was created to kill, to extinguish life wherever I find it, and I have accepted that responsibility" ("Who Are You?"). This both mirrors and conflicts with *Buffy*'s representation of responsibility as taking up a role (such as the Slayer), since this always involves a sacrifice of self and saving or helping others (Adam sacrifices others). As religious leader and "evil messiah guy" ("Superstar" 4017), Adam recruits vampires to his cause by offering the elimination of fear and the reclaiming of "masculine" bravery and courage (as with Jack O'Toole), and most of his recruits are male. Adam promises to free demons from their subordination to "men" and to free "men" from their human weakness (their "feminine" qualities?). He combines the apparent opposites of science and religion, though both are masculinized.

Adam's inhumanity is underlined by his lack of emotion, but this can also be read as a tough-guy characteristic (like Clint Eastwood's "man with no name" or Arnold Schwarzenegger's hypermasculine emotionless "cyborg" in the *Terminator* films). Even his claims to family are deadpan. Because of this Adam is categorized as "evil" and is an almost parodic villain, showing up the ways in which traditional masculinity is constructed. Yet Adam cannot be defeated by Buffy the female action hero alone.

The power that defeats him is the female power of the Slayers, but as already mentioned, Combo-Buffy includes both masculine and feminine elements. Adam is thus contrasted with female strength and power and with Xander and Giles, and his male technological power is defeated by female mysticism but by Xander's suggestion. Visually Adam is large and clumsy next to Combo-Buffy in their final fight scene (the hypermasculine made to look hyper), and Buttsworth even suggests that Combo-Buffy's actions feminize him: "Penetration is to pervert and undo masculine warrior identity" (2002: 194). Combo-Buffy easily rips out Adam's uranium core, but he can "never hope to grasp the source of" her power because he only sees clear-cut oppositions and binaries. "I'm the war between man and demon, the war that no one can win," he says in "Who Are You?" The battle is lost by Adam because he does not understand the value of cooperation (as a typical tough-guy leader he dominates rather than encourages his minions).

In "Goodbye, Iowa" Buffy admits to Willow, "I could barely fight him. It was like Maggie designed him to be the ultimate warrior" and concludes, "I think the part where he's pure evil and kills randomly was an oversight." This equates hypermasculinity and "pure evil" with no thought of shades of gray (contrasting the treatment of Riley or Spike in this season) and is reminiscent of Pete's condemnation and Forrest's assertion. From his position of power, Adam is "really not" worried that Buffy might stop him ("Primeval") but it is because he is so "evil" that he is marked for defeat. He ignores Spike's warning that Buffy has stopped "every would-be unstoppable badass" who has come to Sunnydale ("The Yoko Factor"). What seemed a major threat is taken out so easily by Buffy and the gang that the showdown fight with Adam is over in scant minutes,[8] and notably it is *not* the season finale. Adam proves that excessive masculinity is untenable, "evil," and ultimately easily dismissed, but he also proves how attractive and powerful it is to certain groups. And although Adam is clearly a fantasy monster, this attraction is strongest in "real-world" masculinized groups like the military or the scientific community. Adam himself is not split in two, but with Riley he shows the "good" and the "bad" side of constructed and institutionalized masculinity. After all, he is "Mr. Bits" (as Spike calls him in "The Yoko Factor")—a tough guy literally constructed from men and monsters.

The Most Anxious

Even though he may not appear to be a tough guy, Warren follows the pattern set out for tough-guy identity in *Buffy*. He is a geek, a

nerd, the tough guy as bully. As clearly as Daryl and Eric, Warren objectifies women; he is introduced as the creator of the robot-girlfriend
April in "I Was Made to Love You." The same question Xander asked

in "Some Assembly Required" is repeated about April, this time by
Anya: "Why would anyone do that [make a girl] if they could have a
real live person?" Warren clearly could have "a real live person," since
he is dating Katrina at U. C. Sunnydale, but this relationship is jeopar-
dized when April and Buffy seek him out. Warren tries to put Katrina
in her place: "This is important. Wait *in the kitchen* [my emphasis]," but
she resists and walks out. Thus the audience's first view of Warren is that
he is both "sleazy" and "sad," and this is underlined when Spike com-
missions him to make a robot-Buffy, complete with special (sex) programming. Warren later gets Katrina back by hypnotizing her with a
"cerebral dampener" in "Dead Things," and in a similar fashion to April,
Katrina is "programmed" to do what he tells her, becoming a "willing
sex slave." Yet just when the mise-en-scène implies that she is about to
perform oral sex, Katrina recovers her resistance and independence (the
dampener is "out of juice"). She faces her captors down, telling them:
"This is not some fantasy, it's not a game, you freaks, it's rape," and in
calling this rape, the show links male domination, heterosexuality, and
violence. Warren kills Katrina, by accident perhaps, but he shows no
remorse (as both Jonathan and Andrew do) and refuses to accept the
consequences (like Faith, another "human monster"). He uses Katrina's
body to convince Buffy that she has killed a human, neatly foreshadowing the dilemma when Willow kills Warren. Warren is later characterized
by Dark Willow as a woman-killer, and using language recognizable to
the contemporary viewer as misogynist, he tells her, "You really are asking for it, you know that?" while claiming that Katrina "deserved it"
("Villains").

Warren uses his power to dominate, and the need to prove himself
leads to competition with other males and with superhero Buffy. First
he forms a gang, "the Trio," backing himself up with weaker associates
(Andrew's lack of self is highlighted continually here by the fact that
no one knows who he is; he is there to be overshadowed). Warren suggests banding together to "take over Sunnydale" ("Flooded"), and he is
always presented as the driving force behind their schemes against Buffy.
While initially any of the three might be the leader, Warren gradually
takes over through bullying or manipulation, and increasingly he is the
one who "gets to play with all the cool stuff," as Andrew complains in
"Smashed." "Doesn't play well with others" is a deep criticism in *Buffy*

as well as a sign of masculine individualism. Warren shows little loyalty to his allies and is early marked as different; he is "evil," while the other two are just trying to have a (nerdy) good time (Simkin [2004b: 12] points to the "paltry nature of their ambitions, in comparison with the considerable powers they have developed").

Everything about Warren shows that he competitively pursues a tough-guy image. In "Seeing Red" he tries to impress women (Xander notes his lack of success) and also enjoys dominating men (as in his clash with a bully from fifth-grade gym class and with Xander). Warren's reminder to the bully, "This ain't high school," demonstrates how he seeks manhood as part of an adult identity but also as a way of taking revenge. In the inevitable fight with Buffy his power is derived from mystical orbs and as Simkin has noted, the language again overtly connotes "phallic—or, more precisely, testicular" power (2004a: 21). Warren calls Buffy "superbitch" and "kitten," while she states the obvious: "You really got a problem with strong women, don't you?"—a recognizably postfeminist response. Warren repeats the lines of several other tough-guy villains: "*That all you got?* What's the matter, baby, you never fight a real man before?" ("Seeing Red," my emphasis) but is ultimately feminized when he sneers, "Say goodnight, bitch," and Buffy, defeating him, responds, "Goodnight, bitch." (Only the most divided or contested masculine figures have been called "bitch"—Angelus by Buffy during their possession in "I Only Have Eyes for You," and Spike, naming himself "love's bitch" in "Lover's Walk"). Dark Willow later sums up Warren's sense of masculinity and inadequacy relating to women and Buffy in particular: "You get off on it. That's why you had a mad-on for the Slayer. She was your big-O, wasn't she, Warren?" ("Villains").

That Warren's tough-guy masculinity is constructed may not be immediately obvious, since he is not a Frankenstein's monster, a reanimated corpse, or a drug-enhanced super-soldier. He is, like many other tough guys, associated with masculinized science and technology: while Jonathan uses magic and Andrew summons demons, Warren invents gadgets and uses a gun. He tries to valorize this as a masculine quality equal to physical power: "It's not the muscles, baby, it's the brains" ("Seeing Red"). As indicated, language is a factor in constructing his tough-guy identity, just as it was for the Initiative soldiers. Anxiety about sexuality is underlined constantly by the implication that Andrew is not only gay but also attracted to Warren. Andrew's homosexual desire is a clear indication that he is not a "real man"; "real men" are heterosexual. Part of the group's "mission statement" is about "girls," though they never seem to be clear on details, and while conducting surveillance Warren suggests that they might be able to hack into "free cable porn" (a link back to Eric). When the three steal a diamond to complete one of Warren's technical projects, he proclaims, "Size is everything" (and he is literally larger and heavier than the other two, enabling him to physically dominate them; "Smashed"). Warren belittles the others in terms designed to bolster his own sense of masculinity, treating them like children or "girls" ("when you girls are done touching each other," in "Dead Things").

Like Adam and Forrest, Warren's emotions are restricted to anger, and his lack of emotional connections or remorse is what ultimately makes him a villain (Andrew has an emotional investment in Warren himself, and Jonathan feels remorse and tries to help the Scoobies). Warren is frequently characterized by Buffy as a "boy"—he lacks emotional maturity and (like Willow) has gained too much power too quickly,[9] taking out his insecurities on those weaker than himself. Warren chooses to be a bad guy ("you guys are so immature, we're *villains*" in "Gone" 6011). Although Simkin suggests that for all three "masculinity is associated with their degree of evil" (2004b: 12), I would argue that Warren alone makes this connection, as did previous tough guys. But he fails to heed the warning about Superman and Lex Luthor: although he points out that Luthor never kills Superman "because it's Superman's book, you moron," it is left to the viewer to conclude that this is Buffy's show.

Warren's presentation emphasizes that his idea of masculinity is related to domination and power because these compensate for his perceived weakness and inadequacy. The binary morality of masculinity does not fit Warren: he has no "good" and "bad" side, but the gap between his inadequacy and his power is itself a binary of masculinity. Moreover, his constant attempts to maintain his tough-guy façade demonstrate that it is not "natural." "He's just as bad as any vampire you sent to Dustville," says Xander to Buffy, yet Warren does more damage to Buffy and the Scoobies than any other villain because he is "real." When Willow kills a human, just as Warren did, he has won, as Buffy points out ("Villains"). Hence the significance of Willow's phallic power being tamed by the feminized Xander and Giles. Like Adam, Warren is defeated by a combination of female and male power. Nobody gets to be a tough guy anymore, not even Dark Willow, and the new men save the day.

It seems strange, then, that season 7 of *Buffy* presents a very obvious male villain in Caleb. Caleb may not immediately seem to be a tough guy but he too displays their characteristics. He is both an individualist (a lone male) and part of hierarchical evil (he works with the First Evil and the Bringers). His introduction as a preacher and his use of biblical/Christian rhetoric ally him with patriarchal institutionalized religion, and this seems to inform his misogyny (with the exception of the Dagon monks in season 5, traditional religion has always been "bad" on *Buffy*, and many popular culture representations equate religious values and traditional gendering). His power is not natural; the First awarded him superhuman strength, and thus he too is "made" a tough guy. Although Caleb asserts that he is "beyond concepts like" God, when the First responds, "You still wear the outfit," he replies, "A man can't turn his back on what he come from," affirming that his version of masculinity is behind, not beyond the times ("Dirty Girls"). Finally, the narrative of the show constructs him as a polarized male villain, allied with the three "powerful" men who created the First Slayer through a sexualized violation, and set against the feminized power of the Slayer and the pre-Christian female Guardians.

Caleb's exaggerated nature, like Adam's, immediately and undeniably identifies him as "evil." Again he is easily killed, but his defeat is not the finale. Indeed, Caleb is not the season villain; the First is. Caleb's power is used to dominate others: he is able to command the Bringers, and his references to "dirty girls" demonstrate that he objectifies women and associates them with sexual misconduct. There is even a broad hint that his past includes violence against women ("Dirty Girls"). Caleb generally shows only aggression or religious fervor, and his religious rhetoric serves as a distancing mechanism that many viewers recognize as extreme and misogynist. That he does not appear until the eleventh hour ("Dirty Girls" is 7018) demonstrates his unimportance. The hypermasculine Angel standing aside as Buffy kills Caleb merely reinforces that tough guys no longer demand a team effort—they can be dispatched solo by a female hero. The defeat of the tough guy is finally a necessary but relatively unimportant part of the battle to dissociate female power from "masculine" individualism and patriarchal control.

Out of Juice

In addition to gothic monsters, hypermasculinity has been rep-

resented on *Buffy* in other forms, particularly by athletes (what Simkin
[2004b: 3] describes as "traditional models of masculinity in the high
school/college context"). An older version of Daryl the football hero is
shown in "Him" (7006), living on his past glories but useless in the real
adult world, like Tom Buchanan in *The Great Gatsby*.[10] It is also notable
that another apparently hypermasculine character from early seasons,
Larry, turns out to be gay. Larry was such an aggressive masculine predator that the Scoobies suspected him of being the werewolf in "Phases,"
but later he is shown as both a happy "out" gay ("Earshot") and as a
"good" fighter of evil (in "The Wish"). Larry's character thus implies
that being a tough guy is a way of compensating for "unmasculine"
weakness or behavior.

The tough guys, with their violent and predatory hypermasculinity,
form a threat to civilization. Generally women control these "real men":
as already noted, the Slayer plays the "traditional" female role of civilizing influence. Those who represent tough-guy masculinity are generally monstrous because they try to prevent development, and notably,
many of them are dead (and, moreover, need to be "raised"). They cannot adapt, and as Adam, Warren, and Caleb demonstrate, they cannot
see that it is no longer their story: the dominance of the traditional male
is challenged in postmodern society, and inevitably all the tough guys
are defeated, though rarely by female power alone. Thus their stories
are used to contrast other males, such as Xander, Oz, Angel, and Spike.
That both Riley and Warren are attracted to independent young women
is an interesting contradiction that serves to valorize the agency of the
"girls" and to underline the static macho masculinity of these tough
guys—they cannot or will not change, therefore they cannot keep the
girl. This inability of tough guys to negotiate new gendered identities
verges on essentialism (men are "naturally" aggressive) but also points
to the strength of social conditioning in forming gendered identities,
literalized in the tough guys of the Initiative. The lingering influence
of more traditional ideas about gender is linked with the privilege and
power of patriarchy, and in most of the tough guys this is reinforced by
their identity as white, middle class, and heterosexual. Changing gender
roles are a threat to this power. The show aligns gender with morality
in the case of the tough guys, offering its most obvious ideological representation of gender—old masculinity is "bad."

The failure of the tough guys undermines not only the irrelevance of tough-guy masculinity but also the increasing irrelevance of a season villain. Adam, the hypermasculine villain, is succeeded by Glory, the supernatural and parodic female villain discussed in chapter 3, and then by Warren, the human geek as wanna-be tough guy.[11] As the doctor in "Normal Again" notes, once Buffy had "grand villains to battle against. And now what is it? Just ordinary students you went to high school with. No gods, or monsters, just three pathetic little men who like playing with toys" (6017). Tough-guy masculinity is seen to *be* a fantasy, and one indulged in mostly by boys (most of the tough guys are young, and even Adam is presented as a child), who cannot grow into men unless they adapt to changing ideas about gender. Tough guys don't want to escape binary definitions of gender; they pursue and uphold them. But if being a man no longer means being a tough guy, then growing up means changing into something else. *Buffy*'s alternative, the new men, is discussed in the next chapter.

5 New Men "PLAYING THE SENSITIVE LAD"

It follows that in trying to destabilize traditional representations of feminity, especially through role reversal, *Buffy* must offer a concomitant alternative version of masculinity. Producer Fran Rubel Kuzui articulates this when she says, "You can educate your daughters to be Slayers, but you have to educate your sons to be Xanders" (in Golden and Holder 1998: 248). In 1995 Thomas suggested that the British television detective series *Inspector Morse* demonstrated "the extent to which feminist influences are discernible in this example of quality popular culture, particularly in its representations of masculinity" (1997: 184). Television melodrama and soap in particular have addressed masculinity because they are concerned with family and the domestic, traditionally "feminine" areas (Torres 1993: 288). Saxey notes with some surprise that in *Buffy* fan fiction "it is the males who are persistently tortured by doubt" and wonders why "slash readers and writers wish to explore the suffering of these often sensitive, non-traditional male figures, while female characters more often enjoy less emotionally painful treatment" (2001: 201), and I would suggest that it is partly because masculinity is being so visibly renegotiated in pop-cultural forms. As noted in the last chapter, "good" new masculinity contrasts with "bad" tough-guy masculinity by being "feminized," passive, sensitive, weak, and emotional, and this contrast is partly about the separation of gender and behavior in the new men.

Like the young female characters, the new men are very aware of how gender is constructed but are often shown repressing their "real" masculinity (perhaps a recognition of powerful social conditioning). In this way, the new men's identities are shown to be unstable rather than fixed since they too work hard to construct and reconstruct postfeminist gendered identities. In line with the show's heteronormativity, these male characters are depicted as nonhomosocial and were identified early on as heterosexual. Victoria Robinson notes that "[t]he hegemonic model of masculinity" is heterosexual and that many (male) writers on gender both "problematize masculinity and recognize the social constructed nature of male heterosexuality" (1996: 119, 113), highlighting the contradiction here. In addition to Oz, Giles, and Xander, this chapter will use less central characters such as Owen, Ford, Parker, Ben, and Principal Wood to discuss the representation of new masculinity. The contradictions and ambivalences inherent in these characters demonstrate that what *Buffy*'s new men represent is not a successful new masculinity but a detailed portrait of the many anxieties surrounding binary constructions of gender.

Lie to Me

Bill Clinton was elected president in 1992 after presenting himself as "the grandson of a working woman, the son of a single mother, the husband of a working wife" and telling voters, "I have learned that building up women does not diminish men" (in Woloch 2000: 591). This points to the ways feminism has caused changes in the presentation of masculinity, and here I examine three apparently sensitive males who are presented as potential partners for Buffy but prove to be unsuitable because they cling to more traditional masculinities.

OWEN

The first, Owen Thurman, is introduced in "Never Kill a Boy on the First Date" (1005) as "sensitive yet manly," and he shares some characteristics with Angel ("He hardly talks to anyone. He's solitary, mysterious. He can brood for forty minutes straight," says Willow). Owen's "manly" credentials are established both by Cordelia's pursuit of him and his rejection of her, while his sensitivity is established by his admiration of Emily Dickinson's poetry.[1] Further, Owen finds "most girls pretty frivolous" and tells Buffy there are "more important things in life than dating," perhaps indicating that he rejects heterosexual romance, and certainly coding him as different from the typical testosterone-charged male teen. When Angel comes to The Bronze to discuss the latest crisis and discovers that the Slayer is "on a date," Owen and Angel face off— the first in a long line of such confrontations for Buffy's potential partners. Although Buffy confesses that she "almost feels like a girl" with Owen (a gendered articulation of how romance exposes her "split personality"), her Slayer duties inevitably intrude. She leaves Owen at The Bronze but, unhappy in a passive role, he follows the Scoobies and attempts to "protect" Buffy from a vampire. This assertion of traditional male heroism is punctured by his lack of awareness and being promptly knocked out but the definitive undermining of Owen comes in the final act. The next day he asks Buffy when he can see her again, saying, "Last night was incredible, I never thought nearly getting killed would make me feel so alive!" and Buffy confesses to Giles, "He wants to be Dangerman. . . . Two days in my world and Owen really would get himself killed." Buffy is compelled to reject Owen because he displays "masculine" aggression, getting off on the danger of slaying (like Riley and some of the other tough guys) and because he refuses to "be careful" (in contrast with the other Scoobies).

FORD

Another potential new man is Billy Fordham (Ford) from "Lie to Me." Ford's sensitivity is based on his closeness to Buffy: they went to school together in L.A., and he tells the gang that he is now enrolling at Sunnydale High because his father has relocated. This gives Buffy the chance to nostalgically invoke a shared past, as Willow and Xander often do. Ford suggests cheering Buffy up with "a box of Oreos dunked in apple juice but maybe she's over that phase," and their bond is highlighted by his nickname for her ("Summers"). Ford's manly attractions are also clear (Xander complains, "Jeez, doesn't she know any fat guys?"), Buffy admits that Ford was her "giant fifth grade crush," and shots frame Buffy and Ford close together (she often holds his arm when they are walking). When Ford tells Buffy, "You can't touch me, Summers, I know all your darkest secrets," this seems to indicate that his intimacy has limits—he cannot know about her other life. Yet shortly afterward he is with Buffy when she rescues someone from a vamp attack, and he tells her, "You don't have to lie. . . . I know you're the Slayer." Ford's sensitivity thus extends to knowing and accepting Buffy's other role (and her power), and even participating in some of the action, without the fear or excitement that Owen displayed.

This perfect playing of the old friend/new man is punctured when subsequent scenes reveal that Ford is a member of a vampire wannabe club and show him bargaining with Spike and Dru to become a vampire, offering them the Slayer in exchange. He is simply a selfish individualist. It also becomes clear that Ford is willing to sacrifice the other "true believers" to get what he wants. That Ford is terminally ill problematizes things: he offers it as an "excuse" or justification of his behavior. Throughout his conversation with Buffy his face is in shadow, while

Buffy's is in light, polarizing them even as their discussion raises doubts about clear-cut morality. Giles' frequently quoted closing speech in response to Buffy's request, "Lie to me," begins to break down certainties about good and evil in *Buffy*: "Yes, it's terribly simple. The good guys are always stalwart and true, the bad guys are easily distinguished by their pointy horns or black hats, and we always defeat them and save the day. No one ever dies and everybody lives happily ever after." The presentation of a villain invested in fantasy foreshadows the character of Warren, the male character most anxious about projecting a tough-guy image, and Ford similarly demonstrates the "badness" and violence of old masculinity.

PARKER

The next apparently new man is presented more simply because he only features in the "real world" of Sunnydale and knows nothing about vampires or Slayers. In her first weeks as a freshman at U. C. Sunnydale, Buffy meets Parker Abrams in the lunch queue ("Living Conditions" 4002). Later in the same episode Parker pops round to Buffy's dorm room, and by the next episode Buffy and Parker have spent "all week" together. Parker makes several emotive speeches, demonstrating his willingness to admit and articulate his feelings. He tells Buffy that his father died recently and that this brush with mortality has changed his outlook; he is now more interested in "living for now." Naturally, Buffy can relate to this, and Parker tells her very seriously, "It's cool to find someone else who understands." Parker maintains that history is really about "regular people trying to make choices" (keying in to the language of contemporary individualism and popular postfeminism) and when the two finally kiss, the concerned "new man" asks Buffy, "Is this OK? Because I can stop if you wanted, it's your choice." Buffy makes her "choice," and she and Parker end up having sex ("The Harsh Light of Day").

The encounter now replays what happened when Buffy had sex with Angel but without the allegory. Her time with Parker is loaded with reminders of Angel, from Parker's remark about "dark and brooding" guys to Spike's explicit comment, "Guess you're not worth a second go" ("Seems like someone told me as much. Who was that? Oh yeah, Angel"). The two worlds of *Buffy* conflict in a montage of Buffy pursuing her Slayer duties and checking her messages to find that Parker has not called, while the melancholy soundtrack contrasts the previous upbeat music of their developing intimacy. Eventually Buffy catches up with Parker as he talks with another female student and in this scene she seems uncertain and girlish, the freshman Buffy ("feminine") rather than the strong, independent Slayer ("feminist"). When she asks if she did "something wrong," he replies, "Something wrong? No, of course not. It was fun. Didn't you have fun?" before brushing her off. As in "Family," Spike offers a "feminist" explanation, albeit couched in rather unfeminist language: "Did he play the sensitive lad and get you to seduce him? Good trick if the girl's thick enough to buy it." "Playing the sensitive lad" is a strategy that Parker adopts in order to make his conventionally masculine conquests. The success of this strategy relies on traditional moral and sexual values: if the girl thinks *she* seduced *him*, then she is likely to blame herself, as indeed Buffy does.

Buffy's rejection by Parker is shown again in succeeding episodes, and during "Fear, Itself" Buffy tells her mother: "I'm starting to feel like there's a pattern here. Open your heart to someone and he bails on you." In "Beer Bad," Buffy daydreams about saving Parker from a vamp attack. That this daydream occurs in a lecture on the pleasure principle while Parker is chatting up yet another female student is not lost on the viewer. Willow persists in dissuading Buffy: "He's no good. There are men, better men, where the mind is better than the penis," highlighting the changing priorities of postfeminist young women. Riley, Buffy's future boyfriend, disapprovingly tells Buffy that Parker "sets 'em up and knocks 'em down," and when Willow goes to confront Parker, he attempts to charm her too. This time his performance of "the sensitive lad" is deflated by Willow's awareness: "Just how gullible do you think I am? I mean, with your gentle eyes and your shy smile and your ability to talk openly."

Meanwhile Buffy and some other college students have regressed into Neanderthals and a fire has started, trapping Willow, Parker, and several others. As in her fantasy, Buffy saves Parker from mortal danger, and a pensive piano plays in the background as he tells her, "I'm sorry for how I treated you before, it was wrong of me." This fantasy of romance is undercut when Cave-Buffy merely whacks him with her improvised club, leaving the other Scoobies to look down on him, the camera giving a low shot from Parker's prone body.[2] Viewers here get the satisfaction of Parker being rejected through a device that frees Buffy from her contradictory "feminine" and "feminist" positions on romance and sexual behavior. Parker is finally dismissed by Riley when Parker tells Forrest that Buffy is "kinda whiny" and "clingy," concluding with a crack about "freshman girls" and "toilet seats." Riley punches him out, apparently establishing his own credentials as a "sensitive lad" ("The Initiative").

SCOTT

Scott Hope has a brief relationship with Buffy in season 3, but this is complicated by Buffy's Slayer duties and Angel's return from hell, and Scott is not entirely discredited as a new man. Much later the ex–Sunnydale High vampire Webs (Holden Webster) tells Buffy that Scott said she was gay and continues, "He says that about every girl he breaks up with. And then, last year, big surprise, he comes out" ("Conversations with Dead People"). This is the only instance in *Buffy* where sensitivity and (homo)sexuality are related, possibly resolving the complicity between heterosexuality and patriarchy. Yet Scott himself does not reappear. All of these failed partners contribute to undercutting the myth of romance in *Buffy* and highlight romance relationships as the one area in which changes to masculinity are needed and looked for.

Feminized Males

OZ

Oz is figured primarily as the love interest of one of the main characters (generally a female role) and was seen by some viewers as a successful paradigm of new masculinity, combining both "masculine" and "feminine" characteristics. Oz is often identified by his role as rock guitarist and is described by *The Watcher's Guide Volume 2* as "the definition of cool and composed" (Holder, Mariotte, and Hart 2000: 69), two major factors in his appeal. In one way his habitual silence is part of this cool composure and can be read as a trait of "old masculinity" (the strong silent type), yet simultaneously it can be identified as a passive "feminine" characteristic. From the beginning Oz was presented as sensitive and thoughtful, refusing to allow his relationship with Willow to develop before they were both ready (in contrast to Parker's pretence). Kristine Sutherland, who plays Joyce Summers, remarks on the attractions of this: "It was the scene in the van where she asks him to kiss her and he says, 'I don't want to kiss you until you want to kiss me.' That is the kind of man that every woman is looking for" (in Golden and Holder 1998: 215). Once again a new man is one who appears be sensitive to young women's anxieties about relationships. The connection between Oz's wolf cycle and the female menstrual cycle is explicitly referred to in "Phases" and further feminizes Oz. Oz also proves that it is possible to be both a nerd and, as Xander puts it, "more or less cool" ("The Zeppo"), or that social success need not be dependent on particular versions of masculinity. Of all the primary male characters in *Buffy*, only Oz is a dissimilar physical type and an atypical male lead in that he is short and slightly built. (Willow's next partner, Tara, is also an atypical lead.) This allows the show to present variants of masculinity even in appearance.

On the whole Oz appears "very much at ease with his masculinity" (Simkin 2004b: 5) and seems adaptable and free of the anxieties that plague other characters. Oz is willing to stand in for best friend Willow when the Scoobies are worried about Buffy in "Living Conditions." "If it wasn't for this English paper, I'd be right there, listening, doing the girlie best friend thing," Willow worries. "I can do that," responds Oz, going on, "Well, I'm not saying we'll braid each other's hair, probably, but yeah, I can hang with her." Yet his characteristic stoicism can cause problems, and at times friction in his relationship with Willow is exposed. In "Earshot," when Buffy can read thoughts, Willow panics because Buffy knows what Oz is thinking and Willow believes their intimacy will never stretch that far. Another exchange seems to suggest tension when Oz expresses the hope that Buffy has not been encouraging Willow to practice magic ("Fear, Itself"). By the end of a three-way exchange between Buffy, Oz, and Willow, Oz emerges as "supportive boyfriend guy," his reluctance dispelled as concern for Willow's safety. "Just know that whatever you decide, I'll back your play," he concludes, leaving Buffy and Willow to marvel over his "sweet" nature.

Episodes focusing on Oz tend to be either about his relationship with Willow or about the werewolf. In "Fear Itself" he tells Willow and Buffy, "I know what it's like to have a power you can't control and every time I start to wolf out I touch something—deep, dark. It's not fun." Later in the episode this fear is played out in the Halloween "haunted house" when he starts to wolf out for no apparent reason. Oz leaves Willow (to "protect" her) and huddles in an empty bathtub telling himself, "You're not going to change." Thus although Simkin suggests that Oz does not suffer from the anxieties about masculinity that other male characters display (2004b), I argue that Oz's anxiety about the wolf *is* his anxiety about masculinity. Carolyn Korsmeyer notes that Wolf-Oz demonstrates "anger and aggression as brutish elements of the emotional range" and concludes that this "seems especially apt for the male of the species" (2003: 164). Oz's sensitivity is proved by his realization that he needs to restrain this side of himself.

It is no coincidence that his crisis concerns another young woman, Veruca, who comes between Oz and Willow because she too is a were-wolf and a musician ("Wild at Heart"). Veruca disturbs Oz's peaceful surface: "You're the wolf all the time, and your human face is just your disguise. Ever think of that?" Veruca's animal/sexual magnetism seems to affect other men (both Xander and Giles are riveted by her stage pres-ence), and physical/sexual desire is highlighted in her liaison with Oz, so that despite the "cuddly" nature of his relationship with Willow he is sexualized. Dyer observes that white sexuality is often seen as "bes-tial and antithetical to civilization" (1997: 26), and Oz as werewolf lit-eralizes this view. Challenged by Willow, he maintains, "I don't know what Veruca and I have done. When I change, it's like I'm gone and the wolf takes over," but Willow points out, "You wanted her. Like, in an animal way." Significantly, Veruca, not Oz, carries most of the blame for their sexual transgression (and Willow describes Veruca as dressing "like Faith," another sexualized bad girl). Following Veruca's death, Oz leaves Sunnydale to try and control the werewolf. As mentioned in chap-ter 2, he is an aggressive intruder when he returns to Sunnydale and disrupts Willow's new relationship with Tara, sexual jealousy calling out the wolf he thought he had tamed. After escaping the Initiative, he again leaves Sunnydale, Willow, and the series, establishing a pattern in his behavior.[3]

Robinson identifies an "ambiguity around male sexuality," noting that seeing it as "simultaneously both vulnerable and powerful" is nec-essary to changing definitions of masculinity (1996: 115). Oz in particu-lar exemplifies this ambiguity. External factors (actor Seth Green's other commitments) meant that Oz lasted only around two seasons as a *Buffy* regular, but the manner of his departure underlines the tension between competing versions of masculinity. All the Scoobies are presented as flawed in some way, but many male characters' flaws or mistakes are related to gendering or gendered behavior. Although Simkin suggests that Oz's departure "offers only a puzzlingly abrupt, incongruous and unsatisfactory resolution" (2004b: 7), I am more inclined to agree with Mendlesohn, who argues that it signals a reluctance to allow Willow agency (2002: 55)—something I see as fitting an overall tendency. Sayer's observation that "[o]ver the course of the show it is primarily the men (Angel, Oz, Riley and to some extent Spike) who have left" (2001: 112), together with Buffy's comment on men "bailing," point to the frequency of men leaving women. All of the characters Sayer picks out demonstrate a contested masculinity, and I argue that their leaving undermines their apparent sensitivity, highlighting the tension within them.

GILES

Another important male character, Giles, was early described as "a decidedly feminized male" (Owen 1999: 24). As an adult, Giles is exceptional: in a show where almost all adults and authority figures are proved "bad," he is not only fully aware of the teen characters' heroism, but supportive of it. This is largely because, as Christine Jarvis has noted, Giles begins as the school librarian and honorary teacher, and "where good teachers are portrayed in popular culture, they usually stand against the system" (2001: 264). Giles stands out against the system of school and of hierarchy. In terms of age, and origin (he is British), Giles is presented as different. Yet he shares certain characteristics with other new men.

Giles' new-man sensitivity may be difficult to pinpoint, since he is presented as a reserved character and since age separates him from the teens. Although vampires like Angel are effectively older than Giles, he is generally seen as the oldest character in the team, highlighted by his traditional dress and speech (also related to his British-ness). Even in the early seasons, however, when he is at his most tweedy, Giles (and the show) is aware of this. When Jenny Calendar asks him, "Did anyone ever tell you you're kind of a fuddy duddy?" he responds, "No one ever seems to tell me anything else" ("The Dark Age" 2008). The fact that he has two "first" names (Rupert Giles) allows him to be regularly called "Giles" by the teen characters, without this ever sounding strange (as it might if they called him "Smith"), and suggesting a degree of intimacy while not quite putting them on the same footing. Giles' position as the only adult in the group offers a different perspective to the viewer but still allows his emotional side to be revealed in a number of ways. First, and perhaps most obviously, his emotions are shown in his fathering of Buffy, as discussed in chapter 7. But he also demonstrates a keen sense of responsibility for the safety of the other teens and displays emotion and affection when they are threatened (as when they think Willow has been killed and turned into a vampire in "Doppelgangland").

Giles takes his responsibility as part of the team very seriously. When Willow asks him, "How is it you always know this stuff? You always know what's going on. I never know what's going on," Giles replies, "Well, you weren't here from midnight to six researching it" ("Angel"). Giles is always a key member of the Scoobies and their communal efforts.

He is presented as hetero- rather than homosocial, and his few adult friendships or affinities are with both males and females (Angel, Ethan Rayne, Jenny Calendar, Joyce Summers, Olivia). After the school is destroyed and he loses his job as librarian, Giles is allowed to shed his reserve, and the teens unexpectedly find common ground with him. His position in the team is reinforced as he also "grows up," briefly acquiring a British girlfriend, Olivia, and doing his own thing. He is never set up as the leader, though his knowledge and experience are often useful and are respected by the others. His role as Buffy's Watcher (trainer and researcher, as well as mentor) means that Giles is inevitably a passive rather than an active character. Despite his "generic roots . . . in the von Helsings [sic] of British horror" (Whedon in Lavery 2002a: 50), like Xander, Giles is rarely involved in the physical aspects of slaying. But this does not negate his heroism. In "The Zeppo" he is a key player in the mostly off-screen attempt to avert another apocalypse, and when Buffy says, "It was the bravest thing I've ever seen," Giles merely responds, "The stupidest." In this way, Giles' heroism is presented as team effort and self-sacrifice rather than "masculine" individualist heroics.

Giles also allows the teen Scoobies independence and agency. His positions of authority (as Watcher and as a kind of teacher) are traditional patriarchal roles and encourage him to try and take charge early on, but this is resisted by Buffy and the others. J. P. Williams has argued that Buffy's "knowledge of Slayers and slaying is filtered through" Giles, "who, in his dual roles of Watcher and librarian, controls Buffy's access to knowledge and parcels out information on a 'need-to-know' basis" (2002: 62). I would point out that although it is rarely articulated, the show demonstrates that a Watcher must learn as much as a Slayer, since s/he has only theory and no practice. That Giles lacks practical authority is shown in Buffy's frequent insubordination, and he supports her rejection of the Council. Buffy's relationship with Giles can be problematic, but generally Giles allows female characters active agency. Ms. Calendar takes the lead in their romance, and Giles generally encourages both Buffy and Willow to develop their particular skills and rarely implies that they are not strong enough to face potential challenges.

Thus Giles seems to fit the profile for a new man. Yet Giles' position as adult makes him initially the only member of the Scoobies to work, and he is a protector and provider. This role as provider places others in a dependent position, though this is never spelled out. Giles provides transport and, more important, space: three of the four Scooby meeting places are "his" (the library in early seasons, his home in season 4, and The Magic Box in seasons 5 and 6). That Giles' identity crisis in season 4 focuses on his decline to useless, unemployed drunk (part of the larger disintegration of the Scooby Gang in this season) merely highlights how his identity is tied up with wage earning and providing. The male character Giles has most in common with in early seasons is Angel (also an older male, a displaced European, well traveled and well read), and the two meet often over their concern to protect Buffy. As season 5 develops, Giles acts as protector of Dawn and Buffy and provides financial support when they are in difficulty. (Since viewers know Buffy managed to get Giles reinstated as a Watcher with full back pay in "Checkpoint," it might not be such an invidious position. It is also clearly designed to show Buffy's inexperience in the "real" world and her need to rely on someone else.)

Giles displays other traditionally masculine characteristics—aggressive sexuality and physical violence—though these are often displaced onto his alter ego, Ripper (figure 9). Ripper is constructed deliberately to contrast the traditional Giles of early seasons,[4] demonstrating the binary nature of masculinity in *Buffy* and the split personality of many characters. He thus offers similar viewing pleasure to the alternative versions of Willow. In "The Dark Age" viewers and characters discover Giles' past as a university dropout who dabbled in dark magic. Ripper is first hinted at when Buffy discovers Giles at home, neglecting his Watcher responsibilities and apparently drunk. She reports that he was acting "very anti-Giles" and Xander observes, "Nobody can be wound as straight and narrow as Giles without a dark side erupting" (foreshadowing similar comments on Willow and Buffy). Although the Ripper aspect of Giles is more aggressive and assertive (telling Buffy, "Hey, this is not your battle and as your Watcher I am telling you unequivocally to stay out of it"), he remains feminized. "You're like a woman, Ripper," the demon Eyghon tells him, wearing Ms. Calendar's body. "You never had the strength for me."

Ripper surfaces at subsequent points, most notably in "Band Candy" (3006), and is always associated with aggression and violence (I see him as a strategy for the use of violence in an otherwise intellectual character). In general the violence of Ripper is used by Giles as part of his role in protecting Buffy and the Scoobies. His language, like Giles', signals his difference, but it also signals a difference *from* Giles: the received pronunciation of the privileged and educated Brit is replaced in Ripper by a (rather exaggerated) generic southern English working-class "accent." I would argue, therefore, that along with Jack O'Toole and Spike, Ripper

FIGURE 9: *Ripper the "anti-Giles" ("Band Candy").*

links a certain type of masculinity with certain types of men: middle-
class men may be new men, but working-class men are real men. It is
also suggestive that some business with Giles' glasses often heralds the
return of Ripper, and Ripper does not wear glasses, a classic signifier of
the wimpy swot. His costuming in "Band Candy" associates him with
either a working-class hero (like early Marlon Brando) or, perhaps, a
middle-class would-be rebel like James Dean in *Rebel Without a Cause*
(1955). This visual presentation of Ripper as a 1950s rebel does not match

his actual rebellion in the 1970s, but it does draw on intertexts that are classic representations of masculinity and a period of American cultural history much concerned with asserting masculinity in the face of femi-nization (books from the 1940s like Philip Wylie's *Generation of Vipers* and Edward Strecker's *Their Mother's Sons* influenced this view).

Ripper first appears in an episode where Giles' relationship with Ms. Calendar is about to become sexual, though his violence is not di-rectly related to or triggered by sexuality in the narrative (as with Oz and Angel/us, for example). Giles' position as a forty-something who hangs out with a group of teenagers could be slightly dubious, as Buffy points out: "So, you like to party with the students? Isn't that kind of skanky?" ("Welcome to the Hellmouth"). Initially, Giles' role as nur-turer defuses any sexual attraction (within the narrative), and age divides him from Buffy and her peers, even when the teen characters themselves become adults (see also Levine and Schneider 2003: 308). Outside the narrative, Anthony Head, the actor who plays Giles, "was surprised by the strong reaction to Giles as a sex symbol" (Golden and Holder 1998: 210), though he had played the romantic lead in a series of successful coffee adverts, and this "sexy" image is subsequently played up.[5] In-deed, Ms. Calendar's follow-up to her "fuddy duddy" remark was "Has anybody ever told you're kind of a sexy fuddy duddy?" Part of Giles' loosening up in season 4 is about acquiring a kind of "cool," as when the Scoobies witness his "gig" at the coffee shop and Willow admits that she had a crush on him ("Where the Wild Things Are"). Given the perhaps unexpectedly broad demographic of *Buffy*'s audience, Giles offers view-ing pleasure to female and male viewers of the show, in a similar way to characters like Inspector Morse (see Thomas).

Giles' relationships with Jenny Calendar, and later Olivia, work in several ways: to establish him as heterosexual, to remove him from sexual connections with teen characters, and to further emphasize his age difference (the teens generally see it as "gross" and inappropriate that older people have a sex life). They also show that he is sexually attractive. Ripper has sex with Joyce in "Band Candy," and when Buffy can read thoughts in "Earshot," she overhears her mother thinking that Ripper was like a "stevedore" during sex (another reference potentially relating class and sexuality). Edwards also suggests that Giles' sexual prowess is "proved" by his black girlfriend, Olivia (2002: 95)—he can satisfy an "exotic" lover. (Furthermore, it could be argued that this interracial re-lationship links new masculinity with liberal values.)[6] Although Giles is characterized primarily as a new man, he is far from weak and effeminate—he is a desirable heterosexual partner. Again *Buffy* has the best of both worlds. Matching the apparently contradictory combination of "femininity" and "feminism" in the young female protagonists, Giles is both a sensitive new man and a virile lover whose heterosexuality upholds rather than challenges patriarchal structures and gendering.

Dyer argues that the "divided nature of white masculinity . . . is expressed in relation not only to sexuality but also to anything that can be characterized as low, dark and irredeemably corporeal" (1997: 28). I would suggest that Ripper's other more traditional masculine qualities such as aggression and physical violence are corporeal (physical) and presented as uncharacteristically "low" or "dark." These emerge at other times, as in the season 4 chainsaw-wielding scene ("Fear, Itself"). Being turned into a Faryl demon ("A New Man"—the title is open to all kinds of interpretations) seemed to imply the return of the dark side for Giles, and this episode features Ethan Rayne, an acquaintance from Giles' Ripper days and a recurring villain. The episode highlights Giles' sense that he is losing his role in the group when Professor Walsh undermines his special relationship as a father figure and mentor to Buffy. This is partially resolved by the fact that Buffy later recognizes Giles within the demon, yet demon-Giles is shown deliberately scaring Professor Walsh, whom he called a "harridan." Here the show articulates debates about changing masculinity, encouraging a "feminist" explanation of Giles' behavior. Walsh clearly evokes anxieties about Giles' masculinity, verbalised in the company of a male friend and while engaging in the "masculine" pursuit of drowning his sorrows. "Twenty years I've been fighting demons," Giles slurs to Ethan, "*Maggie Walsh and her nancy ninja boys* come and six months later the demons are pissing themselves with fear. They never even noticed me." He continues, more explicitly, "She said I was an absent male role model. Absent my arse, *I'm twice the man she is* [my emphasis]." Like the tough guys, Giles uses language to preserve gender distinctions and to shore up his own masculinity.

At the episode's conclusion Buffy tells Riley that she does not want to speculate on what might have happened if demon-Giles had killed Ethan. She means largely that they might not have been able to turn Giles back, but bear in mind the cardinal sin on *Buffy* is to kill a human. This potential violence is always within Giles, though arguably the comic aspects of Giles' transformation here work against a serious view of his behavior. As the pressure to defeat Glory heightens in season 5 and Buffy insists on protecting Dawn at the possible expense of ending the world, Ripper begins to reemerge. In one episode Giles threatens

Spike with such vigor that the vampire is for once left speechless ("I Was Made to Love You"), then Giles wreaks unspecified off-screen violence on one of Glory's demon minions in order to get information ("Tough Love"). In the showdown Buffy defeats Glory, who withdraws, leaving Ben, her human host, battered but intact. Buffy makes Ben promise that he/Glory will never again pursue her and Dawn, then lets him live. Giles, however, suffocates Ben, explaining that Buffy "couldn't take a human life. She's a hero, you see. She's not like us" ("The Gift"). Thus the apparently civilized Giles will kill a human when he believes that it is morally justified. Giles' statement also sets up oppositions ("she" and "us"; his use of "hero" might imply "villain"). Certainly his use of violence to protect the female Buffy allows him to take on a conventional masculine role as her protector, and Jacob M. Held even describes Giles as the only one "strong enough" to kill Ben (2003: 237). As I argued in chapter 1, Giles' killing of Ben allows Buffy to preserve her moral purity.

During seasons 6 and 7 Giles is absent for much of the time and generally reverts to a father figure.[7] I have already mentioned that Giles clashes with Buffy over Spike (as with his killing of Ben, he sees this as being for the greater good) and she rejects his advice. Later in "Chosen," however, he supports Buffy's "radical" final solution ("it's bloody brilliant!") and joins the original Scoobies for the last battle. Giles displays some potential as a new man, but his negotiation of gender and gendered relationships is often complicated by his role as a parent figure, as I have indicated. Not until Principal Wood does the show offer a further, more mature version of a new man, this time uncomplicated by parental anxieties. I discuss Wood at the end of this chapter.

BEN

"Gentle Ben," as Glory calls him, implying another "sensitive lad," is a hospital intern who features in season 5. He takes an interest in Buffy and her mother's illness while they are at the hospital. This positions him in a caring profession sometimes associated with women, and he is contrasted with the older male doctor who is presented as a distant professional. He looks after Dawn at various points, further reinforcing his "feminine" nurturing qualities, though his heterosexuality is established by his interest in Buffy. He might even have been a partner for her, but she puts off a date with him after her encounter with Warren and April ("I Was Made to Love You"). Ben is trusted enough to help the Scoobies when Giles is seriously injured as the gang try to escape Glory and the Knights of Byzantium at the end of the season. He betrays them because Glory inhabits his body and takes over at inappropriate times. Ben is thus further feminized, especially by sudden reappearances (from Glory) when he ends up wearing dresses as in "Spiral" (notably, this does not masculinize Glory). Dawn sums up Ben's nature when, abducted as the Key, she tells him that she prefers Glory because she does not pretend to be anything other than a monster ("The Weight of the World"), implying that Ben too is only "playing" the new man.

Make Me Feel Like a Man

Xander demonstrates characteristics of a new man, though at times the implication is that he is a new man because he cannot be a real man. Xander's emotional ties to the group are obvious: his long-lasting friendship with Willow is a core element and his position as the "heart" of the group is emphasized more than once. It is his bond with Willow that saves the world at the end of season 6: despite Dark Willow's sarcastic remark "You're going to stop me by telling me you love me," this is almost exactly what happens. Xander tries to reconcile Buffy and Riley when their relationship becomes distant. He refuses to be caught between Willow and Anya when they vie for his attention, and again his loyalty is proved when he refuses to choose one of "his women" to die at the hands of a troll in "Triangle" (5011). That Xander represents emotion, love, and friendship is part of the project of dissociating gender and behavior: more conventionally the "heart" of the Scooby family would be female. In this way Xander demonstrates typically "feminine" competencies in relationship management (though his romance relationships threaten to disrupt the Scooby family) and a willingness to articulate emotion.

Xander is eager to play a part in the communal efforts of the Scoobies, even if his role tends to be passive and he often has to be rescued by Buffy. He is not physically up to fighting evil, and though keen, he is most often knocked out or incapacitated. Indeed, his high point in fight scenes is the slow-motion slap-fight with Vamp Harmony in "The Initiative" (mentioned in chapter 3). In a less exaggerated but similar way to hapless male "hero" Joxer from *Xena: Warrior Princess*, Xander's lack of physical prowess affords pleasure to the viewer through role reversal (the opposite of Buffy's strength and action). Despite this apparent lack of "real masculinity," the show makes much of Xander as a soldier, first in "Halloween" when he "becomes" his soldier costume, and later in episodes relating to this. This may simply be a useful plot point, but it also asserts some "real" masculinity in Xander, and Buttsworth suggests that his transformation invokes "the ways in which the military claims to 'make men out of boys'" (2002: 187). Xander initially wants to be a hero, and developments like "The Zeppo" mean that by season 4 he is comfortable telling Buffy, "You're my hero" ("The Freshman" 4001). Notably Xander's version of heroism, like Giles', involves self-sacrifice and a willingness to put others before himself, as well as personal risk, demonstrated in his face-off with Dark Willow (Wendy Love Anderson [2003: 226] points out the potential religious allegory in this scene). This self-sacrifice is further underlined in the fight with Caleb in season 7, where Xander is seriously wounded in the eye ("Dirty Girls"). Relating gendering to Christianity, Dyer suggests that suffering is almost *an assertion of* white masculinity (1997: 17).

Like Giles and Oz, Xander is primarily heterosocial; at high school he seems to avoid the company of other males. He gets along with girls and is accepted by them as an unthreatening, equal companion: "You're not like other guys at all," Buffy tells him. "You're totally one of the girls" ("The Witch" 1003). In the second ever episode he says, "I'm inadequate, that's fine. I'm less than a man" ("The Harvest"). Much of Xander's appeal in early seasons was based on the fact that he is very conscious of being "less than a man," part of what Simkin calls "his endearingly self-deprecating nature" (2004b: 18). When Xander is discovered as a crasher at a frat party, he is forced to dress as a woman and is ridiculed for his lack of "real" masculinity ("Reptile Boy"). Later Anya is attracted to him because he's "not quite as obnoxious as most of the alpha males" ("The Prom"). Thus I would agree with A. Susan Owen that Xander consistently "makes ironic and self-mocking commentary on the perils and challenges of masculine social scripts" (1999: 26), offering a variant of masculinity and perhaps eliciting recognition from the viewer. Simkin argues that Xander "does not fall into the same category as Jonathan, Andrew and Warren" (2004b: 11), but the comparison with the Trio does much to clarify Xander's sense of inadequacy: the way he deals with it differs radically from the way they do. All this may seem to prove that Xander's character is a new representation of masculinity, one that complements the show's strong female protagonists.

Yet Xander is far from the perfect new man. Like Giles, he eventually has paid employment, making him a wage earner and provider. His job in construction establishes a traditional kind of masculinity related to physical work, akin to an earlier American ideal that Michael Kimmel calls "the Heroic Artisan" (1997: 16). This relates to Xander's uncertain class positioning: he is the only teen character in early seasons who is not clearly middle class. In season 3 his brief liaison with Faith ties him to another character who is differentiated in class terms, and I suggested in the last chapter that one of the less obvious undercurrents of "The Zeppo" is that Xander rejects tough-guy masculinity because he is trying to escape the working-class identity represented by Jack and his gang. Similarly, in season 4 Xander's series of minimum-wage jobs and perhaps even the unfounded rumor that he might join the army imply a future as a working-class nobody. His success in the construction industry establishes him in a working-class "trade" (rather than a middle-class "profession"), but his rapid rise through the ranks shows him moving toward middle-class managerial status. "Lessons" cuts from Giles telling Willow that "we all are who we are, no matter how much we may appear to have changed" to Xander emerging from an apparently new car, wearing a suit and tie (figure 10). As a kind of self-made man, Xander is another example of shifting identity. He becomes a provider, highlighted through his relationship with Anya, as discussed in chapter 1, and season 7 shows Xander acting as "man of the house" for the Summers women. Initially he wished to be a protector, and now he is cast in this role, though not quite in the heroic way he imagined. Xander is often called upon to protect Dawn, and in the final battle Buffy sends him away to do just that, telling him, "I need someone I can count on, no matter what happens" ("End of Days"). Notably, Dawn asserts her independence and sabotages the plan: Xander is "not man enough" to stop her.

But as I see it the real problem with Xander's representation as a new man is sexuality, especially given the contradiction already outlined between new masculinities and heterosexuality's complicity in patriarchal structures. Sexual prowess is again called on to demonstrate that a new man is in fact a real man. Xander's uninhibited (hetero)sexuality can be read as another trait attributed to the working class by the middle class. Early on he appeared to be sexually innocent, if eager for experience. Xander's unrequited love for Buffy is emphasized in season 1 by his transformation in "The Pack," when, possessed by the spirit of a hyena, he attempts to force himself on her. Giles comments, "Testosterone is a great equalizer. It turns all men into morons," but it is made clear that Xander is only acting this way because of the spirit possession and therefore that he is *not* a typical adolescent male. This sexual naïveté is highlighted again in season 3, when he has a one-nighter with Faith ("Consequences"). Despite complaining about having "bounced back to being

FIGURE 10: *Xander rises from tradesman to professional ("Lessons").*

a dateless nerd" in "Beneath You," Xander's relationships with Cordelia
and Anya and Willow's long-unrequited love for him prove his desirability. Whedon's admission that Nicholas Brendon (who plays Xander)
is "way too hunky" to be a nerd (in Lavery 2002a: 38) underlines this
as potentially another source of viewing pleasure, and the show played
it up with the "Speedo moment" of "Go Fish" (2020). All of Xander's
relationships are based on physical attraction (Cordelia, Faith, Anya),
and he finds them problematic.

Xander's romances and sexual liaisons almost seem designed to "make
up for" his other shortcomings. Early on his fascination with sex was
seen as an integral part of his geek teen boy behavior: "I'm seventeen. Looking at linoleum makes me wanna have sex" ("Innocence").
Xander's (and the show's) self-awareness thus asserts his typical behavior *and* his difference. Anya's insistence on discussing their sex life in
public has been highlighted as part of her characteristic difference, but
it serves another function as well. That Xander is a "Viking in the sack"
("The Yoko Factor") adds a twist to his apparently new masculinity:

just as Giles is able to "satisfy" a black woman, Xander is able to satisfy an ex-demon. Like Giles, Xander is not just desirable—he is virile. And despite the many subtexts of *Buffy*, Larry's assumption that Xander is gay, and some of Xander's own more unguarded comments (particularly about Spike), Xander's liaisons have always been firmly heterosexual. So much so that his "Willow, gay me up" speech in "First Date" is clearly a joke stemming from his disgust at attracting more "demon women." Saxey suggests that fan fiction often presents Xander as gay because his "problems as they are currently presented—worries about his role in life, struggles with his notions of masculinity, sex and relationships— don't contain within them a recognizable solution" (2001: 202). That is, fans see heterosexuality, consciously or not, as a stumbling block to reconciling the "problems" in constructing contemporary masculinity. To Xander his relationship with Anya is a strong affirmation of his mas- culinity, and Simkin notes that the "real crisis [in "The Replacement"], however, is centred on Anya" (2004b: 21). "You make me feel like I've never felt before in my life," he tells her, "*like a man*" ("Into the Woods," my emphasis), and before the showdown at the end of season 5, Xander asks Anya to marry him. Xander's high school fantasies never disappear, and even in season 7 he dreams about young innocent Potentials offering themselves to his sexual experience ("Dirty Girls"). This is presented as comical, and Xander's function as a comic character tends to play down his flaws; they are laughable foibles that add to his character.

Xander and Willow's male-female friendship is a core element hold- ing the gang together, but notably Xander is never shown in a non- sexualized relationship with a female character. As Korsmeyer observes, even "Xander's steadfast friendship for Willow has an early erotic as- pect" (2003: 167), and as I mentioned earlier, he is initially attracted to Buffy. In the season 2 finale, Xander chose not to tell Buffy that Wil- low had a chance of returning Angel's soul, and Buffy was forced to kill Angel rather than Angelus (this is raised again in "Selfless" but not ad- dressed). Clearly this is motivated by Xander's jealousy of Angel, and Gregory J. Sakal notes the "hubris of his presumption to know what is best for" Buffy (2003: 246), a removal of agency from the female. Xander also told Riley about Buffy and Angel's sexual relationship ("The Yoko Factor"). When Xander finds out that Spike and Anya consoled each other sexually after the wedding fiasco, Xander pursues Spike with an axe ("Entropy" 6018). Here sexual jealousy (of Anya and Buffy) is Xander's downfall (the same jealousy he displayed to all potential part- ners for Buffy in high school): his condemnation of Anya, "I look at you and I feel sick because you have sex with that," also includes Buffy, his "hero" and unattainable idol. (Both Sakal 2003: 248 and Levine and Schneider 2003: 306 read Xander as idealizing Buffy, as "femininity" has traditionally been idealized.) Xander's behavior is consistently motivated by sexual jealousy—a typical "masculine" quality.

Furthermore, despite his attraction to strong women (shared with almost all male characters, regardless of their gender "politics"), Xander has problems allowing his partners equality and agency. Granted, in his early relationship with Cordelia she appeared to be dominant, largely because of her higher status in the high school world, but Xander's relationship with Anya is a key example of inequality. Xander jilts Anya at the altar after receiving a "nightmare vision" of their future together ("Hells Bells"). His vision is very similar to his version of Angel and Buffy's future in "Surprise,"[8] but Xander is now in the position he imagined for Angel, "dreaming of the glory days," while Anya works to support their family. Xander's feelings for Buffy are still creating tension, while the mixed heritage of their children also causes friction. Although Xander's background here is not as ambivalent as in previous seasons (since his family are shown), domestic violence and drinking again imply working-class behavior (as noted in chapter 3, these tend to be attributed to the working class). Xander's violence and aggression in the vision are clearly modeled on his own father (see chapter 7), but he uses his new-man sensitivity as an "excuse": although he still appears to love Anya, he runs away, implying that this is to protect her. Once again a new man demonstrates a capacity for violence, cannot cope with the situation, denies the female partner agency, and leaves. And, as with Oz, Xander is not really blamed, in this case because Anya is still an outsider.

Xander's anxieties throughout *Buffy* have concerned his inability to contribute to the group with a special talent (superpower): even in season 7 he discusses this with Dawn ("Potential"). In "Checkpoint" Buffy answered this criticism from the Watcher's Council by pointing out, "'The boy' has clocked more field time than any of you put together," countering the belittlement of "the boy" with a military metaphor and underlining Xander's willingness to contribute. I would point out in conclusion that Xander does in fact have a special status: he is, as the show underlines, the normal one. Despite his ambivalent class background and his geek status, he is a white heterosexual male and is thus the *only* Scooby who is also a member of the historically dominant sector of American society. Dyer notes of the character Prendergast in *Falling Down* (1993) that his "very unobtrusiveness . . . allows him to occupy more comfortably the position of ordinariness that is the white man's prerogative" (1997: 221), and this is an apt description of Xander.[9] This may be exactly *why* Xander has so many problems negotiating a new masculine identity. Although his version of masculinity is not exactly "hegemonic," his position as white American heterosexual male allows him to "benefit without really trying, from a patriarchal dividend" (Johnson 1997: 15).

Principal Man

In season 7 Sunnydale High School opens again, and its new principal is a departure from previous incumbents—he is young and black. Like other nonwhite characters on *Buffy*, Principal Robin Wood is whitewashed, assimilated: he is a middle-class professional who tells Buffy he is from Beverly Hills, not "the 'hood" ("Help" 7004). Wood is an interesting development in *Buffy*'s representation of race, but he is also, I would argue, the most uncompromised new man. He is the son of Nikki Wood, the subway Slayer killed by Spike in 1977 New York ("Fool for Love"). This means that Wood is from a matriarchal line; he remembers a strong mother and no father (a typical characterization of black families based on post–World War II demographics and employment patterns [Woloch 2000: 524, 582]). As Spike points out, Wood finds it hard to accept that although Spike may have taken his childhood away by killing his mother, his mother had to balance "the mission" and her responsibility to him ("Lies My Parents Told Me").

Wood is also one of very few "good" adults, and unlike most other adults on *Buffy*, he does not function as a parent figure (except for his role as a teacher), perhaps because he enters when the original teens are themselves adults. Furthermore, because he is Other, Wood is not implicated in white male supremacy: he accepts Buffy as an equal (though he is still her boss) and later a "general" and supports Faith as a leader. Like Xander, he has no superpowers, though he has been trained to fight vampires: "I'm just a guy. Granted, a cool and sexy vampire-fighting guy, but still" ("First Date"). In this way he offers a similar "ordinary" subject position to the viewer, though like other characters of color on *Buffy* he remains a minor character. His scenes do allow him some development apart from the main protagonists, as when the First appears to him as his mother, but he is primarily used to illuminate the role of Slayer and the newly souled Spike. He has little interaction with the other Scoobies; he opposes Spike, the dead white European male, and allies with Giles, the only other "man" in the group and someone also marked by difference.

His vendetta against Spike is related strongly to emotional reactions,[10] and his sensitivity is shown through the articulation of emotion that the show values. In connection with his mother, in his interaction with Faith (he is part of her redemption), and even in his early conversations with Buffy he is not afraid to admit to being scared ("Beneath You") or to needing love and reinforcement. When he tells Faith how the First appeared as his mother he says he knew it wasn't real, "but I still wanted my mother to hold me like a baby," adding, "In a manly way, of course" (this awareness of gendered constructions further links him to other new men). His connection with Faith reinforces his presentation as a "pretty decent guy." Furthermore, his assertion that "nobody wants to be alone" ("Touched") proves that he is not an individualist. Wood shares the communal ethos of the group—he is willing to work beside them, even Spike, to fight evil.

Like other new men Wood displays violent aggression and heightened sexuality. In his case these are "justified" by the show's narrative and can also be related to his representation as a nonwhite character and to age (in "First Date" Xander says he must be at least ten years older than Buffy, but the show's chronology puts him at around 30, rather young to be a high school principal). His aggression is directed at the "right" targets, and if he initially resents Spike, this is understandable given his history, and it is eventually resolved. Wood's history allows him more subjectivity than any other character of color and sufficient emotional articulation to qualify as a new man. Like Kendra, Wood is sexualized and presented as a sexual object rather than a sexual threat, though like many other male characters he offers a further source of viewing pleasure to a "female gaze." There is a sexual tension between him and Buffy from their first meeting. Eventually he asks her out on a date, and in "First Date" Buffy describes him as "a young, hot principal with earrings" (I read his earrings as a signifier of the exotic; see also chapter 6 on Mr. Trick). He becomes even more sexualized through his interaction with Faith, and liberal values are connoted by his interracial relationships (Gill [2003] notes that by season 7 all the main characters are or have been interracially dating). Yet he does not display the sexual jealousy that marks Xander and Oz; he endorses romance relationships between equals and allows Faith to take the lead in their sexual encounter. This may be partly owing to age: he admits that he has grown out of some of his younger, more aggressive behavior (such as an "avenging son phase" in his twenties ["First Date"]).

Gill offers an insight into fan interaction with the show when she describes how a Web site called The Principal Wood Deathwatch was set up by black female viewers after Wood's first appearance on *Buffy*, in the expectation that, as a character of color, he would shortly be killed (2003). The show also intimates that Wood may be a villain. His early appearances are often accompanied by menacing music, he is shown finding Jonathan's body in the school basement and then burying it in secret ("Never Leave Me" 7009), and, as Buffy says, "He's got that whole too-charming-to-be-real thing going on" ("First Date"). These expectations are reversed, as regular viewers might expect, when Wood reveals to Buffy that he is the son of a Slayer.[11] Unlike Giles, Wood's presentation is uncomplicated by a "parental" role, and his late appearance means that he has an openness that allows his character great potential (as with some of the bad girls): he is both a man and a new man, perhaps the first in *Buffy*. Notably, however, he is also still a real man, and he remains Other since he is allied with Others (Giles, foreigner; Faith, working class); again openness is a consequence of marginality.

You Men and Your Man-Ness

Some representations of masculinity in *Buffy* seem able to transcend gender binaries, but on closer examination their masculinity retains traditional elements, and almost all of the new men display a split personality or tension that reinforces a binary structure. New men try to repress "natural" masculine tendencies in themselves (Korsmeyer [2003: 165] describes Giles as "[h]abitually on guard against the resurgence of his old 'Ripper' self"), though this is not always successful. Male characters can either retain their masculinity and be classed as the enemy and be defeated by the Slayer, or they can give up their power and be classed as allies and become feminized (Slayerettes—changed later to Scooby Gang). Many new men relate to Buffy as potential partners, and because of this, just like the tough guys, they are in competition with Buffy and with each other (especially with Angel) and their very heterosexuality marks them as complicit with patriarchal structures. Even Jonathan demonstrates this in "Superstar" when he uses an "augmentation" spell to construct a new-man superstar version of himself but unwittingly creates its antithesis, a monster that violently attacks innocent people (mainly women): the new man cannot exist without the old monster masculinity. All the new men are aware of how masculinity is constructed and therefore of how they differ from its traditional form.

This does not prevent every new man from simultaneously being presented as a real man who has to/is able to prove this, especially through sexual prowess or aggression. Masculinity is further asserted by wage earning: of the males in the group, Giles, Xander, and Wood all have paying jobs. Just as Parker and others did, Xander, Oz and Giles may "play the sensitive lad," but they are as capable as tough guys and monsters of unbridled sexual appetite, damaging sexual jealousy, unthinking violence, or removing female agency. The presentation of "uncharacteristic" traditional masculine behavior in new men is often deflected by comedy. All of this may be a strategy to show that new men do not have to "lack" the attributes of real men, and therefore to make them more appealing to viewers, but it also closes down some of their potential for a revisioning of masculinity. The audience may laugh at Xander's difficulties in trying to be a new man, but there is no real indication that he will ever become one; Wood retains his potential only through his limited development. The new men are valorized through their contrast with "bad" tough guys, but they are clearly not a solution. They demonstrate again the difficulty in negotiating a new type of gender identity, in trying to construct a masculinity that fits the postfeminist age.

6 *Dead Boys* "WE LIKE TO TALK BIG"

The majority of vampires on *Buffy* are merely stake-fodder, though some are also traditional villains or henchmen. Other vampires retain idiosyncratic "human" personalities because it serves a convenient function in the narrative. The inclusion of Angel (who has a soul and no longer feeds on humans) also allows the show to poke some fun at the Ricean "vampire with a conscience," and both Spike and Angel function to blur morality and the boundaries between human and monster. As noted in chapter 3, *Buffy*'s most popular and most highly developed vampire characters are male. I have called this chapter "Dead Boys" because many longer-running vampire characters are "young" so they can more readily interact in the lives of the teen protagonists, as Whedon admits (in Lavery 2002a: 37). Although Angel and Spike count their age in centuries rather than decades, they are rarely separated from the teen protagonists by age. The title of the teen vampire film *The Lost Boys* (1987) invoked the Peter Pan ideal of never growing up, and the youthful appearance of the male vampires I discuss here includes them in *Buffy*'s competing versions of masculinity.

Although vampires, being nonhuman, need not take on socially constructed gender, they usually do: female vampires are generally masculinized, while male vampires are almost always feminized. Creed suggests that male victims in horror films may be feminized—"a consequence of placing a male in a masochistic position"—but adds that "in the process of being constructed as monstrous the male is 'feminized'" (1993b: 121). Since horror is constructed around violation of binary divisions, this may not be surprising, but because *Buffy* is about a vampire slayer the monsters (vampires) in the show are also the victims, and thus doubly feminized. Spike may be the most obvious example, but all the male vampires discussed here can be read as feminized. In the context of action, Stacey Abbott suggests that *Buffy* manipulates the conventions of the vampire "by emphasizing the physical over the spiritual"

(2001: 3). I would add that this emphasis relates to the physical nature of masculinity and that for vampires the physical body is a site of anxiety and change as well as desire (Ford's statement in "Lie to Me" that vampires "die young—and stay pretty" also points to this). Here I discuss Angel and Spike's significance within the visual and generic context of screen horror and look at other vampire males, such as Luke, Dalton, Mr. Trick, and Dracula.

Getting Away From the Dark Prince

I begin my discussion with vampires who seem to clearly fit the conventions of genre and gender.

LUKE

Luke is integral to *Buffy*'s reversal of vampire representations, and though Abbott describes them as nineteenth-century vampires (2001: 16), both he and the Nosferatu-like Master avoid the prevalent Dracula image (which *was* used in the *Buffy* movie). Luke is a typical second-in-command henchman, that is, a tough guy. Size alone makes him formidable, and his strength is underlined by his age—he has been undefeated in combat since "1843. Madrid" ("The Harvest"). He comes close to killing Buffy at the end of "Welcome to the Hellmouth" but (inexplicably) doesn't. She kills him fairly easily in "The Harvest," distracting him by breaking a window and reminding him about sunrise, only to conclude, "It's in about nine hours, moron." Luke is simultaneously a (feminized) subordinate to the Master, the leader; he acts as the Master's "vessel." Whedon has even noted that in "an unintentionally provocative shot in 'the Harvest' in which Luke pledges his allegiance, the mise-en-scène appears to suggest that the disciple is performing fellatio on The Master" (in Lavery 2002a: 35). The actor who played Luke (Brian Thompson) returned in season 2 to play the Judge, a similarly hulking and invincible demon villain who was killed by Buffy with a little help from her friends and a rocket launcher ("What's that do?") in "Innocence." In both cases the character's failure to move with the times leads to death, suggesting the anachronistic nature of this type of masculinity.

JESSE

Anachronistic it may be, but the desire for such tough-guy monster strength is played out in the story of Xander's male friend, Jesse, who appears in the same episodes as Luke. Jesse is presented as similar to

Xander: he is a nerd, a failure at traditional masculinity.[1] After Jesse is picked up by Darla at The Bronze, Xander and the others assume he is dead, but later in "The Harvest" he meets Xander and Buffy and they discover that he has been turned into a vampire. As with Vamp Willow, Vamp Jesse's behavior is a clear reversal. Cordelia, who had previously rejected him, is now attracted by his assertive behavior (he tells her to "shut up" as he leads her to the dance floor), but she is then taken from Jesse to feed Luke in the ritual. Jesse is thus forced to submit to both tough guy Luke and the patriarchal Master, complaining, "I don't get one?" When Xander says he is sorry to see his friend changed, he responds, "Sorry? I feel good, Xander, I feel strong" ("The Harvest"). Like demon-Forrest, Jesse sees his transformation as boosting his masculinity: "Jesse was an excruciating loser who couldn't get a date with anyone in the sighted community! Look at me! *I'm a new man* [my emphasis]." This enacts the vampire's ability to reflect not just hidden fears but also desires (Silver and Ursini 1993: 55). Ironically, Jesse is dusted by Xander when a fleeing Bronze-goer jolts him into the stake Xander holds.

DALTON

Another vampire who appears in season 2 is the bookish Dalton. Very little information is given about him: he works for Spike and Drusilla, and Spike points out, "He's a wanker, but he's the only one we've got with half a brain" ("Surprise"). Dalton has very little screen time but functions as simple contrast to further the characterization of Spike (and to a lesser extent Dru), and Spike uses the line quoted above to prevent Drusilla from killing him. He operates almost as a vampire Watcher, assisting Spike with research until he is killed by the Judge in "Surprise." He is coded as a nerd: he reads a lot, wears glasses, and is nervous around Spike. In other words, he displays none of the aggressive masculinity of other male vampires. Dalton is further distinguished from season 2's more youthful and modern vampires by his clothing (wing collar, cravat, waistcoat). (With hindsight, this appearance links him to the human who became Spike—William the "bloody awful" poet, a rather feminized figure.) The apocalyptic Judge has the power to burn the life out of all who display humanity or goodness. "This one is full of feeling. He reads," he says of Dalton, and Dalton's death proves that male vampires are neither exclusively tough guys nor exclusively evil.

Dark Prince Envy

Having avoided the Dracula type for so long, the opening episode of season 5 finally allows *Buffy* to "do" Dracula, though its tongue-in-cheek spirit is summed up in the title, "Buffy vs. Dracula." The episode makes many references to the myths and representations of Dracula and other pop-culture vampires, as when Buffy tells Dracula, "I've fought more than a couple of pimply overweight vamps who called themselves Lestat," and Xander derides him, "Look who's got a bad case of dark prince envy." Dracula takes up residence in a castle that no one has ever noticed in Sunnydale before; he transforms into bats, a wolf, and mist, and the details of his appearance are traditional (he is tall, with a white face, a cloak, and abundant dark hair). Arguably Dracula is presented as a new man; he seems to be sensitive and lacks the violent physical aggression of tough-guy vamps like Luke. This is partly because Dracula, as an archetypal vampire, can easily be seen as a feminized monster, Other than the human male heroes who resist him. Yet at the same time *Buffy*'s Dracula is masculinized through a powerful sexuality that threatens not only Buffy but also the male characters. Dracula, like the tough guys, is in competition with other males and with the Slayer.

His sexual power is deliberately presented as penetrative and aggressive (Buffy defensively says, "There was no penetration" after she and Willow discuss Dracula's "dark penetrating eyes"). Although Dracula is called "master" by Xander (taking the role of the "bug eater" Renfield), he is far removed from the ancient and sexless Master of season 1, who was gendered by age and his position as a patriarch. Steps are taken to differentiate Dracula—Willow tells the Scoobies, "Dracula's modus operandi is different from other vampires. He will kill just to feed but he'd rather have a connection with his victims. And he has all these mental powers to draw them in"—but he is a type viewers have seen before. Dracula is a sexual predator, a demonic Parker Abrams who manipulates his female victims into "choosing" him not by "mental powers" but by playing on the conventions of heterosexual romance. Daugherty even suggests that "Dracula comes close to defeating Buffy, not through a display of force, but by appealing to the romantic side of Buffy's nature" (2001: 163).

The episode focuses on the attempted seduction of Buffy and her realization that she has further exploration of her role "to come," yet it also pits Dracula against every regular male character, throwing most of them into anxiety about their manhood. Spike and Dracula do not meet, but Spike's dismissal of Dracula is clearly bluster, motivated partly by jealousy, and his parting comment to Riley—"You'll never find him. Not before he gets to her"—acknowledges Dracula's threat. Giles, feeling that he should leave Buffy to develop independently, tells Willow at the beginning of the episode that he intends to return to England. Although he meets Dracula only briefly, Giles is overwhelmed by the highly sexualized "three sisters" (in a scene parodying *Bram Stoker's Dracula* [1992]) and has to be rescued by Riley. Riley is directly threatened by Dracula's seduction of Buffy, and as mentioned in chapter 4, the teaser for this episode implies that Riley cannot physically satisfy Buffy (he is also forcibly reminded of her relationship with Angel). Xander seems the most threatened by Dracula's presence. Anya has "hung out a few times" with Dracula, and Xander is clearly uncomfortable with this sexual competition. He is then dominated by Dracula and calls him "master." At the end of the episode he complains in revealing gendered and sexualized language about being turned into "a spider-eating man-bitch" and concludes, "I'm tired of being everybody's butt-monkey."

In the final analysis, the male characters are more threatened by Dracula than Buffy is. She successfully resists him, makes the males' rescue attempt unnecessary, and returns to form, telling Dracula, "You know, I really think the thrall's gone out of our relationship," before fighting and staking him. As Giles points out, "Although [Dracula] goes through the motions of an intimate seduction, the end result is the same"—that is, the end result of Dracula in *Buffy* is that she slays the vampire. For the male characters this sameness works on another level. Riley says early on, "He's still just a vampire," but Dracula is also just a male: he never wears vamp face, even when feeding on Buffy. Like Parker, Dracula manipulates gendered responses to seduce women, but in this case the combination of his success and his feminization as a monster (Otherness) creates anxiety in men.

Hello, Darkness

Mr. Trick is not the first nonwhite vampire to appear in *Buffy*,[2] but unlike most other dead boys he is emphatically modern and urban, and he is one of very few American vampires to appear regularly at this stage.[3] Robyn Wiegman argues that masculinity for the black male is marked as "racially produced excess" (1993: 180), and in comparison with Forrest and Principal Wood's assimilation into the predominantly white middle-class culture of Sunnydale, almost everything about Trick is excessive. Ono points out that in early seasons Trick was the "longest-running character of color" (2000: 178). He is the first character on *Buffy* to even mention racial difference:

> Admittedly it's not a haven for the brothers, strictly the Caucasian persuasion here in the Dale, but you know you just gotta stand up and salute that death rate. I ran a statistical analysis and hello, darkness. Makes D.C. look like Mayberry, and ain't nobody saying boo about it. We could fit right in here. Have us some fun. ("Faith, Hope and Trick" 3003)

Ono argues that this speech "overtly clarifies the racial metaphor underlying the show's narrative," suggesting that it "collapses together into one character the racialization of vampires and the racialization of actors who are people of color on the show" (2000: 178; this strategy is not unusual for speculative fiction on television [see also Bernardi 1998: 12]). Similarly, Boyd Tonkin claims that "the ethnic marking of a demonic troublemaker becomes exuberantly in-your-face (even over-the-top) in the figure of the African-American vampire hoodlum, Mr. Trick" (2001: 45).

Cultural stereotyping has represented black males as "feminized" in contrast to white males. Although young and powerful, Mr. Trick is slight, shorter than most other male characters, and does not physically match Angel or even Spike. Trick's role is largely as a subordinate to white male power, first to Kakistos and then to the Mayor. When he asks the Mayor, "What if I don't want to be part of the team?" the reply is simply, "Oh, that won't be an issue" ("Homecoming"). Thus Trick functions both as a foil for the Mayor's provincial charm (as Faith does subsequently) and as "the faithful servant of the white master" (Ono 2000: 178), and he calls Kakistos "the master" ("Faith, Hope and Trick"). Like Kendra and Forrest, Trick is used primarily to highlight white characters, in this case the Mayor and Faith. This male black vampire is supplanted by female white working-class Slayer, Faith, and it is not Buffy who kills Trick, but Faith (he is not important enough to merit death from a major player). During his final fight Mr. Trick manages to catch Buffy (she has been knocked out) and reaches for her neck, but at the last minute he is staked by Faith ("Consequences"). In a subsequent conversation, Faith dismisses Trick as the Mayor's "boy" ("You sent your boy to kill me"—both a dismissal of his masculinity and a nod to the language of American racial history), concluding, "He's dust," and taking over his role herself. Mr. Trick's death is significant not in itself but for what it tells us about Faith.[4]

Trick's association with technology could also be read as a feminization, something for unmanly nerds and geeks (in early *Buffy* technology is associated with women, though the male Initiative later use high-tech equipment). I see Mr. Trick as a postmodern vampire, having more in common with the pseudo-science of *Blade* than more traditional representations. During Trick's second appearance he talks to his vampire "boss," Kakistos, in techno-babble—"fiber optics . . . 25 hundred megs per"—and comments, "We stay local where the humans are jumpin and the cotton is high but we live global—on the net" ("Faith, Hope and Trick"—a knowing reference to *Porgy and Bess*). Just as early seasons of *Buffy* made much of the contrast between postmodern teens and ancient vampires, the same contrast is now evident between the ancient, demonic Kakistos (he has cloven hooves) and the postmodern technological Trick. At the end of the episode, when Kakistos' revenge on Faith is going badly, Mr. Trick observes how anachronistic tough-guy violence now seems ("There's a reason these vengeance crusades are out of style") and describes himself as "the modern vampire" who sees "the big picture."

Left to his own devices, Trick organizes "SlayerFest '98," a competition to kill the two Slayers ("Homecoming"). The hijacked Buffy and Cordelia (mistaken for Faith) find a video message from Mr. Trick on a laptop, and throughout the episode Trick is shown with the favorite in the competition, the older controller of two German assassins, who uses the latest high-tech equipment to track and target victims. When the controller tells Trick, "You're about to see why Daniel Boone and that idiot demon [other competitors] are creatures of the past. I am the future," this clearly echoes Trick's own sentiments and again points to the need for a different kind of masculinity in a postindustrial society. All the hunters are male (except Candy, "wife" of vampire Lyle Gorch), thus enabling the typical female victim/male predator scenario that *Buffy* often plays with, but also putting Trick firmly in the male predator camp.

Mr. Trick does not act like other dead boys because he is business-like and professional. This is one thing he and the Mayor have in common: they embrace not just demonic evil, but also American values such as individualism, capitalism, and self-improvement (complicit in patriarchy). At the close of "Homecoming" Trick is taken away by Sunnydale police officers and ends up in the Mayor's office. Overturning assumptions and the subtext of institutionalized racism ("If this is the point where you tell me that I don't fit in here in your quiet little neighborhood you can just skip it because that all got old long before I became a vampire"), the Mayor offers him a job. In the following episode, "Band Candy," Mr. Trick shows initiative by "subcontracting" Ethan Rayne to produce the magical candy that will transform everyone who eats it into irresponsible teenagers. While touring the production line, Trick celebrates American capitalism, stating, "The reason I love this country" is that "[y]ou make a good product and the people will come to you." He acknowledges the violence of the system when he continues, "Of course, a lot of them are gonna die but that's the other reason I love this country." After telling a worker, "Don't sample the products," he snaps his neck as a warning to the others.

In my reading, Trick is far from the kind of "hoodlum" Tonkin implies (recall that Principal Wood told Buffy he was from Beverly Hills, not "the 'hood"); his suits and ties reflect his sense of himself as a businessman. Changing employment patterns in the mid–twentieth century were seen to feminize white middle-class American males, making them passive men in gray suits, lacking individuality or active masculinity. Mr. Trick's suits are far from conservative, since his ensembles are usually in shades of one primary color and he also wears earrings (a signifier of exotic Otherness that he shares with Principal Wood). The effect of Mr. Trick's suits is to mark him as an urban visitor to provincial Sunnydale and to negate the presentation of him as "young." Trick's colorful suits both reinforce and overturn his feminization.

Trick has been characterized as "a survivor" (Holder, Mariotte, and Hart 2000: 98). In his first episode he left Kakistos fighting two Slayers and saved himself. During "Band Candy" he tells Buffy, "Ordinarily I like other people to do my fighting for me, but I just gotta see what you got." (This has a sexual undertone in keeping with Trick's nature as a vampire invested in penetration.) Yet despite his adaptability, sophisticated manner, and general refusal of action, Trick is still presented as a brutal killer, a monstrous male. In his very first scene, Mr. Trick kills a fast-food attendant with full vamp face, and his attempt to kill Buffy is a savage attack with vamp face and animalistic growling. These acts of violence are in direct contrast to his killing of the worker in "Band Candy," which was premeditated and cool, motivated by business sense (intimidation of the workforce) rather than animal appetite (the need to feed). Ono has noted that the demonic face of the vampires is itself a racialization (2000: 172), and he points to "Mr. Trick in vampireface" (179) as simply an updated version of the minstrel's blackface. As minstrelsy did for white males in the previous century (see Lott 1995), Trick's vamp face allows him to display excessive or unacceptable masculine behavior.

Wiegman argues that historically representation of the black male has been "reliant on sexual difference: from nineteenth century images of the bumbling, ineffectual minstrel 'coon' . . . to the mythologized black rapist of both centuries, whose hypermasculinization begets and nourishes the many cinematic trajectories of 'Shaft' and 'Superspade'" (1993: 175). At first glance, Trick is not obviously a sexual predator. Yet in "Homecoming" he and the old controller visually monitor the progress of SlayerFest, and Mr. Trick identifies Buffy "[i]n the nubile flesh." During "Faith, Hope and Trick" Mr. Trick's speech on abandoning Kakistos is delivered to a young, white, blonde female vampire, who leaves with him, and I have already mentioned his comment about what Buffy has "got" in "Band Candy." In this light, Mr. Trick's attack on blonde middle-class Buffy rather than brunette working-class Faith clearly does invoke racial stereotypes: he is a powerful and aggressive young black male about to penetrate a young white female, and he dies for it. Gill notes that his quip, "I hear once you taste a Slayer, you never go back" is a direct reference to the phrase "Once you go black, you never go back" (2003), an even more telling sexualization of this moment.[5] Mr. Trick fits the cultural stereotype of an aggressive and violent black male who physically and sexually threatens white "civilization" (see also Ono 2000: 168). Trick's conjunction of masculinity and race is underlined by his name—he is always "Mr." Trick (compare the famous "They call me MISTER Tibbs" from *In the Heat of the Night* [1967]).

The Man I Am Today

One of the primary examples of masculinity's split personality in *Buffy* is Angel/us. He is either very good (new man Angel) or very bad (real man Angelus); a conscience-stricken, Romantic vampire like Louis in Anne Rice's *Interview with the Vampire*, or a remorseless inhuman predator. At first Angel appears to be hypermasculine and traditionally gendered, and he is recognizable as many stock male figures: the action hero, the Romantic hero, the older boyfriend, the dangerous lover, and the mysterious stranger. As an action hero, Angel is equal to Buffy in strength and physical power (though he does not actively compete with her) and is the one male character who successfully uses physical means to rescue her from danger.[6] Angel's masculinity functions as a benchmark in that almost every male who appears in early seasons of

Buffy is measured against, and fails to match, his exaggerated gendering. Riley is unmanned by Angel in "The Yoko Factor" when he loses a
physical fight, loses his cool, and appears less manly because less mature
than Angel (he becomes hysterical and childish). Admittedly Angel also
has his childish moments (from "He started it" to "I don't like him"),
but when he calls Riley "boy," he invokes age and the symbolic power
of the patriarch.

Angel/us' vampirism encompasses physical male aggression, and even
before his return from hell as a "wild" man, Buffy is presented as a civilizing influence on his monstrous masculinity (see DeKelb-Rittenhouse
2002: 151). This aggression is seen more clearly in Angelus, who "has a
flamboyance in word and deed that comes with complete self-assurance"
(Shuttleworth 2001: 231). The "self-assurance" of Angelus is an enjoyment of physical and sexual power, and although Angel embodies the
same power, like other new men, he chooses to repress it. Angelus accepts his nature (just as Darla did) and thus escapes Angel's alienation.
This alienation, along with his new-man sensitivity, makes Angel recognizably a Romantic hero. Rose notes that "such heroes had to assert
their masculinity in the face of all this sensitivity," and this role combines
"masculine" and "feminine" characteristics. His "Irishness" merely adds
to the effect. Rose cites Riley's comment from "The Yoko Factor" that
Angel is "all billowy coat, King of Pain, and girls really [go for that]"
(2002: 142, note 3). That the character was popular enough to merit his
own spin-off show indicates that viewers felt the attraction too.

Yet Angel also takes on traditionally female roles: he is the love interest. Owen sees him as "primarily a plot-enabler. In relation to Buffy
Angel's presence enables various clichés of heterosexual romance, such
as the redemptive power of dyadic love, the agony and angst of star-
crossed lovers, the allure of secret trysts, and the deflowering of the
female virgin" (1999: 27). In this reading Angel's significance lies in his
relationship with Buffy and his upholding "clichés" of gender (and, I
would argue, genre). I noted in chapter 2 that Buffy is the younger
partner, matched to an older and more experienced male. His attraction to her fits the Romantic hero—dark older man drawn to young
innocent girl—but the contrast between them also brings to mind more
comedic contrasts, such as Emma and Mr. Knightley in Jane Austen's
novel *Emma*. Like Knightley, Angel sees the "essence" of Buffy and encourages her to leave behind the petty aspects of society and take her
place in the world. He offers advice and acts as a kind of mentor to
Buffy, both in her personal and her professional life, apparently the ideal

match for a postfeminist protagonist. On reflection, however, Angel's age brings into question his motives in pursuing a relationship with Buffy, as Levine and Schneider note: "Angel is at one and the same time a Prince Charming catering to a young girl's fantasies, a forbidden object, and also a 'dirty old man'" (2003: 307).

Contrasting Buffy's "good" influence on Angel, Joyce and the Mayor point out Angel's "bad" influence on Buffy. Although Milavec and Kaye suggest that Angel and Buffy's parting at the end of season 3 is mutual and equal (2003: 181), when Joyce persuades Angel to leave Sunnydale and Buffy behind, this demonstrates Angel's dominance, removing agency from Buffy. The only point at which she seems more dominant is briefly in "I Only Have Eyes for You," through role reversal, after Angel's transformation into Angelus. Buffy and Angelus are the last in a series of hapless by-passers possessed by the ghosts of pupil James and teacher Grace Newman, who reenact the break-up of another taboo relationship. (Grace's rejection of James is a foreshadowing of Angel's own leaving: as the older, more responsible partner, she does it "for his own good.") Buffy, in the male role, memorably tells Angelus, "Don't walk away from me, bitch!" and this scenario plays on Angel's "feminine" sensitivity, Angelus' rejection of Buffy, and Buffy's reaction to it. Of course, it offers viewing pleasure in the reversal of this previously romanticized relationship.

His function as love interest and his nature as a vampire make Angel highly sexualized, and every challenge to him, from Xander's initial dislike, through the triangle with Drusilla and Spike, to Riley's physical fight, is motivated by sexual competition. Angel is dangerous and a sexual threat in the teen narrative (because of his age, the stereotyped older boyfriend) and in the vampire narrative; he is old *because* he is a vampire. Likewise, Angel/us embodies sex as a part of both narratives.

The episode where Angel and Buffy consummate their relationship ("Surprise") caused some controversy among parents whose children watched the show. One of the executive producers acknowledges this: "We were not endorsing [teenage sex] or trivializing it. When Buffy and Angel have relations, it is not a good thing" (Berman in Moy 1999: 86; any viewer familiar with teen slasher movies knows that sex is never "a good thing").

Because he has experienced a perfect moment of happiness with Buffy, the curse on Angel is lifted, his soul is removed, and he reverts to evil Angelus. Angelus is more explicitly threatening and plays out the bad-older-boyfriend scenario: after sex with Buffy he wakes, leaves her sleeping, and goes out and feeds on a lone woman, blowing out "smoke" as if from a post-coital cigarette (Wilcox 1999: 21). Later he is coded as a stalker (predatory and sexual).

In network television and teen drama terms, Angel and Buffy's relationship was always challenging, and Lavery notes that the "words Angelus scrolled in blood on the wall at the scene of his murder of Uncle Enyos ('Was it good for you too?') prompt Whedon to speak of his amazement at what Buffy is sometimes able to 'get away with'" (in Lavery 2002a: 44).[7]

This sexual nature is a weakness: Angelus' relationships with Darla and Drusilla led to his divided nature (in a further undercutting of his hypermasculinity, Angelus was "sired" by a female), and when, as Angel, he falls in love with Buffy, his sexual nature leads to a return of his vampire nature. On Angel's return from hell in season 3 everyone except Buffy sees him as a threat, with discussions of this hinging on his sexuality. In other words, as with Oz, Angel's sexual desire may lead to a return of his violence, but both are manifestations of his disturbing physical masculinity. As he says himself, "It's not the demon in me that needs killing, Buffy. *It's the man*" ("Amends" 3010, my emphasis).

Abbott suggests that "vampires in *Buffy* are, like the humans that surround them, singularly defined by their bodies" (2001: 10), and another contributing factor to Angel's hypermasculinity is his physical presentation. Marcia Shulman, casting director, said that she "was looking for the sexiest, most mysterious, every-hyperbole-you-can-think-of guy" to play Angel (in Ogle 1999: 2). Like Mr. Trick, Angel is excessive. Whether Angel or Angelus, I agree that he was "the most sexualized and eroticised of all the characters in the series" (Owen 1999: 27) — at least until Spike's return. *Buffy* offers other males as spectacle, as in Xander's parody of male desirability during "Bewitched, Bothered, and Bewildered" and in the later "Speedo moment" ("Go Fish"). The presentation of Angel's body as spectacle is less parodic but just as self-conscious.

From very early on Angel's body is displayed for the female protagonist, Buffy, and for the viewer. In "Angel" he is injured fighting alongside Buffy, she takes him home to tend his wound, and he has to undress in the process (figure 11). The display of Angel's body and the sexual reaction it provokes lead to the revelation of his vampire nature: as he kisses Buffy, he shows his vamp face (a displaced physical manifestation of male desire?). The tension inherent in this display of the masculine body is that it actually has the effect of feminizing the character by positioning the male as sexual object to be looked at. Interestingly, an

FIGURE 11: *The first of many times that Angel's body is displayed ("Angel").*

earlier version of Angelus' rejection of Buffy, filmed outside the Summers house, was reworked because Whedon found it unsatisfactory. The
scene finally takes place in Angel/us' "bedroom with Angelus shirtless"
(in Lavery 2002a: 22). I suggest that this second version is more successful because it displays the male body, reflecting the content of the scene
but undercutting Angelus' treatment of Buffy as sexual object by presenting him as a sexual object too. Lavery notes Whedon's film studies
background and the implication that Whedon fully understands "the
terrible objectifying male" gaze Laura Mulvey posited (2002b: 7). This
male to-be-looked-at-ness is demonstrated most by Angel and Spike,
two characters marked as Other from the start since they are vampires
(and European).[8] Dyer notes that this contradiction is almost an aesthetic tradition: "Within Western art the dead white body has often been
a sight of veneration, an object of beauty" (1997: 208).

The exercise of sexual power draws out some of these ambivalences
and throws Angel/us into crisis. "The important thing is," Angelus

taunts Buffy in "Innocence," "that *you made me the man I am today* [my emphasis]." The *male* is transformed by this sexual encounter, and Beth Braun suggests that after Angel's transformation "Buffy's goal is to penetrate Angel's body with a wooden stake to kill the demon she had brought to life," in a reflection of "the sexual penetration that caused Angel's rebirth as a vampire" (2000: 91). Creed's reading of the monstrous male body in horror films can be useful here: "They assume characteristics usually associated with the female body: they experience a blood cycle, change shape, bleed, give birth, become penetrable, are castrated" (1993b: 118). Angel, and later Spike, exhibits all or most of these, again a relation to their function as always already Other. Angel drinks blood and bleeds, he "breeds" new vampires, he changes shape (vamp face), his body is made vulnerable, he is often wounded, and he fears penetration (staking). In fact, his body is displayed semi-naked at least as often in scenes of wounding or torture as in "bedroom" scenes (season 2 scenes with Drusilla conflate the two through S/M). As Saxey observes, "Angel spends a ludicrous amount of time in chains, shirtless" (2001: 203).

Alternatively Dyer suggests that white Western masculinity is modeled on Christ, entailing both opposition and suffering, "in men the model is of a divided nature and internal struggle between mind (God) and body (man), and of suffering as the supreme expression of both spiritual and physical striving" (1997: 17), noting the traditional representation of "dignity and transcendence in such pain" (28). Applying this theory, Angel's suffering can be read as an assertion of masculinity.

Most clearly, because of the curse, Angel is emasculated: castrated through his impotence as a vampire (he is cut off from his true nature, as Spike later is, though the term *castration*, used explicitly for Spike, is not used for Angel), and rendered sexually impotent with Buffy for fear of losing his soul (regaining his true nature).[9] Thus Angel embodies neatly the idea that "the muscular body functions as a powerful symbol of desire and lack" (Tasker 1993b: 242). Angel is manly but *not a man*, and his display of masculinity points to the ambivalences that surround gender.

Angel's vampire nature makes him the man he is today but also feminizes him. Gender and genre serve to overdetermine Angel at every point, and this contested position is continued and developed in *Angel*. Here his character is reinvented as a(n almost) celibate dark superhero, assuming a more obvious patriarchal role. He even manages to become a father, simultaneously the ultimate "proof" of masculinity and of his new-man status. Angel's hypermasculinity restricts his role in *Buffy* (he cannot overshadow the postfeminist hero), and this is even more obvious in his brief returns, when he is given very little to do. Although on *Buffy* he appears to blend new-man qualities with traditional masculine power and sexuality (and this may be *why* he inspires anxiety in real men and new men alike), Angel's masculinity is so excessive that he does not really present an alternative mode of gender, as his Otherness (even uniqueness) underlines. These contrasting representations only exist in polarity: he does not negotiate a mixture of these identities; he can be one or the other but not both at the same time.

Treat Me Like a Man

Since his appearance in season 2, supposedly as a fill-in villain until Angel turned bad, Spike has become one of the most popular *Buffy* characters and one of the most frequently discussed in recent scholarship. This may be due to his many contradictions: Spike blurs boundaries between good and bad, "masculine" and "feminine," hetero- and homosexual, man and monster, comic and tragic, villain and hero. Spicer argues convincingly that "it is his very liminality—the impossibility of consigning him to a predetermined gender category—that empowers him in the Buffyverse, enabling him to navigate the complex gender inversions that mark a community oriented around a heroic, female Slayer" (2002: 1).

At first, Spike is almost a parody of real masculinity: strong, aggressive, sexual, a real bad-boy rebel.[10] His challenge to the old order— "Now, any of you want to test who has the biggest wrinklies round here, step on up" ("School Hard")—conflates vampirism and masculinity (this is an obvious way of saying "who has the most balls," but "wrinklies" could also mean vamp face). With Drusilla he was "one half of a symbolic whole," the masculine lover and protector (Spicer 2002: 7). Spike pits himself against other males, equating badness and masculinity like anxious tough guys Forrest, Warren, and Jack O'Toole. He also sets himself in direct competition with Buffy, as he has with other Slayers. This element of parody is related to his comic function, but I would argue that Spike consciously "puts on" or (borrowing a term from queer theory) *performs* masculinity. "Spike" is a persona of powerful masculinity adopted by the dithering poet William after his rejection in love by the human Cecily and his transformation into a vampire by Drusilla ("Fool for Love"), and as with Vamp Willow, Spike is everything William was not. The gap between William and Spike is highlighted by the way the flashback narrative is constructed, moving between the two, and by the apparently unreliable nature of Spike's narrative (Michele Boyette calls him "a legend in his own mind" 2001: 15). James Lawler suggests that "temptations of sensuous gratification and physical power" lure Angel and Spike to their vampiric transformation (2003: 110), perhaps unconsciously highlighting the "masculine" power to be gained from this re-creation. In season 6 the vampire leaves his signature coat behind in Sunnydale. Returning in season 7 with a soul, he is no longer Spike the leather-clad tough guy; in early episodes he answers to both Spike and William.

This performance of masculinity is, as with Ripper and Jack O'Toole, also related to class. In discussing the replicants of the film *Blade Runner*, Nick Heffernan observes that

> They are given all the disturbing and unappealing qualities frequently attached to the working class by the middle-class guardians of morality and professional agencies of regulation: they are without proper family socialization and etiquette; they are "irrational," violent and over instinctive, particularly in sexual matters; their subjective life is more intense because it is insufficiently mediated by introspection and internalised interdictions. Yet these are also qualities that the narrative . . . in some senses longs for and valorizes positively precisely because they are deemed absent from the restrained and highly self-disciplined modes of professional existence. (2000: 161)

I suggest that not only is Spike (and many other vampires in *Buffy*) imbued with these same qualities but that his position as a vampire is similar to the position of the replicants in *Blade Runner*: they appear to be human but are not, and they have a complex relation to feeling ("empathy" in *Blade Runner*) and morality. I would also note that the white-blond Roy Baty, leader of the replicants, can be read as a figure who blurs distinctions of race, gender, and sexuality, just as Spike does.[11] Roy and Spike display stereotypical working-class attributes that are valorized in a climate of anxiety about what constitutes masculinity.

Buffy's strong women are transgressive because they are relatively new representations; Spike is transgressive partly because he presents an older, no longer politically correct version of masculinity. Part of his contradictory nature is the gap between his sensitivity and the way his observations are often racist ("Pangs") or sexist, and this may be a consciously adopted characteristic that middle-class William associates with the working class. In a slightly different way than with Giles/Ripper, class is denoted by Spike's language and accent. I suggested that Ripper's "rough" speech is somewhat exaggerated, and this is even more noticeable in Spike's case, perhaps unintentionally (since Giles is played by a British actor but Spike is not). The fact that James Marsters does not always reproduce an authentic British accent actually works *for* Spike, rather than against him, since it reinforces his "performance" of masculinity.

Spike embodies, as Owen puts it, "danger and desire" (1999: 27). He is a "bad boy," his image styled as British punk and played up in the show by clothes and music.[12] This is where his attraction lies, as Milavec and Kaye point out: "Spike is irresistible to Buffy because he is a monster: monsters are evil, evil is dangerous, and danger is exciting" (2003: 178). Again class intersects with sexuality—in British idiom, Spike is "a bit of rough." Spike styles himself as a rebel (*"I'm* the rebel, you're an idiot," he says in "All the Way"), and Wall and Zryd call him "anarchic" (2001: 55). Peter Biskind and Barbara Ehrenreich's description of the "defiant" working-class male hero in certain 1970s films fits Spike almost exactly: he too is "the underdog who beats incredible odds, the sullen adolescent who kicks beer cans (and clingy girls) out of his path, the tough guy who doesn't take shit from anyone" (1987: 214–215). Although Biskind and Ehrenreich conclude that this type of masculinity is already "an anachronism," it continued as "a metaphor" for another decade or so (Traube 1992: 159) and matches Spike's role as a 126-year-old vampire. That the black-and-white "sideshow" poses Spike strikes in Giles' segment of "Restless" were included in the subsequent season's opening credit sequence demonstrates the power of this iconography, as well as drawing attention to its performativity.

Yet while Spike performs tough-guy masculinity, he is never directly presented as powerful or particularly evil. Despite fearsome descriptions of Spike as a killer, his own comments, and his threats to key characters like Joyce and Willow, Spike's reputation often seems to exceed his actions, and he does not often kill humans on-screen.[13] Spike is all mouth and no trousers, as it were, and he admits, "We like to talk big, vampires do. 'I'm gonna destroy the world'—just tough-guy talk, strutting around with your friends over a pint of blood" ("Becoming Part 2"). This heightens Spike's value as a comic villain (he can be laughed at because he never wins), and in season 3 he is presented as pathetic and lost without Drusilla. Dru has split up with Spike because he was "not demon enough for the likes of her" ("Lover's Walk"), and his comment

"I may be love's bitch, but at least I'm man enough to admit it" demonstrates the confusion in his gendering. Spike's impotence is increased in season 4, which sees him "castrated" by the Initiative's microchip: "Hostile Seventeen can't hurt any living creature, in any way, without intense neurological pain." This is introduced into the narrative in sexual terms when Spike tries to attack Willow in an initially chilling "rape" scene that degenerates into comedy as she responds to his failure to perform, saying, "Maybe you were nervous. You're probably just trying too hard" ("The Initiative").

Spike also has his "feminine" side. He cannot hide this even from Harmony, who exasperatedly comments, "You are *so* sensitive" ("Fool for Love"). Spike is sensitive not only in that he is easily hurt but also in the "feminine" way of being attuned to situations, relationships, and underlying emotions, as his frequently perceptive comments demonstrate. This ability to articulate his emotions also explains why his character fits so well into *Buffy*, a show that consistently values this trait; Boyette observes that Spike's conversation with Joyce about Dru is reminiscent of "one of the soap operas he likes to watch" (2001: 9), invoking emotional articulation, traditionally "feminine" competencies, and a female address. Across several seasons Spike is shown sharing his problems with Joyce, Willow, Anya, and even Riley, and supporting Dawn and Buffy (like Xander and Giles, he is heterosocial). Spike is "man enough" to admit and discuss his problems, generally relating to his masculinity or lack thereof, and is thus positioned as a self-aware new-man.

This is revealed in other relationships with women, as well as through his characterization as a "fool for love." His first defining relationship is with his mother (unlike Angelus, whose defining human relationship was with his father). "Lies My Parents Told Me" even reveals that Spike turned his mother into a vampire in an attempt to save her life (she is dying of consumption) and keep them together. While a Romantic hero like Anne Rice's Lestat manages this successfully (*The Vampire Lestat*), Spike does not: as a vampire his mother mocks his emotional weakness, so he stakes her. Spike and Dru's relationship seems to be based on "real" love, and this distinguished him early on from other dead boys. I have already argued that Spike allows Buffy agency in their relationship. Notably, in her rejection she calls him William, a name that invokes his human (and feminized) side ("As You Were"). Spicer observes that his choice of adversary, the Slayer, demonstrates that Spike acknowledges female power and that even Spike's signature coat is, "figuratively if not literally, an article of female clothing" (2002: 14; Spike took it from Nikki Wood in "Fool for Love").

As with Angel, sex is shown to be Spike's weakness. He is injured by Buffy in an attempt to restore Dru to full health and is further "unmanned" when Angelus returns and is reunited with Drusilla.[14] His jealousy leads him to make a truce with the Slayer. Later the show details Spike's crush on Buffy, and although he is presented as a stalker, the viewer is encouraged to sympathize with him because he is so pathetic. This position is made almost tenable by the fact that viewers know Spike is harmless because of his chip. Spike also retains his comic value since, as he says, "At least I've still got the attitude" ("Shadow")—that is, he keeps up the performance, despite its transparency. The disturbing aspects of Spike's presentation return when he moves from pathetic reject to attempted rapist, failing only because Buffy can match his strength ("Seeing Red").

Shot partially from above in glaring white light, this scene is disorienting and uncomfortable. In "Dead Things" the mise-en-scène suggests that Spike is taking Buffy from behind. She insists, "Don't," while he retorts, "Stop me." Throughout the relationship Spike has ignored Buffy's denials, even though it was fairly clear that Buffy's "no" didn't mean no and ambivalent scenes such as this paved the way for the "real" violence of the attempted rape. As noted in chapter 4, there are strong links between love, sex, and violence, and Spike uses romantic heterosexual love as a "defense" of sexualized violence. In contrast to Spike's "passion," Buffy invokes "trust." The attempted rape is a betrayal of the "trust" Buffy and the viewer may have placed in Spike following his apparent rehabilitation, and fans argued over how to react to it (see Fossey 2003: 13). It may also indicate that Spike's hypermasculine persona and his monstrous nature remain (they are intertwined), and Mimi Marinucci points out that "Spike's attempt to rape Buffy resembles an ordinary attempt to suck her blood" (2003: 71). Yet Spicer suggests that this scene merely reinforces Spike's gender ambivalence, since it simultaneously shows "the feminine convention of the clingy lover and the masculine convention of violent lover" (2002: 23).

This moment of sexual violence is what loses Spike the careful performance of tough-guy masculinity, so closely related to his monstrosity. Spike's rejection of Buffy's assertion of "trust" during the attempted rape is a rejection of the moral values Buffy represents, and it has been suggested that she "gradually transforms and ennobles him" (Spah 2002: 2)—in other words, that she civilizes him. Even before the at-

tempted rape, Spike believes that Buffy's (unnatural) influence is erod-
ing his monstrosity (something he sees as integral to his identity): "This,
with you, it's wrong, I know it. . . . Do you think I like having you in here
destroying everything that's me?" ("Crush"). This is part of Buffy's role
as upholder of morals, and Sakal notes how Buffy is "a feminine ideal
to be worshipped but, of whose affections he is not completely worthy"
(2003: 248). This was seen earlier in Spike/William's history through his
interactions with both Cecily and Drusilla, his "black goddess."

Spike is further feminized by his passive role as sex toy in season 6. Although he tries to build on the sexual relationship (as in "Dead Things"),
Buffy rejects him as a "person" while using him for sex. (In "Wrecked"
she accuses him of just wanting to "do a Slayer," and it is unclear whether
Spike's interest is in Buffy or the Slayer.) Despite his initial establishment
as heterosexual, Spike has been a favorite character for slash and sexual
speculation. This may be a measure of his popularity and attraction,
but it is also indicative of his ambivalent representation and Whedon's
"bring your own subtext" invitation.[15] In season 2, Spike was involved
in both S/M and a "triangle" with another male. Superficially Spike is
cast in sexual competition with Angel (presenting them both as heterosexual), but the notion of alternative sexuality may also imply that the
triangle of sexual desire works in other directions. Dyer suggests a clear
link between homosexuality and death: "The pervasive use of homo-
eroticism in consumer culture gives spice to the vanilla of straight sex,
but homosex is also the sign of the spectre of sex as death, because of the
association of AIDS and also because it is a non-(racially) reproductive
form of sexuality" (1997: 219). This is especially apt for a vampire. Both
Spike and Angel are presented as aggressively heterosexual, but context
and subtext encourage other readings.

I have already argued that Angel's function as the "love interest"
led to the display of his body as an object to be looked at and desired.
When Angel leaves, Spike takes over this function (in a way that Riley
or Buffy's other human partners never do). Spike's body began to be displayed through his relationship with Harmony, and increasingly he was
shown bare-chested in "bedroom" scenes. The muscular masculine body
is also marked by class, since it may be "built" through physical work
or through sport/the gym. Tasker pushes this further when she suggests
that if "muscles are signifiers of both struggle and traditional forms of
male labor, then for many critics the muscles of male stars seem repulsive
and ridiculous precisely because they seem to be dysfunctional, 'nothing
more' than decoration, a distinctly unmanly designation" (1993b: 239),

pointing out that a display of the masculine form can actually be seen as "unmanly." The spectacle of masculinity further indicates Spike's appropriation of masculinity through performance. Steven Cohan suggests that "[s]creen acting in particular blows the cover of a 'natural' man in its technical acknowledgement that gendered sexualities are constituted out of fakery and spectacle" (1993: 221). Even as a character, Spike is involved in constituting a gendered identity through performance, and his ambivalent position in terms of both gender and sexuality, coupled with the attraction of his character to male and female viewers, can be disturbing.

Spike's body is also displayed in scenes of violence and torture, making him the feminized, passive victim as well as the erotic object of the gaze. Spike's body is vulnerable. He is frequently beaten up and often retains his cuts and bruises across several episodes, as when he is tortured by Glory in "Intervention" (5018) or beaten by Buffy in "Dead Things." On one hand, it has been argued that torture and sadism help repress attraction and disqualify the male body as an object of desiring looks (Neale 1993: 14) but on the other, that same torture and sadism subject the male body "to humiliation and mockery" (Tasker 1993b: 237). The beatings are further proof of Spike's "humiliation," the level to which he has sunk, and a physical sign of his vulnerability. But they are also "sexy wounds" (as Buffy playing Robot-Buffy says in "Intervention"), since Spike's body is displayed to be looked at. Further, as with Angel and Dru, Spike and Buffy's relationship uses pain/violence *as* eroticism (when Spike tells Buffy, "I'm in love with you," she responds, "You're in love with pain" ["Smashed"]). Mulvey's association of voyeurism, sadism, and narrative is useful here.

> Voyeurism . . . has associations with sadism: pleasure lies in ascertaining guilt (immediately associated with castration), asserting control and subjecting the guilty person through punishment and forgiveness. This sadistic side fits in well with narrative. Sadism demands a story, depends on making something happen, forcing a change in another person, a battle of will and strength, victory and defeat, all occurring in linear time with a beginning and an end. (1989: 21–22)

As much as Buffy, if not more, Spike demonstrates the sadistic tendency of narrative. Spike has changed because of his chip (forced on him) and his "love" for Buffy; his position as a vampire makes retaining his position a battle of will and strength, and he has suffered both victory and defeat, punishment and forgiveness, sometimes at the same time. *Buffy's* serial format ensured that he continued to suffer, and the same contrasting interpretations that apply to Angel also apply to Spike; this both underlines and subverts his "masculinity."

Another factor in Spike's complex gendering and position in the show is his relation to Angel. He competes with Angel in a typical anxious tough-guy way, but he also becomes Angel, however unwillingly. Angel, the unique vampire with a soul and Buffy's lover, is overtaken by Spike, another ensouled vampire who has a relationship with Buffy. *The Watcher's Guide* even implies that Spike is a bleached blond because James Marsters' dark hair made him look too much like Angel (Golden and Holder 1998: 226): the visual contrast constructed between these two parallels the one constructed between Buffy and Faith. Yet rather than directly threatening Angel, this competition undercuts Spike, since Angel was there first. The show itself suggests that Spike's real function is to be a bad boy, not a hero. From season 5, Buffy relies on Spike's strength, at once a characteristic of real masculinity and a symptom of his monstrosity. Before the battle with Glory, Spike tells Buffy, "I know that I'm a monster, but you treat me like a man" ("The Gift"). However, in "Get It Done" Buffy implies that Spike's strength lies in his bad-boy persona, telling him, "What I want is the Spike who's dangerous" (he later retrieves his leather coat, beats up a demon, and smokes a cigarette). Although, using Spicer's term, Spike may be the most "hybridized" character in terms of gender, within the show he is presented until the last moment as a failure. He is aware of the binaries of gender but cannot transcend them because his role (villain, lover, or hero) depends on "being a man." These identities further reinforce him as masculine and heterosexual.

Spike was a huge success outside the show, becoming more popular than Angel and at least as popular as Buffy (the character's move to *Angel* may be another indication of his popularity). Although Victoria Spah states that it is "tremendously satisfying to see our favorite Big Bad reinvented" (2002: 18), invoking the viewing pleasure to be had from reversals, I suggest that Spike's popularity was based on his transgressive appeal as a bad boy. This is finally undermined by his admission to Buffy (backed by romantic strings and piano) in "End of Days" that watching her sleep was the best night of his life. Spike may well be "terrified" by what this means and notably he suggests, "let's just leave it," deferring the moment when he must give up his bad-boy persona and all its allure. As Claire Fossey concludes (2003: 18), in Spike's own words, Spike as a "good" hero "wouldn't be nearly as interesting, would it?" ("Wrecked").

As vampires the dead boys demonstrate the outdated nature of violent tough-guy masculinity, thus they also show the need to adapt to changing gender roles. Most male vampires are ambiguously gendered: traditionally as monsters they are Other than male human protagonists; here in *Buffy* they are opposed to a female Slayer (masculinized) but also staked by a "girl" (feminized). Angel and Spike are distinguished from the other dead boys by their new-men characteristics, and their old masculinity is explicitly shown to be tamed or civilized by good girl Buffy. Their roles as villain, hero, and lover seem to masculinize and heterosexualize them, but as male monsters, passive victims of torture, and objects of the desiring gaze they are also feminized and queered.

Both Angel and Spike are generally discussed in terms of morality rather than masculinity. Ian Shuttleworth notes that Angel "bases his function . . . on concepts of divinity and damnation" (2001: 232), implying that because Angel accepts these moral concepts, they come to define him. Similarly, it could be argued that because Angel accepts the cultural binaries of masculinity and femininity, he restricts himself to being one or the other. Both Angel and Spike blur boundaries of morality and gender through their liminal position as vampires. "A man can change," Spike argues in "Smashed," but Buffy's response is "*You're not a man, you're a thing* [my emphasis]." It is also interesting to note that these male characters do not function strictly in the postfeminist American society of the Scoobies. As vampires they need not adapt to changing social conditions like other tough guys, but their very liminality also makes them ideal figures to disrupt gender constructions that rely on boundaries. Anne Rice has stated that she wished to create a "gender-free perspective" characters in the protagonists of her *Vampire Chronicles* (in Ramsland 1991: 148), but readers and scholars have noted that her most "androgynous" vampire characters are "male." The same applies to *Buffy*'s vampires. Transgression is the attraction of any dead boy, but as with the openness of other more minor characters, this functions both to enlarge and restrict their potential as alternative gender representations. Dead boys exist *through* binary opposition; they are always already Other.

7 Parental Issues

Buffy's early seasons show a clear generational divide, though this blurs as the original teen characters grow older. The show does not have many "real" parents but abounds in parent figures, and generational conflict sets all these older parent figures against the teen protagonists. The generational divide is integral to many teen dramas, and *Buffy* reproduces anxieties about adult authority and parental absence or neglect which pervade both teen and slasher films.[1] It has been pointed out that horror films invariably show unsupervised teenagers doing things they are not supposed to and that supernatural or horrific elements enforce the authority and social regulation parents and other adults fail to offer (Lewis 1992: 67). The very fact of teen protagonists undermines any sense of adult authority or responsibility (it is not they but the teens who save the world). It is thus difficult to present adult characters positively, and there are progressively fewer as the teen characters age.

Buffy's representation of parents and family is inflected by genre, but it is also situated in a postfeminist context. Changing social trends and the impact of feminism meant that family and parental roles also changed. The so-called backlash of the 1980s saw politicians endorsing "family values," yet the traditional post-war American family no longer really existed. The marriage age rose during the last decades of the twentieth century, and the number of single women rose too; both figures reflected rising numbers of cohabiting unmarried couples, homosexual as well as heterosexual. By the end of the 1980s, two-thirds of married women held jobs, and so did 68 percent of women with children; in effect, working wives and mothers became the norm (in Woloch 2000: 573). As the emphasis for women shifted from domestic to professional, the shift for men was in the other direction. Men who increasingly felt that they could not successfully base masculinity on work and breadwinning were told that they could assert it simply by being a dad (see Kimmel 1997: 247), and this emphasis on fatherhood continued into subsequent decades. While one-parent families were usually headed by women, several popular films (especially in the 1980s) represented men as single parents and indeed as being both "mom" and "dad" to their children (*Three Men and a Baby* [1987] was one of the most successful). Jeffords therefore suggests that "fathering was a key characterization and narrative device for displaying the 'new' Hollywood masculinities" (1993: 254), and this can be seen to permeate domestic television serials like *thirtysomething* and even genre shows like *Star Trek: Deep Space Nine*.

As already suggested, *Buffy* uses serial form to undercut the traditional patriarchal structure of the family. Busse notes that "[t]raditional nuclear families in the Buffyverse are mostly corrupt" (2002: 209), and Buffy's family is the only one that is finally shown in a positive light. Like other television serials, *Buffy* "strive[s] to maintain a sense of 'community' which is often modeled on the family, but does not necessarily equate with a 'real' family" (Geraghty in Hollows 2000: 91). Miller has stated that "Buffy's sense of self is deeply relational" (2003: 38), and I have noted before how *Buffy*'s construction of the alternative Scooby family encourages complex relationship patterns. This problematizes the representation of parent figures and family and also exemplifies the shift from teen drama (with its subtext of generational conflict) to soap/melodrama (emphasizing "family" groupings and emotion). The representation of parent figures in *Buffy* offers several popular types, like the nurturing dad and the stressed-out single mother, but it also airs some of the tensions inherent in negotiating the new family and roles within it.

Patriarchal Villains

The villains of seasons 1 and 3, the Master and the Mayor, are both authority figures in positions of hierarchical power (indeed, their titles function as their personal names), they punish or reward those below them in the structure, they are both very old and set apart by the language they use (as many older characters are), and they both threaten Buffy as the Slayer (reinforcing the teen/teen horror theme of generational conflict). The evil of the Master is clear and unambiguous (he is an ancient vampire who never wears a human face), but in the Mayor it is masked by humanity. The demonic nature of the Master makes him an ideal opening villain, while the Mayor features in a season where moral complexity is highlighted in relation to growing up.

The earlier discussion of Faith (chapter 3) touched on her relationship with the Mayor, and here I explore in more detail how he is presented as a father figure. He is an elected official and thus has to convince the electorate that he is doing the right thing for them—a kind of paternalism. This "Fifties-sitcom-dad demeanor" (Pasley 2003: 257) is highlighted in his relationship with Faith, and the Mayor demonstrates a traditional authoritarian attitude tempered by an apparently caring motivation. The script for "Homecoming" states that he "couldn't be more unassuming" but continues, "One feels that this man has not raised his voice in years, and although he is mild enough in demeanor, one hopes he won't" (in Holder, Mariotte, and Hart 2000: 100), hinting at underlying menace. The Mayor dispenses folksy wisdom and kindly reprimands (Jeffrey L. Pasley [2003: 257] comments that he upholds "Middle American virtues") even to "enemies" like Buffy and Angel. He becomes as much a father figure to Faith as Giles is to Buffy, and the two are similarly mismatched: the streetwise, sexualized Faith is teamed with the traditional, family-values local politician. Just as Giles does with his Slayer, the Mayor nurtures Faith's talents and allows her to gain a sense of identity and self-assurance after her defection from the Scoobies.

As I have already suggested, while everyone else compares Buffy and Faith, the Mayor never does, and this validates Faith. The show implies that she has experienced neither a stable family background that provides for her material needs, nor parental support and discipline, nor an environment in which she feels accepted and valued. The Mayor offers all of these, thus absence and neglect on the part of Faith's real parents are shown to create her weakness. She readily accepts financial and material support, making her dependent on her "father." She is given a new apartment, fully furnished with luxuries as well as basics (she gets a Playstation), and the Mayor's gift of a knife takes on significance in the unfolding narrative.

The Mayor rejects any implication of a sexual relationship when Faith calls him "sugar daddy," telling her, "I don't find that sort of thing amusing. I'm a family man" ("Doppelgangland"), and Tjardes (2003: 74) notes that fan fiction "surprisingly" retains the family construction (though Keller [2002: 173] points to "the typical mythological blurring of father/daughter/lovers" in Faith's dream during "This Year's Girl"; figure 12). I suggest that this lack of sexual interest is essential to the success of the relationship: Faith's sexuality is another weapon to her and not related to love and loyalty, while sexuality in older characters is generally threatening. Thus Faith becomes the Mayor's child, drinking milk

FIGURE 12: *The Mayor as picnic pal in Faith's dream ("This Year's Girl").*

and trying on a flowered dress to please him. Their bond ensures that she carries out orders with similar obedience. Unable to even give a reason for killing geologist Lester Worth in "Graduation Day Part 1" (3021), she tells him simply, "The boss wants you dead." Arguably, Faith's vengeful return in season 4 is another example of the Mayor's bad influence.

Although he calls himself a "family man," the ageless Mayor has no extant family (in "Choices" 3019 he speaks of a dead wife, Edna Mae). This highlights the Mayor's position as an older character: his values are those of a previous generation, and it is later revealed ("Enemies") that he has lived through three generations (he is Richard Wilkins I, II, *and* III). The Mayor is in many ways a ("masculine") individualist, but his relationship with Faith changes this, and the affection he feels for her seems genuine. When he finds Faith in a coma after Buffy's attack, he is, as Angel says, "crazed" with grief ("Graduation Day Part 2"). But while the affection Buffy and Giles share is seen to be a good thing, the affection between Faith and the Mayor is presented in contrast as "bad."

In a sense the Mayor lets Faith down by allowing her to become dependent on him. He tells her, "You'll always have me" ("Enemies"), but that promise is broken by his death soon thereafter (Angel's promise to Buffy in "Earshot," "No matter what, I'll always be with you," echoes the Mayor's vow and is similarly proved false). No parent can truly promise to "always" be there, and the implication is that no parent should want to. The Mayor is ultimately a "bad" father because he upholds the status quo: like the Master before him, he is a powerful patriarch who wants to maintain his position at the top, and the children of such parents will never be able to grow up. The postfeminist narrative ensures that two "girls" achieve his downfall, and the "good" parallel, Giles, demonstrates that he can allow his "daughter" to achieve independence (see below).

The Stepford Stepdad

Ted Buchanan appears in only one episode ("Ted"); Buffy discovers him and her mother in a clinch in the Summers' kitchen. At first Ted appears to be, as Joyce says, "a wonderful man" who can make time for teens as well as adults (he talks computers with Willow and pizza with Xander) and seems keen to get on with Buffy. Buffy, and probably the viewer, thinks that he is rather too good to be true. But her reaction to Ted could simply be "separation anxiety, the mother figure being taken away, conflict with the father figure," as Willow suggests, linking to the "primal scene" of the kiss and using popular psychology to give a rational explanation. Likewise, when Buffy complains to Angel, he gently asks, "There's a guy out there that would satisfy you?" and Buffy is left to lamely respond, "My dad." Ted highlights Buffy's family situation—her father's absence and her mixed feelings about it. He also serves to remind Buffy that her mother may want to have a "normal" life but has her own difficulties ("it's not exactly like men beat down the door when you're—" begins Joyce and "—a single parent," finishes Buffy). Buffy's apparently unfounded resentment becomes an obstacle to Joyce's happiness, articulated when Willow asks Buffy what she means by Joyce's behavior changing since Ted's appearance, "Different. Like happy?" Buffy's reply, "Like Stepford," points to less attractive aspects of Ted's character, brings in the possibility of a step*father*, and hints at his true identity.

Ted seems to be a new man; he cooks and bakes for everyone, is willing to date a single mother with a teenage daughter, and is able to communicate with the younger generation. Yet like the Mayor, Ted combines these "new" masculine and fatherly qualities with conservative, patriarchal values: he has what Cynthia Bowers describes as a "father knows best" attitude (2001: 16), again a return to more traditional 1950s notions of parental roles. Like previous patriarchs, Ted's language sets him apart from younger characters, and it reveals something of his perspective on gendered relations. He calls Buffy "little lady," uses the diminutive "Joycie," and begins to speak for Joyce, answering questions addressed to her and contradicting what she says. Furthermore, his authoritarian nature is revealed early to Buffy and the viewer. During a game of miniature golf he catches Buffy cheating, reprimands her, and eventually threatens to slap her.

This threat is developed when Buffy returns from patrol to find Ted in her room reading her diary. In a chilling scene, Ted tells Buffy she is delusional and warns her that if she doesn't stay in line he will have her put in a mental hospital.[2] After waiting for Ted to hit her first, Buffy attacks him; he falls down the stairs and dies. In a show that, despite being based on horror, is not very often scary, this episode stands out, I would argue, because Ted seems to be a real rather than a fantasy threat. Buffy meets the threat as the Slayer and apparently does the unthinkable: kills a human. The undercurrents of this situation (teen allegory) are also disturbing: Ted is in a serious relationship with Buffy's mother, but he is not being honest, and because he is an adult, everyone believes him. The threat of an adult male in a young teenage girl's bedroom is never made explicit but nevertheless carries overtones of sexual abuse (apart from the kiss with Joyce, Ted is not really sexualized, though displays of sexuality in adults are almost always threatening).[3] David Greenwalt, who co-wrote this episode with Whedon, has said:

> The soft and sweet side of him [Ted] is what is so scary; that *other* people don't see that this is a monster. There are a million families in America like that, where Mom and Dad look so good on the outside and go to church on Sunday, but you get inside that house and it's . . . terrifying, because Dad is an abusive totalitarian. (In Golden, Bissette, and Sniegoski 2000: 363; ellipses in original)

Thus Ted is clearly situated as a commentary on American family relationships, and the link between the "ideal" family and the perpetuation of male violence is demonstrated.

Having shocked the viewer with domestic violence in the "real" world, the show moves us into more familiar territory, and Buffy and the other teens (significantly, Giles is not involved) prove that Ted is a "robot" constructed by a man whose wife left him. This defuses the "real" emotional situation without lessening Ted's power as a threatening male figure. Ted returns to the Summers' house and, having knocked Buffy unconscious, tries to persuade Joyce to leave with him. "Don't I always tell you what to do?" he asks rhetorically, and when she resists he snaps, "I don't take orders from women." Ted tells Joyce, "You left me once but I keep bringing you back. Husband and wife is forever," a scary affirmation of the married state and a sentiment that Joyce has already rejected, having separated from Buffy's father. Buffy finally subdues Ted, the invading and controlling patriarch, in a telling exchange, hitting him with his own cast-iron skillet, and responding to his comment "I don't stand for that kind of malarkey in my house" by reclaiming the house as female space—"Teddy, this house is mine."[4]

That the original Ted was able to make a convincing replica of a man (not as easily detected as April, for example) suggests again that certain types of masculinity and gendered relations are programmed and constructed, not "natural." Ted's apparent niceness is another version of the Mayor's folksy charm: it masks a sense of security in patriarchal power, and both date back to an earlier period, when women were expected to know their place. Although Bowers mentions Ted's "warped expectations" (2001: 18), his expectations, though dated, are traditional, even conventional; it is *Buffy*'s postfeminist context that makes them unacceptable and presents them as "evil." Buffy and Joyce appear to reject heterosexual romance for a while after their experience (they are shown talking about renting a movie, and Buffy concludes, "I guess we're Thelma and Louising it again"), but the episode is careful not to reject the idea of romance among older people—it ends with Giles and Jenny Calendar kissing in the library, witnessed by the other Scoobies.

The Real Deal?

As noted in chapter 5, Xander appears to have the most "dysfunctional" family background of the young characters (except Faith). Throwaway comments reveal that he has spent more time at Willow's house than his own and that holidays and celebrations at his house become drunken riots. Perhaps paradoxically, Xander mentions family members more often than anyone else (Uncle Roary in particular) and, like Angel before he was turned into a vampire, his relationship with his father is often seen to define his identity as a man.

Xander's father debuted in "Restless" as a silhouette at the top of the basement stairs, largely characterized through his angry voice. The scene is threatening and appears to be a typical family argument (his father implies that Xander is "ashamed of" his parents, and refers to Xander's mother's crying). This father figure rips Xander's heart out (paternal threats are followed by physical violence), turning only then into the First Slayer. In "Hell's Bells" Xander's family seem to be as bad as he ever described them. Despite efforts to control him, Mr. Harris drinks constantly at the bar and is abusive to all comers. His interactions with his wife are clearly skirmishes in an ongoing domestic battle. Twice the waiting wedding guests become involved in a brawl at Mr. Harris' instigation, and even the mild-mannered demon Clem is provoked into complaining. The wedding (and the couple) is broken up by Xander's fear of what he might become, implicitly based on his experience of family life and his parents' marriage. Korsmeyer comments that the "the weight of his unhappy family history" means that Xander "deeply loves but cannot marry" (2003: 169). I have less sympathy for Xander here, but he is in a no-win situation. He wishes to reject the model of masculinity and parenting offered by his father, but trying to do so produces equally hurtful consequences. This episode is much later than those featuring the other "bad" parent figures discussed in this chapter and as such it is more characteristic of soap/melodrama than teen drama. The show is consistent in presenting violent masculinity negatively and offering "bad" examples of married and family life and of parenting.

Evil Bitch-Monsters of Death

Buffy's young female characters initially struggle to define their postfeminist identities in opposition to, rather than in emulation of, the show's older women (this is also inflected by the generational conflict of teen drama). Owen notes that "Buffy's strength and confidence are not learned from the vast experiences of past generations of women; rather, they are her mystical birthright as a slayer" (1999: 30–31), implying that Buffy rejects or bypasses the legacy of second-wave feminism and the example of older women.

JENNY CALENDAR

Jenny Calendar arguably is the only sympathetic older woman in early seasons of the show. She is presented as a professional woman but is also relatively young, fashionable, au fait with both technology (a computer teacher) and the supernatural (a techno-pagan), sexually attractive and independent (more assertive in these matters than Giles), and thus in many ways closer to the teen characters than the adults. Her power lies in her postfeminist confidence and her abilities. Some have argued convincingly for Jenny as a model or mentor for Willow, but Jenny is never a surrogate parent. Lacking a developed subject position, she is important mainly because of her relationship with Giles, and she adds impact to Angel's change (Angelus kills a familiar, recurring character who is sympathetic and valued). Her admirable qualities are undermined by her presentation as Other (she is a gypsy, Janna Kalderash) and betrayer of the core group when it is revealed that she has been sent to ensure that the curse on Angel is still secure. In maintaining her loyalty to one family (her own people), Jenny betrays another (the Scooby "family"), and although she works to redeem herself, eventually finding a way to reverse Angel's transformation, her significance is in her death. Jenny became independent by leaving her oppressively patriarchal family behind her, as Tara later does, but she too falls victim to a violent male, and J. P. Williams concludes that she "is a victim of the patriarchy she criticized" (2002: 71).

MAGGIE WALSH

Professor Maggie Walsh is presented as an almost stereotypical strong woman who appears to be tough, professional, and in control. Stage directions for "The Freshman" describe her as "a down-to-earth, likable woman in her fifties. As smart as she is strong willed" (in Holder, Mariotte, and Hart 2000: 99). As Buffy's psychology professor, Walsh seems at first to be presented as a possible "real-life" mentor or role model. Later she is revealed as an Initiative scientist and a potential ally for the Slayer. Like many male characters, Walsh is a figure of authority and power in hierarchical institutions (the university and the military Initiative), and Early even suggests that she "symbolizes the male-identified woman par excellence" (2002: 25). Such readings imply that although Walsh is of the right age to be a second-wave feminist, her actions do not identify her as one. Walsh is further masculinized by her roles as professional, scientist, and leader; she has no husband or family, and she has short hair (rare for female characters on *Buffy*).

Walsh's "masculine" authority is transformed into parenting when she becomes the unnatural mother of Frankenstein's monster Adam (altering the typical male mad scientist role); she asks a fellow Initiative scientist, "How's our baby doing today?" ("The I in Team"). Walsh is soon presented as an antagonist, vying with Buffy for Riley's affections. The ultimate controlling mother, Walsh literally sees a threat to the status quo when she watches Riley and Buffy have sex via Initiative surveillance. She also demonstrates the kind of competition between women that characters like Cordelia and Faith showed. "I've worked too long to let the little bitch threaten this project," she says, "Once she's gone, Riley will come around" ("The I in Team"). Thus Walsh's introduction to her Psych 101 class is borne out: she really *is* "the nickname my TAs use and don't think I know about: the Evil Bitch-Monster of Death" ("The Freshman"; Muntersbjorn [2003: 92] also identifies her as a "bitch"). Alongside another manipulative older woman, Faith's pseudo-Watcher, Gwendolyn Post, Walsh appears in *The Monster Book* under the "human monster" (Golden, Bissette, and Sniegoski 2000: 362).

At first Walsh seems to nurture younger characters, but she crushes their individualism, and Jarvis suggests that Walsh and the Initiative embody the "fear of excessive control" that matches the fear of chaos more often represented in teen horror (2001: 264). Notably, this threatening mother is killed first by her "son" Adam and then, after being re-created as a zombie, by Buffy. Coppock, Haydon, and Richter suggest that in certain types of domestic serial drama women "who hold powerful positions outside the family are frequently portrayed negatively, as hard, uncaring, even dangerous" (1995: 117), and in this way Walsh contrasts the earlier, more "positive" character of Jenny Calendar. Alternatively, Walsh could be seen as an androgynous figure; she displays a mix of traditionally gendered characteristics.[5] I would suggest that Walsh's position as a woman among men in the Initiative and her construction as Adam's "mother" underlines her gendering as female rather than her hybridity. Walsh seems to indicate that powerful women are bad—that only *girls* can be presented as heroes—but it is difficult to decide whether it is her gender or her age that makes her most threatening.

CATHERINE MADISON

A more typical representation of older women is as mothers, and particularly as one-half of a troubled mother-daughter relationship. In "The Witch" Catherine Madison, once a Sunnydale High cheerleading star, now apparently a housewife and mother, literally takes over her daughter's life by magic in order to relive her past glories. Catherine not only uses parental pressure to force her daughter, Amy, to try out for cheerleading, she finally swaps bodies with her. Amy reports, "She said I was wasting my youth, so she took it." This powerful mother is shown to stunt her children's life rather than nurture it (Tracy Little [2003: 290] suggests that this allegorizes the very real steps some parents will take to realize ambitions on behalf of their children). After her defeat Amy is free to build up her (by implication) "healthier" relationship with her dad, who had previously left his wife and daughter.

SHEILA ROSENBERG

There is no sense that Catherine tried to balance family and career, but such juggling is presented as a "problem" for the mothers of the main female protagonists, Buffy and Willow. "Gingerbread" (3011) contrasts the two mother-daughter relationships. Willow's mother, Sheila Rosenberg, is a career woman identified by her work and professional interests. She is described in the script as "sweet and well-meaning—but definitely of the woolly intellectual variety" (in Holder, Mariotte, and Hart 2000: 95), but she seems to appear only in order to be demonized (and Willow's father has never featured in any episode). When Buffy complains about Joyce's inappropriately bringing her a snack while patrolling, Willow remarks, "God, your mother would actually take the time to do that with you," while later, at the town meeting orchestrated by Joyce, she assumes that her mother will take no interest and is surprised to see her there. During the exchange between Willow and her mother, Sheila neither notices that Willow has cut her hair nor knows the name of her best friend (she calls her "Bunny Summers"). In the subsequent confrontation over Willow's interest in witchcraft, Sheila dismisses it as "a classic adolescent response to the pressures of incipient adulthood" and implies that Willow is seeking attention. Eventually Sheila does take Willow seriously—but by attempting to have her burned at the stake alongside Buffy and Amy Madison, with Joyce's support.

J. P. Williams calls Sheila "the expert who fails at relating to her own daughter" (2002: 67), and she is certainly presented as allowing her involvement in her career to supersede her "natural" maternal attention to her daughter. In this way Sheila can be read as a more exaggerated version of how Buffy sees Joyce at this stage. The notion of growing up and, as I will suggest, more open subject positions shift this perspective, enabling the viewer to see it with hindsight as the viewpoint of a self-absorbed teenager. Likewise, a later comment from Willow implies that her relationship with her mother is not all bad: after Joyce's death Willow tells Xander that she is visiting her mother "a lot lately" ("Forever" 5017).

The two main "parents" in Buffy are Joyce and Giles, and tension between them is developed in season 3. During "Anne" (3001) Joyce blames Giles for Buffy's running away, claiming that he could have influenced her to do otherwise, but she goes on, "You had this whole relationship with her behind my back. I feel like you've taken her away from me." Later, in "Gingerbread," Joyce begins a campaign against witchcraft as an unwholesome teenage activity and, albeit acting under the influence of a demon, attempts to have Buffy burned at the stake. Meanwhile, "Helpless" (3012) has Giles sacked by the Watcher's Council and replaced as Buffy's Watcher because his "father's love" for her is seen to interfere with objective execution of his duties. It is this contrasting representation that leads Busse to remark that Giles' "loving care" of the Scoobies is "in glaring opposition to their biological parents' lack of concern" (2002: 209). The focus of the series inevitably makes Giles more important than Joyce, and *Buffy* scholarship has tended to valorize Giles over Joyce. Since Owen stated that "Joyce is emblematic of parental and feminine limitation in the series" (1999: 30–31), almost all commentators have read Joyce as a "bad" mother (though Bowers [2001: 20] convicts both of "equally poor parenting"). Such representation (and how viewers interpret it) may be influenced by the contemporary context of pop-culture representations of parents, the way "the appropriation of women's roles by men is now a widely distributed theme, familiar from Vietnam films to television sitcoms about male single-parenting" (Jeffords in Traube 1992: 120). Traube suggested that "[m]ost 1980s movies construct good, nurturing fathers as substitutes for bad, overambitious mothers," concluding that "such constructions have strong anti-feminist implications" (1992: 25). The serial representation of Giles and Joyce develops from this simple contrast.

JOYCE

At first Joyce seems to be a typical teen-horror parent, very like the single mother Lucy in teen vampire movie *The Lost Boys*. She is caring and supportive, but because she has no idea what is really going on, she cannot help her teenage child effectively. That Joyce is not "in the know" makes for many comic moments in early seasons, highlighting Buffy's double life as both regular teen and superhero. During "The Harvest," blissfully unaware of the literal meaning of her words, Joyce says to Buffy, "I know, if you don't go out, it will be the end of the world." In this way J. P. Williams suggests that Joyce "is *Buffy*'s Lois Lane, her intelligence and love for the hero called into question by her inability to perceive the hero's superpowers" (2002: 64). Williams also notes that while the show "has Joyce continually stating just how much she loves Buffy" (discussed further below), "these conversations usually take place in the Summers' house, reinforcing Joyce's relegation to the private space of the home" (64–65). When Joyce is forced to recognize that Buffy is the Slayer, Buffy tells her, "Open your eyes, mom. What do you think has being going on for the past two years? The fights, the weird occurrences. How many times have you washed blood out of my clothing and you still haven't figured it out?" ("Becoming Part 2"). Buffy puts her mother in her place—washing clothes—and shortly afterward, in a brief struggle, demonstrates that Joyce is not physically capable of enforcing her parental authority. Joyce is most often referred to as "mom," "Mrs. Summers," and then "Joyce." Traube notes that in popular representations "motherhood is essential to women in a way that fatherhood is not to men" (1992: 131) and in *Buffy* Joyce is always and only Buffy's mother, never just another person or a member of the team.

Joyce also exhibits parental pressure—ironically, especially *after* she finds out that Buffy is the Slayer. In season 3 Joyce worries about where Buffy is going and what she is doing, brings snacks to Buffy while she is on patrol ("Gingerbread"), gets together with Giles to work out a slay-and-family schedule ("Band Candy"), and, when Faith arrives, suggests that since Buffy is not in fact the only Slayer, she could have a future at an out-of-town college (Helford reads this as class prejudice). Joyce's helplessness in the Slayer side of Buffy's life is demonstrated in "Gingerbread." She meets Buffy on patrol and discovers the bodies of two young children, whereupon mother and daughter roles are reversed: Buffy tries to comfort Joyce, telling her, "I'm so sorry that you had to see this, but I promise everything is going to be okay." Sarah E. Skwire further suggests that "[a]ll of Joyce's actions and choices will be governed by her desire to respond to these murders in a responsible and adult way. All of her choices will be wrong" (2002: 199). In contrast, Giles and Buffy's interaction over this incident maintains a more conventional adult/child dynamic—Giles is more in control than Joyce.

Yet Joyce is not so easily dismissed. She lacks character development because of her position in the narrative (Buffy's mother, not part of the team). She cannot protect or understand Buffy, but she is aware of this limitation, and it can be read as an extension of regular teenage alienation (as discussed in relation to Dawn). Joyce nurtures the other younger Scoobies and shows an intuitive understanding of her daughter. The show demonstrates that she tries to help and protect Buffy (as Buffy does for others) and is concerned about her education, lifestyle, and relationships. In the Slayer argument mentioned above, the viewer may acknowledge Joyce's side, particularly when Buffy dismisses her, saying, "Just have another drink," yet because Buffy is the protagonist and viewers know that the world really will end if she doesn't save it, audience sympathy is inevitably with Buffy. The viewer is privileged to see Joyce regret her reaction both immediately (as Buffy leaves the house, the camera shows Joyce close her eyes and cover her face with her hands) and later, when she finds a note from Buffy. Despite what might initially seem a "negative" presentation, Joyce increasingly offers, perhaps especially for older viewers, a valid subject position that can critique the younger characters. The recognition viewers feel at some of the clashes between Joyce and Buffy arises from our familiarity with the way teenage "cultural forms and practices exist and take shape outside the controlling and defining gaze of otherwise more powerful others, including parents" and how this "also accounts for the feelings of anxiety, fear and powerlessness experienced by conventional 'moral guardians' and also by parents" (McRobbie 1994: 174).

The argument in "Dead Man's Party" after Buffy's return to Sunnydale validates Joyce's position as a parent. In this episode zombies are raised by a mask Joyce has brought home (her inexperience with the supernatural is typically pointed out by Giles), but this is presented alongside her negotiation of a tricky family situation. "You just dumped this thing on me and you expected me to get it," Joyce tells her daughter. "Well, guess what? Mom's not perfect. Okay? I handled it badly." Here Joyce expresses emotion and exhibits honest self-awareness, both qualities the show valorizes. Joyce also accepts Buffy back without question and goes on to defend her right to an education (Buffy was expelled from school at the end of the previous season, though it is Giles who effects Buffy's readmission). Now Joyce tries to show Buffy the consequences of her own actions, encouraging her to take responsibility rather than assuming that Joyce will look after it (a quality later valorized in Giles).

Although Bowers suggests that "Joyce's parenting failures" betray "profoundly the mother-daughter bond" (2001: 14), many viewers would argue that this bond is strongly represented in the show. After the trauma of Angel's transformation, Buffy turns to her mother for comfort, and Joyce gives it without needing to understand the situation fully ("Innocence"). *The Watcher's Guide Volume 2* reads Joyce's request to Angel to end his relationship with Buffy toward the end of season 3 as "a mother's plea to the man she thinks is wrong for her daughter" (Holder, Mariotte, and Hart 2000: 97). Later Joyce is shown accepting Dawn unconditionally, asking Buffy to protect her while at the same time reassuring Buffy of her love. Throughout her time on the show Joyce's character regularly articulates her love for Buffy, and although J. P. Williams implies that this is a kind of substitute for understanding and support, I would argue that the emphasis on emotional articulation begins here. The Buffy/Joyce relationship is more positively portrayed in later seasons, through several scenes of family togetherness. When Buffy and Dawn tease Joyce about what to wear for a date, Joyce asks Buffy for advice as if marking a new, more adult phase of their relationship ("I Was Made to Love You")—one that will never be developed because of Joyce's death soon after.[6]

As already implied in my discussion of Tara, I read Joyce as a kind of postfeminist matriarch: she does not focus on home and family alone (though the character's role in the show does), but she remains "the lynchpin [*sic*] of the family—the emotional pivot through which the action takes place" (Coppock, Haydon, and Richter 1995: 114). Joyce is presented as the head of an all-female household that rarely needs a man, a role indicative of the show's historical context. McRobbie notes the appearance of single mothers in pop-culture representations "as a sign of these expanded possibilities of being female, a category which marks a changed society and a changed model of familial organization" (1994: 70). Thus Buffy comes from two female lines, the Summers line and the Slayer line. In later seasons various characters use the phrase "the Summers women": Joyce is the first of the Summers women, increasingly offered as an example of female strength. Joyce is resourceful and independent enough to establish her own life after Buffy's father leaves (she is rarely presented as a victim of this abandonment, though Buffy likes to see herself as one), retaining a career (with a suitably "feminine" aspect of creativity—she runs an art gallery), socializing with other female friends, and dating.

It could be argued that Joyce's sexuality allows her to be more than a mother but there is a tension here. Kennedy suggests that "mothers are sexual beings whose sexuality will not be limited to reproductive heterosexuality" (1997: 320), yet Joyce's sexuality is both displayed and displaced by being represented not through her dates but in her "teenage" encounter with Ripper in "Band Candy" and later in Xander's dream sequence during "Restless."[7] Bowers notes that the handcuffs Joyce lends

Buffy in "Band Candy" "suggest a level of sexual danger and experimentation" (2001: 23) that Buffy may not expect from her mother, and of course such scenes offer the viewing pleasure of reversal and unexpected behavior. My point is that sexual behavior is not expected from Joyce because she is so clearly presented *as a mother*. The parental role inflects the presentation of Giles' character in a similar way. In season 4, Buffy meets a woman (Olivia) at his apartment one morning and is shocked. Giles asks: "I'm not supposed to have a private life?" "No. Because you're very, very old and it's gross," replies Buffy, and it is obviously his role as her "father" that produces this extreme reaction ("The Freshman").[8] Yet Giles is afforded more development because he is a person as well as a parent, and I have already discussed the ways in which sexuality relates to his negotiation of masculinity.

Joyce's influence appeared to recede when Buffy went to U. C. Sunnydale in season 4 and all the young characters began to grow up, but she regains significance through her illness in season 5. When she dies, she is mourned by the whole "family," even black sheep Spike and awkward Anya. The Summers' house remains the "family" center, and Tara briefly takes over Joyce's role as matriarch. After Buffy has discovered her mother's body in the teaser to "The Body" (5016), the scene shifts to a festive meal at the Summers' house, with Joyce and Giles acting as host "parents" to the Scooby family. This situates Joyce firmly as part of Buffy's family life (see figure 13). J. P. Williams notes how "[i]n many television series, characters who leave are simply stricken from the memories of those who remain" and mentions that Jenny Calendar "continues to be a presence" in *Buffy* after her death (2002: 70). This is even clearer for Joyce, though she is remembered not for being Joyce but for being mom. Buffy subsequently refers to how Joyce would have done things, or dealt with problems, how she was always right, knew just what to say, partly in a reflection of Buffy's anxiety about being head of the household. Dawn misses her mother on a more emotional level, to the extent of trying to raise her from the dead by black magic ("Forever") and fighting to speak with her ghost in "Conversations with Dead People."

Joyce represents the "normal" life of the show, and all the Scooby family members look to her to provide them with the comfort of that normal life. After Joyce's death, this illusion is removed, and "normal" life becomes a problem or a trial. Only with Joyce gone, therefore, can the younger characters realize that normal life, with its bills, broken windows, and regular meals, is just as challenging as dealing with the super-

FIGURE 13: *Joyce and Buffy share a mother-daughter moment in the heart of the Summers' home ("The Body").*

natural. As Buffy admits to Angel, "I can stick wood in vampires but mom was the strong one in real life" ("Forever"). Although the show valorizes her as a model of the modern woman who more or less manages to "have it all," Joyce's female strength is represented through suffering (over Buffy's dangerous responsibility, Dawn's alienation, or her own illness), and she eventually dies.

GILES

I have already discussed Giles as a "new man"; here I examine his role as father figure to Buffy. Indeed, the two are related. Giles is a more prominent character and offers a potentially more popular subject position because he is an integral part of the team and someone who understands what Buffy really is. If Joyce resembles the single mother from *The Lost Boys*, Giles has more in common with the single father from another teen vampire film, *Near Dark*, who accepts what is happening to his son and helps rescue him from the vampires. As mentioned in chapter 5, Giles at first appears to represent a more traditional vampire slayer, thus acting as a foil for *Buffy*'s postmodern teens. As Buffy's Watcher, Giles is in a typical patriarchal position of authority. Wall and Zryd suggest that the title *Watcher* "seems tinged with values of supervision and hierarchy" (2001: 71) but note that the relationship between Buffy and Giles actually operates on "a mutual trust and respect" (73): as I indicated earlier, Giles allows the teens agency and independence. Unlike Joyce, Giles is presented as having few outside interests. Most of his adult friends seem to be other "professionals," and others are scared away by his involvement with the supernatural (Olivia in "Hush"). In one way this stereotypes the traditional father—never home, always working or networking. Yet Giles' relationship with Buffy is initially professional. That is, his fatherly role grows out of his professional role; he cannot disentangle his job from the Scooby "family." This means that Giles is never primarily defined as a parent figure (unlike Joyce), and it allows him to be a person and a professional as well as a parent.

Giles often demonstrates that adults aren't perfect and that being grown up is neither easy nor much different from being a teenager. At the end of "The Dark Age" when Giles' past as Ripper is revealed, Buffy tells him, "I'm so used to you being a grown-up and then I find out that you're a person," and though she admits, "It was scary," Giles continues to develop as a person. Wall and Zryd argue that Giles' "authority in the collective comes from his learned knowledge, reasoned judgement and emotional maturity" (2001: 60). These are functions of Giles' age, something that separates him from the other Scoobies throughout and allows him to *be* a father figure. Various (female) characters point out that Buffy "lacks" a father figure, and she is presented as missing her real father and resenting his abandonment of her. As a sympathetic adult in frequent close contact, Giles is positioned as a substitute or surrogate father, and this is acknowledged at various points.

When Angel turns dark after Buffy has sex with him in season 2, Giles knows more about this than Joyce and is able to accept it more readily. I suggest that this is because Giles is not Buffy's parent: were he "really" her father, he would not have such a mild and considered reaction. Angelus reveals to Joyce as part of his harassment that he and Buffy have had sex, and Joyce then has "the talk" with Buffy ("Passion"). "You had sex with a boy you never even saw fit to tell me you were dating," Joyce scolds her daughter before telling her, typically, "Buffy, you can shut me out of your life, I am pretty much used to that, but don't expect me to ever stop caring about you because it's never going to happen." Giles, on the other hand, *did* know that Buffy was "dating" Angel, he is not "shut out" of Buffy's life, and partly because of this he does not feel the shock and protective anger that Joyce experiences on this revelation (he also discovers it several episodes before Joyce).[9] Buffy expects a disappointed "parental" reaction, but Giles tells her, "If it's guilt you're looking for, Buffy, I'm not your man. All you will get from me is my support and my respect" ("Innocence"). Although this scene is as emotional as the subsequent scene with Joyce, Giles is shown treating Buffy like another "grown-up" able to make her own choices, a clear elevation of the nurturing father over the working mother.

The nature of the relationship is pointed out in the subsequent episode, "Passion," when Angelus kills Jenny Calendar and a grief-stricken Giles sets out to confront him. Buffy is distracted from the fight with Angelus, who points out that Giles is in danger: "You gonna let *your old man* just burn? [my emphasis]." Buffy's complex emotions are shown afterward: she punches Giles to the ground and then hugs him tightly, saying, "You can't leave me, I can't do this alone." Giles replaces the father who has left her, but this time she prevents him from leaving and admits her need for his support.

Another signal of Giles' role as nurturing father is paradoxically provided in an episode where he appears to betray his position of trust. At the beginning of "Helpless" Buffy's feelings for her real father are highlighted. He is to take her to the ice show ("a big dumb girlie thing") for her birthday; she tells Willow it's a family "tradition."[10] She is disappointed when her father cancels their arrangement because his "quarterly projections are unraveling"—here he puts career before family—and after refusing Joyce's offer to accompany her, she hints to Giles that "if someone were free they'd take their daughter, or their student, or their Slayer." The situation becomes more sinister when Giles hypnotizes Buffy and injects her using a hypodermic—categorized by Golden, Bissette, and Sniegoski as his "Most Monstrous Moment" (2000: 172). Buffy later tries to explain that she is losing her Slayer power, saying, "I throw knives like—" and Giles finishes, "—like a girl?" This uncharacteristically "sexist" response is disturbing for Buffy and for the viewer, and it signals that something is definitely wrong.

Shortly afterward it is revealed that the Watcher's Council are testing Buffy by stripping her of her superpowers, and Giles eventually confesses this to her. In doing so, Abbott argues, he is "prioritizing Buffy's safety over tradition" (2001: 22), and she notes that Giles also attempted to do this in "Prophecy Girl" (1012). Giles clashes with the Council representative, Quentin Travers: to a suggestion that what happens to Buffy is none of his business, Giles retorts, "This is not business," thus moving his relationship with Buffy out of the professional sphere. Giles' reactions here underline his role as new man as well as nurturing parent. Buffy passes the test, but Giles, because of his "father's love," fails and is sacked as her Watcher. Their final scene together shows her allowing him to clean her wounds, a more literal representation of his parental nurturing.[11]

Early in season 4, Buffy insists that Thanksgiving dinner takes place at Giles' house since he is "the patriarch" ("Pangs"), and when arranging her (spellbound) wedding with Spike, she asks Giles to give her away ("Something Blue")—she says she wants this event to be about her "real family." At the end of the season, in Giles' dream segment of "Restless," he and Olivia (who pushes a baby buggy) are "parents" to Buffy's "child," yet this phase of their relationship is ending. Catherine Siemann notes that Giles is now suffering from "empty nest syndrome" (2002: 126), and as the season unfolded he began to take a back seat as a parent and teacher. "A New Man" features a rival mentor for Buffy (Walsh) and an apparent ally in her Slayer struggle (the Initiative, headed by Walsh). Much is made of Walsh's dismissal of Giles—she tells him that Buffy "lacks a strong father figure" and suggests that Buffy has had to grow up too quickly. Faced with an assertive professional woman close to his own age, Giles is seen to lack confidence and appears conservative (he calls Buffy a "girl," while Walsh calls her a "woman"). The episode is resolved when Buffy recognizes the look in the demon's eyes as Giles: "You're the only person in the world who can look that annoyed with me," she says, clearly indicating his role as her sometimes authoritarian father. On a basic level of contrast, the show's presentation of one possible surrogate parent and role model (Walsh) as "evil" implies that the other (Giles) must be "good."

Because of his more central position in the show, Giles is (at times) able to protect Buffy from emotional or physical danger, but he is also capable of stepping back when appropriate. At the beginning of season 5, Giles confides to Willow that he intends to leave since he is no longer needed as Buffy's Watcher, though Buffy postpones this after her encounter with Dracula. Giles finally leaves when his Slayer is killed at the end of season 5. When Buffy has been successfully resurrected, he returns, but his reaction is ambivalent; as a "parent" he considers Buffy's feelings and the consequences for her. In "Life Serial" (6005) Buffy admits that Giles' presence and support makes her "feel safe, knowing you're always going to be here." At this point, Giles states that he has become Buffy's "mother" as well as her "father" (articulating his usurpation of the maternal, nurturing role), and as already noted, he provides financial support to the two remaining Summers women when they are in difficulty. This might seem to fall into line with "a wider tendency to convert traditionally feminine attributes into an additional index of masculine superiority, thus reconfiguring gender polarity rather than transcending it" (Jeffords in Traube 1992: 24), though earlier in response to the mundane problems Buffy faces in this season, Giles offers Joyce as a role model, telling Buffy that she "dealt with this kind of thing all the time . . . without the aid of any superpower and got through it all. So can you" ("Flooded").

Giles' song in "Once More with Feeling" states that that his time of "play[ing] the father" to Buffy is "past," and he admits, "I'm standing in the way." That is, his support is preventing Buffy from becoming independent, so he leaves again. He returns in the finale of season 6 to lend assistance in defeating Dark Willow (Dark Willow says, "Daddy's home"), and this demonstrates that though they may need his professional expertise, his Scooby "family" no longer need parental care. Early episodes of season 7 show Giles mentoring Willow as he used to teach Buffy, but when he returns to Sunnydale his presence remains generally low-key. I have noted that Buffy rejects his "teaching" role when she clashes with him over Spike, but part of Giles' motivation is concern for his surrogate daughter: "Buffy, I want more for you" ("First Date"; Joyce displayed a similar motivation in wishing Angel gone). Giles may be read as a new father as well as a new man; unlike the strict authoritarian fathers who know best, "the new father is expected to support his children and guide them toward their adult identities" (Traube 1992: 137). Giles' importance as part of the Scooby family is demonstrated in the final episode by his inclusion in the core group, but his dwindling role as mentor and father is also underlined as he watches the younger Scoobies walk away from him to their battle positions.[12] Arguably, he has succeeded in helping his "children" find their adult identities.

Do I Have Mom Hair?

Episodes such as "The Dark Age" and "Gingerbread" show the teen characters and Buffy in particular taking on parental responsibilities and roles, while older parent-figures act like children—another role reversal derived from the teen hero premise. After the death of their mother, Buffy experiences what it is like to be a surrogate parent to her sister, Dawn. Initially Buffy shirks parental responsibility, passing it off onto Giles, and Willow and Tara also offer Dawn parental support (as well as a stable relationship, something rare in the Buffyverse).

In "Gone" Buffy is presented through a visit from social services as an unemployed layabout who cannot organize the household, has a no-good boyfriend, and is an unfit guardian to her sister. I mentioned in chapter 1 that this briefly disrupts the presentation of Buffy's life as comfortable and middle class, but it also keys into contemporary social changes. Nancy Woloch notes that the "new woman of the 'post-feminist' generation might well be the working wife in an upwardly mobile two-career family. But she might also be a single mother, deserted spouse, impoverished family head, or, by choice or circumstance, a woman living alone" (2000: 578–579). Buffy's situation here alludes to a larger context. Since most people resent intervention by social services, sympathy is likely to lie with Buffy (the protagonist), and the viewer can see that a series of coincidences leads to a worst-case scenario for the social worker's visit.

Still, the show has Buffy admit that she has been acting irresponsibly, and she swings from being overprotective to being hostile or irritated. Dawn sees Buffy as putting her career (Slaying) before her family, and in "Older and Far Away" (6014) vengeance demon Halfrek's appearance is explained by her "thing for bad parents," implicating Buffy. "Lies My Parents Told Me" reveals that Slayer Nikki Wood had a child, but rather than opening up new possibilities, this reiterates the same problems: she tells her son, "Look at me. You know I love you but I got a job to do. The mission is what matters, right?" In this way the show seems to equate being a Slayer (or a career woman) with being a "bad" mother. Yet Dawn is also a large part of the reason Buffy does her "job" so well: family and friends are important parts of the world that need saving. At the end of season 6 Buffy notably does *not* save the world, but she *does* make a step forward in her relationship with Dawn. When Buffy and Dawn are trapped under a graveyard in the season finale, Buffy is forced to acknowledge Dawn as a possible ally. Although Buffy does not imagine that she can actually help (and nor perhaps does the viewer), Dawn successfully decapitates a demon with the sword Buffy gives her, saying, "What? You think I never watched you?" (Buffy in turn has become a role model). At the end of the episode, Dawn and Buffy's roles are reversed so that Dawn comforts Buffy (as Buffy comforted Joyce in "Gingerbread"), and Buffy finally realizes that Dawn is growing up.

In season 7, Buffy takes Dawn to school (in an echo of Buffy's first

day at Sunnydale High in the opening episode) and at several points is jokingly referred to as Dawn's mother. The new high school principal is neither a wishy-washy liberal like Flutie nor a strict authoritarian like Snyder but an adult who treats Buffy like an equal and the students like, well, teenagers. Buffy is offered a job counseling teens with problems—something that calls for traditional "feminine" and "maternal" skills such as communication, nurturing, and intuition (all things Joyce demonstrated, though this connection is never stated). While Buffy's abilities as a counselor are later undercut by Wood's admission that he merely wanted her on the Hellmouth, the show presents her as relatively successful in this role. Her later characterization as a "general" in the "war" against the First Evil presents her again in a more "masculine" role, but by this stage Buffy can be read as finally accepting her place not as a girl, but as a young, aging woman.

All About the Journey

Earlier adult characters in *Buffy* almost all demonstrate a lack of responsibility as well as a selfish desire to maintain their own powerful position. Because the show starts out as teen drama/teen horror, it is inevitable that it includes conflict between generations. "Fathers" have typically demonstrated power, either in some kind of institution or hierarchy, or through violence. "Mothers" have been more likely to be emotional or communicative, and when they adopt a "masculine" role they are seen to be "bad" (though fathers are just as bad). But since it is "all about the journey," as Giles says in "Restless," adult roles become more complex as the teens progress into adulthood: strong development across the series means that the status quo *cannot* be maintained.

Giles is almost always an exception, and he is free to leave Sunnydale and allow Buffy to mature independently. Joyce, Buffy's "real" parent, did not have this choice and Buffy, as the Slayer, could not leave the Hellmouth. In the logic of the show, therefore, Joyce had to die for Buffy to be able to grow up. Giles sums up their different roles when he tells Buffy, "I've taught you all I can about being the Slayer. Your mother taught you what you needed to know about life" ("Tabula Rasa"). As a new man Giles is not a traditional patriarch, but the importance of a

liberal father in nurturing independent women is noted in his relationships with Willow and Buffy and in Faith's relationship with the Mayor.
Though they functioned as parents to Buffy and the other Scoobies, the
show refused to literally pair Giles and Joyce, further undercutting the
notions of the traditional family and of romance. However, Joyce remains limited (defined) by her role as Buffy's mother; Giles is allowed to
be much more than a father figure. His presentation as both a new father
and a new man is complex and maps a not entirely successful negotiation
of these roles.

Early suggests that despite Buffy's struggles, "in contrast to her male
friends and lovers, Buffy (almost) always knows who she is and what she
must do" (2002: 21). As previous chapters have shown, I do not agree,
and a striking example of Buffy's *conflicted* identity is shown in "Normal Again," where demon venom causes Buffy to believe that she is in
a psychiatric hospital and that her life as the Slayer is a complex delu-
sion. Buffy could be "normal again" but only by rejecting her power as
the Slayer, losing the alternative Scooby family, and accepting her place
as the little girl in a patriarchal nuclear family (in this reality her father
never left). Dark Willow later reminds Buffy that "an insane asylum"
seemed "a comfy alternative" to the "real" world ("Two to Go"), implying that traditional family roles can offer comfort and erase the need
to struggle for independence. Parents and family remain problematic
in *Buffy*, in part because the show's strong serial form continually resists closure, stable relationships, and "normality." Like other "quality
television" shows (see Torres 1993), *Buffy*'s representation of the family
exposes its ideological tensions: real and traditional parents are largely
demonized, but an alternative family is constituted among the regular characters, so that family values and roles are both denigrated and
upheld.

Conclusion

As I suggested in my introduction, *Buffy* may at first appear progressive in its representation of gender, yet is often contradictory, and at times the strategies taken to try and negotiate problems of gender representation are problematic in themselves. In the context of its historic moment, such ambivalent subversiveness and complicity both responds to and "reflects" changing gender roles in the dominant culture and is typical of contemporary popular culture. Generic hybridity in *Buffy* opens up spaces for new representations of gender, but traditional generic and narrative conventions can be difficult to escape. Adopting different narrative forms allows more focus on emotion and relationships in what might have been seen as an action show, but some types of narrative may be more familiar and therefore more easily read than others. Arguably these aspects depend on what the viewer brings to the show, and more audience response research on *Buffy* could indicate whether particular groups privilege certain types of narrative, generic conventions, or ideological "messages." Recent debates about "quality television" raise questions about consumption and production that I have only begun to address here. Since I started work on this book, it was announced that season 7 would be the last season of *Buffy* and the show is now "finished." As I outline below, the show's concluding season exemplifies some of the patterns and "problems" I have identified in my analysis.

Although *Buffy*'s serial form and its privileging of emotion and relationship arcs challenge resolvable linear narrative, the use of horror conventions invokes narrative resolution and "conservative" moral closures. *Buffy* has been described as "a kind of anti-horror" that "openly mocks the underlying morality" of more traditional horror film (Graber in Anderson 2003: 213, note 1), but it relies on a traditional good-versus-evil scenario, and viewing pleasure is still based on narrative resolutions that destroy or contain disruptive monsters. Season 7 raises some of these contradictions in narrative: it highlights the Slayer as part of a female line by bringing the Potentials to Sunnydale, but it downplays the significance of the Scooby family and emotional bonds in favor of "masculine" war rhetoric (Buffy is often referred to as a "general," for example). The season villain is reinstated (despite my argument that this function had become obsolete) and is revealed as the "First Evil" (incapable of being anything but evil), so the season narrative reverts to a simplistic story of good defeating evil, and characters who were previously morally ambivalent (Faith and Spike) fight on the side of good. Hibbs notes that *Buffy* "has always dealt with the question and problem of Buffy's identity" (2003: 57), yet the series finale does not entirely re/solve the conflict in Buffy's character, which in my reading results in her hybridized gendering. The story of "Buffy the Vampire Slayer" is over, but the "battle" of good and evil goes on and the characters are not positioned in stable situations that indicate closure. In this way the show managed to avoid full closure, leaving the "story" and the characters open.

Elements of "masculine" genres like horror and action are subverted by the way *Buffy* uses role reversal, attempting to separate roles or behaviors from gender. Reversals of horror and action staples are not always successful. Fantasy (the supernatural) allows potentially "alternative" constructions of gender, yet as Spicer observes, "since the Buffyverse is situated in a patriarchal society that utilizes preestablished gender stereotypes, we must acknowledge that it would be difficult for *Buffy* to address issues of gender without engaging with such stereotypes" (2002: 5). Role reversal can be problematic, but the "real-world" setting of *Buffy* also allows for viewer recognition of the problems affecting characters' constant re/construction of gendered identity.

Some have read particular characters as successfully re-visioning gender through genre. Wisker compares Buffy with contemporary women's vampire fiction, and in particular with "the often androgynous figure of the vampire" used "to dismantle patriarchy's reductive binary thought and behaviors" (2001). Certainly the show increasingly suggested connections between Buffy and the "monsters" she was supposed to fight, and I have highlighted the striking similarities between good and bad girls. The vampire is always Other and often a gender hybrid. Traditionally in a linear narrative it functions (like the strong woman) as a problem to be solved, and Tony Williams suggests that "[b]oth female and monster potentially threaten a socially defined male order of things" (1996: 21). *Buffy*'s postfeminist context presents this very much as a story of our time. The teen allegory of early seasons also allows the show to handle gendered issues such as rape, sexuality, domestic violence, and women's self-defense, and in this way genre can open up space for discussion of gender.

However, generic conventions and roles inevitably limit the representation of some characters. Angel really develops only when he moves out of *Buffy* and away from his restrictive role as love interest/object of desire. Tara has great potential as a female-centered character, but because she does not fit the heterosocial model of the show she is sidelined and serves largely to highlight Willow. Drusilla and other bad girls lack extended development because they function as foils for the good girls. These limitations arise partly because of the persistence of gendered narratives in genre. It might initially seem that the show has more success in liberating males from conventional representation than females because males have more generic roles available to them. New men can also be bad boys because rules/roles for males are more flexible and because this makes them more conventionally attractive.

Notably, the two main new men in *Buffy*'s serial narrative, Xander and Giles, are returned to conventional masculinity by normalization, on the one hand, and a diminishing role, on the other. As Xander grows up he becomes more traditionally "masculine" and takes on typical male roles, while as the teen characters grow up, Giles' role as parent and mentor becomes less important and he appears intermittently as a father figure or patriarchal authority. In *Buffy* vampires are liminal gender hybrids, but this transgression too is re/solved by closure in the show's narrative—Angel leaves and Spike dies. (Both reappear in the spin-off show, but *Buffy* and *Angel* differ in their approaches to representing gender and gendered relations within a genre format. It is worth noting that another increasingly complex and liminal male character, Andrew, is transferred, if briefly, into *Angel*.)

The two main female characters are not "solved" by the conclusion of the narrative, and the series presents them as increasingly powerful. In fact, Buffy and Willow become more hybridized and transgressive of gender boundaries as they "grow up." Both retain their power at the end of the final episode ("Chosen"), and Buffy, Willow, and Dawn are in the foreground of the final scene, with Giles, Faith, and Xander behind (figure 14). Buffy's transgressive nature is elided by the ending—she retains her Slayer power but can be a "normal girl" if she wishes. I have argued that Willow is refeminized, but her power is not re/solved. The final episode ends with questions rather than answers, and Faith asks Buffy how it will feel to live "like a person." One possible reading

FIGURE 14: *"What are we going to do now?"—the ambiguous ending of* Buffy *("Chosen").*

of this is that as women who have experienced agency and power, Buffy and Willow (and indeed all the female characters) will never have a "normal" life in the patriarchal world of the contemporary United States. Or, from another angle, Willow and Buffy's experience in negotiating gendered identities that incorporate both "feminism" and "femininity" is typical of young women today.

This lack of resolution reflects the difficulty of transcending the binaries that structure *Buffy*'s (and our society's) premises. These tend toward opposite poles, whether "good" or "bad," "masculine" or "feminine." Morality and gender are inextricably linked, because transgression of gender boundaries is most obvious in "bad" characters and the show cannot always reconcile transgressive behavior in "good" characters. *Buffy* tries to blur clear-cut moral definitions, but characters and viewers tend to identify actions and characters as good or bad, and the many transformations of regular characters make use of binary positions. As I have indicated, viewing pleasure is derived from a transformation that results in the complete opposite of a familiar character (Giles/Ripper, Willow/Vamp Willow, Willow/Dark Willow, Angel/Angelus). Yet characters who resist polarization, such as Faith and Spike, provide the most complex and extended transformations.

Some scholars have argued that Buffy and other characters present "open images" of gender. I have questioned, in the case of Faith and Spike, how useful this openness can be when the narrative resists it. Because their appeal is in their transgression, redemption closes this down and leaves their characters with nowhere to go: they have lost their role and their openness (Faith becomes another good Slayer, Spike becomes another good vampire with a soul).

Open images remain open to traditional readings as well as "feminist" ones and familiar generic trappings might encourage such "easy" decoding. Parpart's analysis of recent audience research points out that many male viewers of *Buffy* remain "clear in their desire to read Buffy's challenges and accomplishments in general, humanistic terms rather than as an effect of or commentary on her gender" (2003: 83). Thus the "open image" of Buffy is liable to elude a "feminist" reading, and Faith's comment "Thank God we're hot chicks with superpowers" ("End of Days") may be taken at face value as a reading of the show.

Of course, female viewers in particular might take pleasure in watching Buffy and other female characters use the power they have; in the transgressive behavior of the bad girls; in the good girls doing bad things; and in recognizing "feminine" concerns about clothes, hair, and style. Such pleasures can be problematic and contingent, as I have indicated. Most tend to convey the notion that women today can be and do anything. The fact that some also apply to male characters ("What is Angel wearing?" or "What have they done to Spike's hair?") seems to demonstrate that gender divisions are broken down through these types of representation. However, one inescapable though perhaps more invisible message of *Buffy* is that women can be and do anything only if they are young, white, middle class, and conventionally attractive. It has often been noted that the "choices" of postfeminist society really only apply to members of the professional middle class, who begin from a position of privilege. The show acknowledges this to some extent with the inclusion of characters like Faith and Nikki Wood, who do not have the same opportunities (choices) as Buffy, and in the tension between Buffy's possession of supernatural power and her lack of "real-world" economic power. Similarly, Buffy's position as heterosexual and as a "mother" to Dawn reinforce a conventional gendered position in the "real" world, at the same time that her action hero role seems to blur gendered characteristics.

If, as Jancovich and Lyons suggest, quality television is marketed at "affluent, highly educated consumers who value the literary qualities of these programs" and its "celebrated formal features" can "work to exclude sections of the viewing public" (2003: 3), then production and reception are marked by exclusivity. Joanne Hollows suggests that some forms of "popular feminism" are exemplary, since "their mode of address seeks to include rather than exclude" (2000: 202). *Buffy* managed to attract large audiences (possibly implying that its "feminist" message was not unappealing), though its "quality television" categorization might demonstrate that it continued to operate in a somewhat exclusive way. I have touched on ways that race and class inflect gender representation but this subject would bear further study. That *Buffy* depicted a long-running lesbian relationship highlights sexual diversity, despite some limitations regarding what is deemed acceptable on primetime network television in the United States. Viewers reacted strongly to Tara's death at the end of season 6, some seeing it as a reversal of the show's representation by having the relationship end in death and "badness," while others argued that heterosexual characters had been "killed off" in similar ways (though the apparently permanent deaths—Tara, Joyce, and Jenny Calendar—are all women).

It would be naive to imagine that commercial television can be entirely "feminist" or radical in its revisioning of gender roles, even if it is classed as "cult television" and is targeted at specific "sections of the viewing public." Both *Xena: Warrior Princess* and *Farscape* presented strong female characters relatively successfully, but camp, comedy, and sometimes almost surreal narrative were used heavily in their representation. Faith's "hot chicks with superpowers" comment is meant to be funny, and humor serves to deflect and mediate the "critique" of conventional gender roles both in *Buffy* and in these other shows. Like *Buffy*, *Xena* and *Farscape* are fantasy or science fiction, not mainstream "realist" television, and the original *Star Trek* demonstrated that genre television is allowed more latitude in what it represents precisely because it is not "real." But commercial television shows must retain popularity if they are to stay on the air (the somewhat idiosyncratic *Farscape* was canceled after four seasons).[1] *Buffy* may have subverted some generic conventions and offered unexpected narrative twists or lack of closure, but it maintained conventional appeal—action, violence, attractive young women, virile male heart-throbs, comedy, tragedy, villains, and heroes. *Buffy*'s binaries inevitably include the conflicting demands of Whedon's "feminism" and the networks' desire for large audiences and high ratings.

I have demonstrated in my reading of *Buffy* that the show does not offer successful alternative gender representations but does raise awareness of the problems inherent in attempting to re-vision gender. Form, genre, narrative, and medium are so closely intertwined with gender that it is difficult to disengage them, in analysis or representation. Buffy may be "Barbie with a kung-fu grip," but she is still Barbie: on American network television, what else could she be? Being "hot chicks with superpowers" does indeed "[take] the edge off," as Faith and Buffy say. This comment, especially coming from a transgressive character like Faith, also exposes the limitations of what a television show can do. I am not claiming that *Buffy* is "better" than, or even different from, other television shows; on the contrary, I have argued that it is a typical example of postmodern popular culture. It is too early to evaluate how influential it might be on future television and whether or how its "open images" of gender will affect subsequent representations. The high, possibly unprecedented, academic interest in *Buffy* and even the many contradictory positions taken about its "value" indicate its success in exposing the difficulties of challenging conventional representation in a popular medium. This, to me, is its "edge." I have argued from the beginning that *Buffy* is both a product of and a response to postfeminist and postmodern culture. Analyzing its transgressions and contradictions can bring us closer to understanding how traditional notions of gender are perpetuated and how new versions are being negotiated. Thinking about gender in *Buffy* while writing this book has certainly made me far more aware of my own preconceptions of, assumptions about, and negotiations of gender and sexuality. As Giles says in "Chosen," "We have a lot of work ahead of us."

notes

INTRODUCTION

1. The amount of academic material produced suggests that *Buffy* is in the process of being canonized. I cannot think of another television show, for example, that has its own dedicated journal (*Slayage*, the online international journal of *Buffy* studies).

2. Thanks to Nick Heffernan for this insight.

3. For instance, feminist theory has varied in different countries, and cultural studies is more inflected by Marxism and class-consciousness in Britain than in America. For a more detailed picture of broadcasting and reception in the U.K. see Hill and Calcutt (2001).

4. This is discernible from the broadcasting of such programs on U.K. television, where they tend to appear on BBC2 or Channel 4.

5. Robin Nelson describes *Ally McBeal* as "a multilayered, self-conscious postmodern text," going on to suggest that "its multi-tracked *bricolage* of televisual and musical styles affords a range of sheer pleasures to be taken. But it also offers a provocation seriously to consider contemporary social issues by transgressing normative codes to disturb traditional sureties and invite quizzical—if not outright oppositional—readings" (2001: 45). *Buffy* does similar things.

6. Rhonda V. Wilcox and David Lavery (2002: xxviii, note 6), and Esther Saxey (2001: 196) have noted in passing the effect of serial television form on *Buffy*'s representation of the family and heterosexual romance, respectively.

CHAPTER I

1. Sara Buttsworth notes that Sarah Michelle Gellar's role in slasher films such as *I Know What You Did Last Summer* and *Scream 2* (both 1997) adds another level to this reversal of victim and Slayer (2002: 196, note 4).

2. *Buffy* bears remarkable similarities to *Mamono Hunter Yôko* (1991).

3. *Xena* also functions as an intertext and is referred to in "Halloween" (2006).

4. The show indicates that Buffy has dreams of the past and of future events.

5. Buttsworth suggests that the Scooby gang "reflects part of a broader Western tradition of the exclusion, and invisibility, of female heroism" (2002: 191). I would argue that *Buffy* has consistently undermined the notion of individual heroism that Buttsworth uses as a model.

6. Buffy's two resurrections (seasons 1 and 6) also play on generic conventions. In a show about vampires the dead frequently return, but *Buffy*'s resistance to the closure of death stems from more than one genre: Whedon has directly alluded to "Patrick Duffy in the shower" (in Nazzaro 2002: 212).

7. Arwen Spicer reads this season as undercutting the feminism of previous narratives (2004).

8. Several Web biographies note that Charisma Carpenter, who plays Cordelia, auditioned for the role of Buffy but took Cordelia after the part was turned down by Bianca Lawson (who later played Kendra).

9. In *Angel* Cordelia becomes a "champion" in her own right.

10. Recently *The TV Genre Book* (Creeber 2001) categorized *Buffy* as teen drama. The show has been compared with other teen dramas like *Dawson's Creek*, as much for its (overly articulate) "teen" dialogue and self-conscious irony as for its focus on teen issues and inclusion of appropriate music. *Buffy* initially rendered many teen issues through horror allegory, and Whedon admits the show afforded him "an opportunity to mythologize [his] crappy high school experience" (in Golden and Holder 1998: 240). Like *Dawson's Creek*, *Buffy* also attracted older audiences.

11. Later Oz has a van, but this is explained in practical terms—moving the band's equipment—rather than status.

12. When Buffy is infected by a demon and starts "hearing" thoughts, Cordelia is unaffected by the embarrassment the other Scoobies feel over this invasion of privacy: she says exactly what she thinks ("Earshot" 3018).

13. In this episode Cordelia is the only woman in Sunnydale to be immune from the love spell. A "magical" explanation is given for this, but I like to read it as awarding her further independence.

14. Thanks to Bronwen Calvert for this observation.

15. An audience member at the *Buffy* Dux and Redux panel of WisCon 27 (2003) used this description.

CHAPTER 2

1. Like Dyer, I find the term *nonwhite* less than satisfactory but use it because of a lack of alternatives (see Dyer 1997: 11).

2. This highlights Drusilla's power but negates Kendra's (see chapter 3).

3. Something that *Angel* began to address. Dominic Alessio notes that Bianca Lawson originally auditioned for the part of Cordelia and remarks, "It is interesting to surmise on the impact a major black character might have had on 'race' depiction" in *Buffy* (2001: 740, note 23). However, given that, as noted in the previous chapter, Cordelia was intended as a short-running foil for Buffy,

Lawson as Cordelia could simply have been whitewashed. Ono also observes that Charisma Carpenter is Latina and that Sarah Michelle Gellar is Jewish (2000: 180), but the show does not use these identities.

4. Candra K. Gill (2003) suggests that the deaths of these two Slayers of color are sexualized, offering a further parallel. The First Slayer is also nonwhite and dead.

5. Paige Moss, who played Veruca, has said, "I love Joss for letting me be different-looking and still be considered sexy" (in Holder, Mariotte, and Hart 2000: 308).

6. Tara's family have been described as "rednecks" (Daugherty 2001: 157), which might imply that class is also a factor. Tara's initial isolation suggests that she did not fit in socially, but she is not presented as having the "lower-class" characteristics of, for example, Faith. Her place at university may be the start of her reclassification, since higher education remains a passport to middle-class professions and salaries. The background Tara transcends is presented more in terms of restrictive ideologies, which are inflected by religious rhetoric (foreshadowing Caleb in season 7). In the context of the episode this works well, but the social stigma and shame Tara feels when the others discover "what kind of people" she comes from can be read as class-based.

7. This and the "previously on *Buffy*" segment serves to remind viewers that Tara once sabotaged a spell she and Willow were working on.

8. Accommodating women, such as Tara's cousin Beth, are also implicated in this control.

9. Although in one argument Tara uncharacteristically invokes male authority, asking, "What would Giles say?" this may simply be a way of reminding viewers of similar warnings from Giles.

10. In *Mamono Hunter Yôko*, for instance, Yôko's power is linked to her virginity.

11. Given my argument here, it is interesting that Buttsworth comments that Buffy survives these events "intact" (2002: 194).

12. *The Watcher's Guide* opens and closes its section on Buffy and Angel's relationship with a line from *Romeo and Juliet* (Golden and Holder 1998: 164), highlighting the "star-crossed lovers" aspect.

13. Spike's motivation for setting out on the quest is ambivalent (he seems to desire the removal of his chip), but in season 7 he is retrospectively assigned the desire to regain his soul. Having a soul appears to be enough to make any vampire "good" in *Buffy*, and Spike's soul also allows the show to present Buffy taking up their relationship again, excusing the attempted rape as committed by another person.

14. Thanks to the *Buffy* Dux and Redux panel audience at WisCon 27 (2003) for this insight.

CHAPTER 3

1. See also Barbara Creed on *The Hunger* (1993a: 59–72).

2. Kristina Busse notes that "[t]hough many different vampire contexts describe the parent-vampire as *sire*, *Buffy* fanfic is singular in describing the offspring as *childe*," but this terminology is not used in the show itself (2002: 214).

3. *Angel* reveals that Darla rejected Angel after his soul returned ("Darla"), but her character is still defined in romantic/sexual relationship to him, even more so when she bears his child. This brings about her redemption: she stakes herself so that the baby can live.

4. Given the teen drama inflections of the show at this early stage, it is interesting how explicit some of this presentation is. Of course, it is designed to characterize these characters as "bad."

5. However, Vamp Harmony says in "The Harsh Light of Day" (4003) that it was a fungus demon.

6. This pose is a striking echo of the pietà, reinforcing Dru as mother to Spike.

7. Dru is quite consciously old-fashioned (traditional), and her clothes on *Buffy* reflect this. An exchange in "Reunion" (*Angel* 2010) highlights Dru's old-world aspects. She says, "The moon showed me. It told me to come into the twentieth century," and when Angel replies, "It's the twenty-first century, Dru," she sighs, "I'm still lagging." See also note 13, below.

8. Angel's response to the news that Spike has killed a Slayer—"Well, I guess that makes you one of us"—could be intended to imply that the other three have also killed Slayers ("Fool for Love"), though Spike's reaction to Kendra's death suggests that this is not the case.

9. Creed suggests a similar opposition between the world of the female vampire and the patriarchal world of the living (1993a: 71).

10. Darla, Drusilla, and Spike do not appear in this parallel universe.

11. It is interesting that neither Dru nor Darla gets to wear leather on *Buffy*, though the Master, Angelus, Spike, and Vamp Willow all do, in a very obvious connotation of "badness" and, in the case of Angelus and Vamp Willow, "deviant" sexuality. In *Angel* ("Reunion" 2010) both Darla and Dru wear leather trousers, an unusual departure in their costuming and a clear indication that they are bad girls.

12. The *Angel* episode "Disharmony" (2017) plays on a confusion of vampirism and lesbianism.

13. See Daugherty 2001: 159 on menstruation.

CHAPTER 4

1. A possible reminder of Xander's time as a hyena in "The Pack" (1006).

2. Like the more masculinized alternative Buffy in "The Wish."

3. As Simkin observes (2004b: note 19), it seems redundant to point out the significance of Sam's masculine name, given Riley's homosocial nature.

4. Although Simkin notes that Forrest calls Riley "brother" after he has been reanimated (2004b: 30), Forrest did it previously too. I see this as conflating both his racial identity and the idea of the Initiative as a family.

5. Forrest's attitude to women (he ogles them in the lunch queue during "The Initiative") underlines the objectification identified in previous tough guys, but it is also, as Simkin observes (2004a: 6), an unfortunate reprisal of the myth of black sexuality. This sexuality is verbally expressed but never visualized. (Gill [2003] notes that other black males on *Buffy* have been coded as rapists.)

6. In early seasons of *Angel*, it is striking how Forrest compares with the character of Charles Gunn. Gunn seems like a deliberate "apology" for previous racial representations, and there are striking similarities and developments from Forrest to Gunn.

7. This is a stereotypical example of a black male posing a physical threat to a white female, and the reference to Buffy as Riley's "girlfriend" adds a subdued sexual overtone (threatening black sexuality). Forrest fights Buffy and seems to be winning, but it is Riley who finally dispatches him. Just as Kendra was killed by Drusilla, Forrest is defeated by a secondary rather than a main character. And as Kendra died but Faith survived, here the black soldier dies, while Graham the white soldier lives and later re-recruits Riley back into the family.

8. The whole confrontation lasts around three minutes, with only around half a minute of physical contact between Combo-Buffy and Adam.

9. "Here we've got all the stuff we ever wanted and we didn't even have to—," begins Andrew. "—Earn it?" suggests Warren ("Flooded"). Peg Aloi pointed out that in this season Willow and Warren share this trait (2002).

10. Tom is described as "one of those men who reach such an acute limited excellence at twenty-one that everything afterward savours of anti-climax" (Fitzgerald 1975: 12).

11. In a similar fashion the hypermasculinity of Arnold Schwarzenegger as the original terminator in *The Terminator* cannot be topped and is contrasted by the geeky but technological T1000 in the second film, and a female terminator is presented in *T3* (2003).

CHAPTER 5

1. A certain naïveté is implied by the fact that he does not understand the "bees"—sexual metaphor eludes him.

2. Given subsequent rhetoric about Spike/William being "beneath" Cecily and Buffy, this positioning is interesting.

3. Thanks to the responsive audience to my paper at WisCon 25 (2001) for raising some of these points in discussion.

4. In this respect Giles also plays out the notion of the repressed Brit.

5. Whedon notes "the sexiness and wit Tony Head brought to the role of Giles. . . . As a result, Giles became much more than 'boring exposition guy' ("Hellmouth")" (in Lavery 2002a: 13).

6. The interracial relationship may have seemed edgy in the U.S. (though not in the U.K.), but that both characters are British distances their relationship from American "norms."

7. Tony Head left the show because he wanted to spend more time with his family in the U.K., but this also fits the "growing up" narrative arc.

8. "It's sad. She's got two jobs: Denny's waitress by day, Slayer by night, and Angel's always in front of the TV with a big blood belly. And he's dreaming of the glory days when Buffy still thought this whole creature of the night routine was a big turn-on."

9. Tom DiPiero suggests that white masculinity itself can be seen as a lack of identity (in Dyer 1997: 212).

10. In the light of Wood's cooperation with Giles and Giles' comment about "personal vengeance," it is perhaps surprising that Giles' similar situation with Angelus in season 2 is never mentioned.

11. Of course, there is precedent for a black vampire hunter, and Wood's hidden cabinet full of bladed weapons may refer to it. The comic book character Blade became widely known via the 1998 movie and its sequel. Blade's mother is highly important in this film: she is also killed by a vampire.

CHAPTER 6

1. The name Jesse might connote a folk hero in the United States, but in northern British vernacular a "jessie" is a sissy.

2. "When She Was Bad" featured a character called Absalom, who acted as a regent for the Anointed One after the death of the Master. Absalom seemed modeled on a southern preacher.

3. Darla is the only longer-running vampire who might be American, but given later developments in *Angel* she too may actually be European: she first appears in the Virginia colony.

4. Tjardes reports that Whedon cited a "lack of chemistry" between Trick and the Mayor and implies that this is why his role is taken over by Faith (2003: 70).

5. Gill notes the sexualization of the Slayers killed by Spike and its relation to race, as well as the representation of black men as rapists in "Get It Done" (2003).

6. In the first few episodes, however, he presents himself as someone who avoids action.

7. It has been suggested that vampire films like *The Lost Boys* and *Near Dark* (1987) are desexualized because they function as teen romance (see Nixon 1997: 122).

8. Chin cites Angel's "oriental" apartment as another signifier of Otherness (2003: 98).

9. He is also impotent in the sense of not being able to have children ("Bad Eggs"). This and his celibacy are later overturned in *Angel*.

10. Visually he resembles David, the vampire gang leader from *The Lost Boys*.

11. Roy's "hyperbolic whiteness" is noted by Kaja Silverman (in Bukatman 1997: 76), and Ono observes that both Spike and Dru appear very "white" (2000: 184, note 24). Neal King compares Buffy's vampires with the representation of Jews under fascism, noting that Spike has a similar " 'dark and 'dirty' " taboo appeal (2003: 202).

12. The Sid Vicious association is so strong that Owen actually refers to Spike as "Sid." Actually, Spike's look may be more reminiscent of Billy Idol.

13. The Master kills Buffy (twice), Angelus kills Jenny Calendar, and Dru kills Kendra. Spike even dissuades other vampires from killing.

14. Boyette notes that in this scenario Spike also puts on a performance, hiding his recovery so that he can outwit Angelus (2001: 9).

15. As mentioned in the introduction (in Saxey 2001: 208).

CHAPTER 7

1. Vampire films of the 1980s and 1990s, such as *Blade*, also used the idea of generational conflict.

2. Foreshadowing "Normal Again," and a real threat if Buffy has already spent time in an institution.

3. Alternatively, Bowers suggests that Joyce's enjoyment of Ted's baking "can be read as a metaphor for sensual indulgence as well as sexual domination and satisfaction" (2001: 15).

4. Notably, these words exclude Joyce.

5. Thanks to Justine Larbalestier for raising the issue of androgyny here.

6. Thanks to Bronwen Calvert for this insight.

7. And, arguably, in "Bewitched, Bothered and Bewildered," where she is one of a few older women who become "bewitched" by Xander.

8. Similarly, Mendlesohn suggests that the revelation of Giles' involvement with Joyce raises "sexual tension" between Buffy and Giles, since Buffy experiences "a complex mixture of adolescent disgust . . . and betrayal that he has had a relationship behind her back" (2002: 49). Mendlesohn actually uses the same words Joyce does when speaking of Giles and Buffy.

9. *The Watcher's Guide Volume 2* notes that while "Joyce is the one to make Angel see that he must let Buffy go — a very parental moment — Giles is present at all her senior milestones" (Holder, Mariotte, and Hart 2000: 80).

10. It is never mentioned, however, on any of her other birthdays.

11. The episode also focuses on mothers. The mortal Kralik was a murderer of women, and Vamp Kralik admits to Joyce that he has "a problem with mothers." He traps Joyce by using her motherly concern for Buffy.

12. This scene is deliberately constructed to echo similar scenes from early seasons.

CONCLUSION

1. In an obvious, if ambiguous, response to its cancellation and a nod to its disruption of linear narrative styles, the final episode of *Farscape* concluded with the words, "To be continued."

BIBLIOGRAPHY

Abbott, Stacey. 2001. "A Little Less Ritual and a Little More Fun: The Modern Vampire in Buffy the Vampire Slayer." *Slayage* 3 (June), 32 pars. 12 June 2002 <http://www.middleenglish.org/slayage/essays/slayage3/sabbott.htm>. Number references given in the text refer to paragraph numbers rather than page numbers.

Alessio, Dominic. 2001. "'Things Are Different Now'?: A Postcolonial Analysis of *Buffy the Vampire Slayer*." *European Legacy* 6.6: 731–740.

Allen, John L., Jr. 1999. "Teens on Screen." *National Catholic Reporter* 35.21 (March 26): 17.

Aloi, Peg. 2002. "Leaves of Dark Willow: Beyond the Metaphor of Magical Addiction." Unpublished paper, "Blood, Texts and Fears" conference, Norwich, U.K.

Anderson, Wendy Love. 2003. "Prophecy Girl and the Powers That Be: The Philosophy of Religion in the Buffyverse." In Buffy the Vampire Slayer *and Philosophy: Fear and Trembling in Sunnydale*, ed. James B. South, 212–226. Peru, Ill.: Open Court.

Ang, Ien. 1997 [1990]. "Melodramatic Identifications: Television Fiction and Women's Fantasy." In *Feminist Television Criticism: A Reader*, ed. Charlotte Brunsdon, Julie D'Acci, and Lynn Spigel, 155–166. Oxford: Clarendon/Oxford University Press.

Appelo, Tim. 1998. "Interview with the Vampires." *TV Guide* July 25: 24–26.

Appleyard, Bryan. 2000. "A Teenager to Get Your Teeth Into." *Sunday Times* (Culture) 10 December: 4.

Armstrong, Stephen. 2000. "An Englishman Abroad: Buffy's Rupert Giles" [interview]. *Sunday Times* (Culture) 10 December: 5.

Asimov, Isaac. 1993 [1954]. *The Caves of Steel*. London: HarperCollins.

Attebery, Brian. 2002. *Decoding Gender in Science Fiction*. New York: Routledge.

Auerbach, Nina. 1995. *Our Vampires, Ourselves*. Chicago: University of Chicago Press.

Austen, Jane. 1996 [1816]. *Emma*. London: Penguin.

Babb, Valerie. 1998. *Whiteness Visible: The Meaning of Whiteness in American Literature and Culture*. New York: New York University Press.

Battis, Jes. 2003. "'She's Not All Grown Yet': Willow as Hybrid/Hero in *Buffy the Vampire Slayer*." *Slayage* 8 (March), 40 pars. 1 May 2003

<http://www.slayage.tv/essays/slayage8/Battis.htm>. Number references given in the text refer to paragraph numbers rather than page numbers.

Bellafante, Ginia. 1997. "Bewitching Teen Heroines." *Time* 149.18 (May 5): 82–85.

Bernardi, Daniel Leonard. 1998. *Star Trek and History: Race-ing Toward a White Future*. New Brunswick, N.J.: Rutgers University Press.

Bernstein, Jonathan. 2001. "Aerial View of America." *The Guide/ The Guardian* 17 November: 98.

Biskind, Peter, and Barbara Ehrenreich. 1987. "Machismo and Hollywood's Working Class." In *American Media and Mass Culture: Left Perspective*, ed. Donald Lazere, 201–215. Berkeley and Los Angeles: University of California Press.

Boris, Cynthia. 1999. "Sharp Spikes." *Cult Times* special 9 (Spring).

Bowers, Cynthia. 2001. "Generation Lapse: The Problematic Parenting of Joyce Summers and Rupert Giles." Slayage 2 (March), 25 pars. 1 May 2003 <http://www.slayage.tv/essays/slayage2/bowers.htm>. Number references given in the text refer to paragraph numbers rather than page numbers.

Boyette, Michele. 2001. "The Comic Anti-Hero in *Buffy the Vampire Slayer*, or Silly Villain: Spike Is for Kicks." *Slayage* 4 (December), 18 pars. 4 August 2003 <http://www.slayage.tv/essays/slayage4/boyette.htm>. Number references given in the text refer to paragraph numbers rather than page numbers.

Braun, Beth. 2000. "The X-Files and Buffy the Vampire Slayer: The Ambiguity of Evil in Supernatural Representations." *Journal of Popular Film and Television* 28.2: 88–94.

Brunsdon, Charlotte. 1997 [1993]. "Identity in Feminist Television Criticism." In *Feminist Television Criticism: A Reader*, ed. Charlotte Brunsdon, Julie D'Acci, and Lynn Spigel, 114–125. Oxford: Clarendon/Oxford University Press.

Brunsdon, Charlotte, Julie D'Acci, and Lynn Spigel, eds. 1997. *Feminist Television Criticism: A Reader*. Oxford: Clarendon/Oxford University Press.

"Buffy's Willow Bends Towards a Girlfriend." 2000. *The Advocate* 28 March: 24.

Buffy the Vampire Slayer *"Once More, with Feeling" script book*. 2002. New York: Pocket Books.

Buffy the Vampire Slayer *The Script Book: Season One, Volume 1*. 2000. New York: Pocket Books.

Bukatman, Scott. 1997. *Blade Runner*. BFI Modern Classics. London: BFI.

Busse, Kristina. 2002. "Crossing the Final Taboo: Family, Sexuality, and Incest in Buffyverse Fan Fiction." In *Fighting the Forces: What's At Stake in Buffy the Vampire Slayer*, ed. Rhonda V. Wilcox and David Lavery, 207–217. Lanham, Md.: Rowman & Littlefield.

Buttsworth, Sara. 2002. " 'Bite Me': *Buffy* and the Penetration of the Gendered Warrior-Hero." *Continuum: Journal of Media and Cultural Studies* 16.2: 185–199.

Buxton, David. 1990. *From* The Avengers *to* Miami Vice: *Form and Ideology in Television*. Manchester: Manchester University Press.

Chin, Vivian. 2003. "Buffy? She's Like Me, She's Not Like Me—She's *Rad*." In *Athena's Daughters: Television's New Women Warriors*, ed. Frances Early and Kathleen Kennedy, 92–102. Syracuse, N.Y.: Syracuse University Press.

Clover, Carol J. 1992. *Men, Women and Chainsaws: Gender in the Modern Horror Film*. London: BFI.

Cohan, Steven. 1993. "Masquerading as the American Male in the Fifties: Picnic, William Holden, and the Spectacle of Masculinity in Hollywood Film." In *Male Trouble*, ed. Constance Penley and Sharon Willis, 203–232. Minneapolis: University of Minneapolis Press.

Coppock, Vicki, Deena Haydon, and Ingrid Richter. 1995. *The Illusions of "Post-Feminism": New Women, Old Myths*. London: Taylor & Francis.

Corner, John. 1999. *Critical Ideas in Television Studies*. Oxford: Clarendon Press.

Creeber, Glen, ed. 2001. *The Television Genre Book*. London: BFI.

Creed, Barbara. 1993a. *The Monstrous-Feminine: Film, Feminism, Psychoanalysis*. London: Routledge.

———. 1993b. "Dark Desires: Male Masochism in the Horror Film." In *Screening the Male: Exploring Masculinities in Hollywood Cinema*, ed. Steven Cohan and Ina Rae Hark, 118–133. London: Routledge.

Daugherty, Anne Millard. 2001. "Just a Girl: Buffy as Icon." In *Reading the Vampire Slayer*, ed. Roz Kaveney, 148–165. London: I. B. Tauris.

"Dawson's Creek." 5 January 2004. <http://www.planetout.com/entertainment/starstruck/feature/spash.html?sernum=192>.

DeCandido, GraceAnne A. 1999. "Bibliographic Good vs. Evil in Buffy the Vampire Slayer." *American Libraries* 30.8: 44–51.

Dechert, S. Renee. 2002. " 'My Boyfriend's in the Band!': *Buffy* and the Rhetoric of Music." In *Fighting the Forces: What's At Stake in* Buffy the Vampire Slayer, ed. Rhonda V. Wilcox and David Lavery, 218–226. Lanham, Md.: Rowman & Littlefield.

DeKelb-Rittenhouse, Diane. 2002. "Sex and the Single Vampire: The Evolution of the Vampire Lothario and Its Representation in *Buffy*." In

Fighting the Forces: What's At Stake in Buffy the Vampire Slayer, ed. Rhonda V. Wilcox and David Lavery, 143–152. Lanham, Md.: Rowman & Littlefield.

Dempsey, John. 1997. "Femme Leads Earn Piece of the Action." *Variety* 367.10 (July 14): 25–26.

Dow, Bonnie J. 1996. *Prime-Time Feminism: Television, Media Culture, and the Woman's Movement since 1970*. Philadelphia: University of Pennsylvania Press.

Dyer, Richard. 1997. *White*. London: Routledge.

Early, Frances. 2002 [2001]. "Staking Her Claim: Buffy the Vampire Slayer as Transgressive Woman Warrior." *Slayage* 6 (September), 29 pars. 18 June 2003 <http://www.slayage.tv/essays/slayage6/Early.htm>. Number references given in the text refer to paragraph numbers rather than page numbers.

———. 2003. "The Female Just Warrior Reimagined." In *Athena's Daughters: Television's New Women Warriors*, ed. Frances Early and Kathleen Kennedy, 55–65. Syracuse, N.Y.: Syracuse University Press.

Early, Frances, and Kathleen Kennedy. 2003. "Introduction: Athena's Daughters." In *Athena's Daughters: Television's New Women Warriors*, ed. Frances Early and Kathleen Kennedy, 1–10. Syracuse, N.Y.: Syracuse University Press.

Edwards, Lynne. 2002. "Slaying in Black and White: Kendra as Tragic Mulatta in *Buffy*." In *Fighting the Forces: What's At Stake in* Buffy the Vampire Slayer, ed. Rhonda V. Wilcox and David Lavery, 85–97. Lanham, Md.: Rowman & Littlefield.

Fitzgerald, F. Scott. 1975 [1926]. *The Great Gatsby*. Harmondsworth: Penguin.

Forster, Greg. 2003. "Faith and Plato: 'You're Nothing! Disgusting, Murderous Bitch!'" In Buffy the Vampire Slayer *and Philosophy: Fear and Trembling in Sunnydale*, ed. James B. South, 7–19. Peru, Ill.: Open Court.

Fossey, Claire. 2003. "'Never Hurt the Feelings of a Brutal Killer': Spike and the Underground Man." *Slayage* 8 (March), 18 pars. 1 May 2003 <http://www.slayage.tv/essays/slayage8/Fossey.htm>. Number references given in the text refer to paragraph numbers rather than page numbers.

Foulkes, Nick. 2001. "Death and the Maiden." *Night & Day* 23 December: 14–16.

Gelder, Ken. 1994. *Reading the Vampire*. London: Routledge.

Geraghty, Christine. 1991. *Women and Soap Opera: A Study of Prime-Time Soaps*. Cambridge, UK: Polity Press.

Gibson, Janine. 2001. "Slay It Again." *Guardian Unlimited* Friday January 5
<www.guardianunlimited.co.uk>.

Gill, Candra K. 2003. " 'Cuz the Black Chick Always Gets It First': Dynamics
of Race in *Buffy the Vampire Slayer*." Unpublished paper, WisCon 27,
Madison, Wisconsin.

Golden, Christopher, and Nancy Holder. 1998. *Buffy the Vampire Slayer:
The Watcher's Guide*. New York: Pocket Books.

Golden, Christopher, Stephen R. Bissette, and Thomas Sniegoski. 2000.
Buffy the Vampire Slayer: The Monster Book. New York: Pocket Books.

Gomez, Jewelle. 1991. *The Gilda Stories: A Novel*. Ithaca, N.Y.: Firebrand
Books.

Gordon, Joan, and Veronica Hollinger. 1997. "Introduction: The Shape of
Vampires." In *Blood Read: The Vampire as Metaphor in Contemporary
Culture*, ed. Joan Gordon and Veronica Hollinger, 1–7. Philadelphia:
University of Pennsylvania Press.

Gray, Herman. 1995. *Watching Race: Television and the Struggle for Blackness*.
Minneapolis: University of Minnesota Press.

Heffernan, Nick. 2000. *Capital, Class and Technology in Contemporary
American Culture: Projecting Post-Fordism*. London: Pluto.

Heide, Margaret J. 1995. *Television Culture and Women's Lives*:
thirtysomething *and the Contradictions of Gender*. Philadelphia: University
of Pennsylvania Press.

Held, Jacob M. 2003. "Justifying the Means: Punishment in the Buffyverse."
In Buffy the Vampire Slayer *and Philosophy: Fear and Trembling in
Sunnydale*, ed. James B. South, 227–238. Peru, Ill.: Open Court.

Helford, Elyce Rae. 2002. " 'My Emotions Give Me Power': The
Containment of Girl's Anger in *Buffy*." In *Fighting the Forces: What's At
Stake in* Buffy the Vampire Slayer, ed. Rhonda V. Wilcox and David
Lavery, 18–34. Lanham, Md.: Rowman & Littlefield.

Hibbs, Thomas. 2003. "*Buffy the Vampire Slayer* as Feminist Noir." In Buffy
the Vampire Slayer *and Philosophy: Fear and Trembling in Sunnydale*, ed.
James B. South, 49–60. Peru, Ill.: Open Court.

Hill, Annette, and Ian Calcutt. 2001. "Vampire Hunters: The Scheduling and
Reception of *Buffy the Vampire Slayer* and *Angel* in the UK." *Intensities:
The Journal of Cult Media* 1 (Spring/ Summer). 15 April 2002 <http://
www.cult-media.com/issue1/Ahill.htm>.

Hinds, Hilary. 1997 [1991]. "Fruitful Investigations: The Case of the
Successful Lesbian Text." In *Feminist Television Criticism: A Reader*, ed.
Charlotte Brunsdon, Julie D'Acci, and Lynn Spigel, 205–210. Oxford:
Clarendon/Oxford University Press.

Holder, Nancy, with Jeff Mariotte and Maryelizabeth Hart. 2000. *Buffy the Vampire Slayer: The Watcher's Guide Volume 2*. New York: Pocket Books.

Hollinger, Veronica. 1997. "Fantasies of Absence: The Postmodern Vampire." In *Blood Read: The Vampire as Metaphor in Contemporary Culture*, ed. Joan Gordon and Veronica Hollinger, 99–212. Philadelphia: University of Pennsylvania Press.

Hollows, Joanne. 2000. *Feminism, Femininity and Popular Culture*. Manchester: Manchester University Press.

Hollway, Wendy. 1996. "Recognition and Heterosexual Desire." In *Theorising Heterosexuality: Telling It Straight*, ed. Diane Richardson, 91–108. Buckingham, U.K.: Open University Press.

Holmlund, Chris. 1993. "Masculinity as Multiple Masquerade: The Mature Stallone and the Stallone Clone." In *Screening the Male: Exploring Masculinities in Hollywood Cinema*, ed. Steven Cohan and Ina Rae Hark, 213–229. London: Routledge.

Inness, Sherrie A. 1999. *Tough Girls: Women Warriors and Wonder Women in Popular Culture*. Philadelphia: University of Pennsylvania Press.

Jackson, Stevi. 1999. *Heterosexuality in Question*. London: Sage.

Jancovich, Mark, and James Lyons, eds. 2003. *Quality Popular Television*. London: BFI.

Jarvis, Christine. 2001. "School Is Hell: Gendered Fears in Teenage Horror." *Educational Studies* 27.3: 257–267.

Jeffords, Susan. 1993. "Can Masculinity Be Terminated?" In *Screening the Male: Exploring Masculinities in Hollywood Cinema*, ed. Steven Cohan and Ina Rae Hark, 245–262. London: Routledge.

Johnson, Catherine. 2001. "*Buffy the Vampire Slayer*." In *The Television Genre Book*, ed. Glen Creeber, 42. London: BFI.

Johnson, Richard. 1997. "Contested Borders, Contingent Lives: An Introduction." In *Border Patrols: Policing the Boundaries of Heterosexuality*, ed. Lynn Steinberg, Debbie Epstein, and Richard Johnson, 1–32. London: Cassell.

Jordan, John J. 1999. "Vampire Cyborgs and Scientific Imperialism: A Reading of the Science-Mysticism Polemic in *Blade*." *Journal of Popular Film and Television* 27.2: 4–15.

Katz, Alyssa. 1998. "Buffy the Vampire Slayer." *The Nation* 266.12 (April 6): 35–36.

Kaveney, Roz. 2001. " 'She Saved the World. A Lot': An Introduction to the Themes and Structures of *Buffy* and *Angel*." In *Reading the Vampire Slayer*, ed. Roz Kaveney, 1–36. London: I. B. Tauris.

Keller, Donald. 2002. "Spirit Guides and Shadow Selves: From the Dream
Life of Buffy (and Faith)." In *Fighting the Forces: What's At Stake in* Buffy
the Vampire Slayer, ed. Rhonda V. Wilcox and David Lavery, 165–177.
Lanham, Md.: Rowman & Littlefield.

Kennedy, Rosanne. 1997 [1994]. "The Gorgeous Lesbian in *L.A. Law*: The
Present Absence?" In *Feminist Television Criticism: A Reader*, ed. Charlotte
Brunsdon, Julie D'Acci, and Lynn Spigel, 318–324. Oxford: Clarendon/
Oxford University Press.

Kimmel, Michael. 1997 [1996]. *Manhood in America: A Cultural History*.
New York: Free Press.

King, Neal. 2003. "Brownskirts: Fascism, Christianity, and the Eternal
Demon." In Buffy the Vampire Slayer *and Philosophy: Fear and Trembling
in Sunnydale*, ed. James B. South, 197–211. Peru, Ill.: Open Court.

Korsmeyer, Carolyn. 2003. "Passion and Action: In and Out of Control." In
Buffy the Vampire Slayer *and Philosophy: Fear and Trembling in Sunnydale*,
ed. James B. South, 160–172. Peru, Ill.: Open Court.

Kristeva, Julia. 1989. *Desire in Language: A Semiotic Approach to Literature
and Art*. Ed. Leon S. Roudiez. Trans. Thomas Gova, Alice Jardine, and
Leon S. Roudiez. Oxford: Basil Blackwell.

Krzywinska, Tanya. 2002. "Hubble-Bubble, Herbs, and Grimoires: Magic,
Manichaeanism, and Witchcraft in Buffy." In *Fighting the Forces: What's
At Stake in* Buffy the Vampire Slayer, ed. Rhonda V. Wilcox and David
Lavery, 178–194. Lanham, Md.: Rowman & Littlefield.

———. 2003. "Playing Buffy: Remediation, Occulted Meta-Game-Physics
and the Dynamics of Agency in the Videogame Version of *Buffy the
Vampire Slayer*." *Slayage* 8 (March 2003), 26 pars. 1 May 2003. <http://
www.slayage.tv/essays/slayage8/Krzywinska.htm>. Number references
given in the text refer to paragraph numbers rather than page numbers.

Larbalestier, Justine. 2002. "*Buffy*'s Mary Sue Is Jonathan: *Buffy*
Acknowledges the Fans." In *Fighting the Forces: What's At Stake in* Buffy
the Vampire Slayer, ed. Rhonda V. Wilcox and David Lavery, 227–238.
Lanham, Md.: Rowman & Littlefield.

Lavery, David. 2002a. "'Emotional Resonance and Rocket Launchers': Joss
Whedon's Commentaries on the *Buffy the Vampire Slayer* DVDs and
Television Creativity." *Slayage* 6 (September), 57 pars. 17 January 2003.
<http://www.slayage.tv/essays/slayage6/Lavery.htm>. Number
references given in the text refer to paragraph numbers rather than page
numbers.

———. 2002b. "'A Religion in Narrative': Joss Whedon and Television

Creativity." *Slayage* 7 (December), 16 pars. 17 January 2003. <http://www
.slayage.tv/essays/slayage7/Lavery.htm>. Number references given in the
text refer to paragraph numbers rather than page numbers.

Lawler, James. 2003. "Between Heaven and Hells: The Multidimensional
Universe in Kant and *Buffy the Vampire Slayer*." In Buffy the Vampire
Slayer *and Philosophy: Fear and Trembling in Sunnydale*, ed. James B.
South, 103–116. Peru, Ill.: Open Court.

LeFanu, Sheridan. 1988 [1872]. "Carmilla." In *The Penguin Book of Vampire
Stories*, ed. Alan Ryan, 71–137. London: Penguin.

Levine, Michael P., and Steven Jay Schneider. 2003. "Feeling for Buffy: The
Girl Next Door." In Buffy the Vampire Slayer *and Philosophy: Fear and
Trembling in Sunnydale*, ed. James B. South, 294–308. Peru, Ill.: Open
Court.

Lewis, Jon. 1992. *The Road to Romance and Ruin: Teen Films and Youth
Culture*. London: Routledge.

Little, Tracy. 2003. "High School Is Hell: Metaphor Made Literal in *Buffy the
Vampire Slayer*." In Buffy the Vampire Slayer *and Philosophy: Fear and
Trembling in Sunnydale*, ed. James B. South, 282–293. Peru, Ill.: Open
Court.

London, Jack. 1994 [1903]. *The Call of the Wild*. In *White Fang and the Call of
the Wild*. London: Penguin.

Longworth, James L., Jr. 2002. "Joss Whedon: Feminist." In *TV Creators:
Conversations with America's Top Producers of Television Drama Volume 2*,
197–220. Syracuse, N.Y.: Syracuse University Press.

Lott, Eric. 1995. *Love and Theft: Blackface Minstrelsy and the American
Working Class*. Oxford: Oxford University Press.

McDonald, Neil. 2000. "*Buffy*: Prime-Time Passion Play." *Quadrant* 44.5
(April): 63–67.

McGuigan, Jim. 1999. *Modernity and Postmodern Culture*. Buckingham,
U.K.: Open University Press.

McRobbie, Angela. 1994. *Postmodernism and Popular Culture*. London:
Routledge.

Marinucci, Mimi. 2003. "Feminism and the Ethics of Violence: Why Buffy
Kicks Ass." In Buffy the Vampire Slayer *and Philosophy: Fear and
Trembling in Sunnydale*, ed. James B. South, 61–75. Peru, Ill.: Open Court.

Mayne, Judith. 1997 [1988]. "*L.A. Law* and Prime-Time Feminism." In
Feminist Television Criticism: A Reader, ed. Charlotte Brunsdon, Julie
D'Acci, and Lynn Spigel, 84–97. Oxford: Clarendon/Oxford University
Press.

Mendlesohn, Farah. 2002. "Surpassing the Love of Vampires: Or, Why (and

How) a Queer Reading of the Buffy/Willow Relationship Is Denied." In *Fighting the Forces: What's At Stake in* Buffy the Vampire Slayer, ed. Rhonda V. Wilcox and David Lavery, 45–60. Lanham, Md.: Rowman & Littlefield.

Milavec, Melissa M., and Sharon M. Kaye. 2003. "Buffy in the Buff: A Slayer's Solution to Aristotle's Love Paradox." In Buffy the Vampire Slayer *and Philosophy: Fear and Trembling in Sunnydale*, ed. James B. South, 173–184. Peru, Ill.: Open Court.

Miller, Jessica Prata. 2003. "'The I in Team': Buffy and Feminist Ethics." In Buffy the Vampire Slayer *and Philosophy: Fear and Trembling in Sunnydale*, ed. James B. South, 35–48. Peru, Ill.: Open Court.

Modleski, Tania. 1997 [1979]. "The Search for Tomorrow in Today's Soap Operas." In *Feminist Television Criticism: A Reader*, ed. Charlotte Brunsdon, Julie D'Acci, and Lynn Spigel, 36–47. Oxford: Clarendon/Oxford University Press.

Money, Mary Alice. 2002. "The Undemonization of Supporting Characters in Buffy." In *Fighting the Forces: What's At Stake in* Buffy the Vampire Slayer, ed. Rhonda V. Wilcox and David Lavery, 98–107. Lanham, Md.: Rowman & Littlefield.

Morgan, Jessica. 2004. "*Dawson's Creek* 'Day Out of Days' Recap." 7 January. <http://www.televisionnwithoutpity.com/show.cgi?show=3>.

Moseley, Rachel. 2001. "The Teen Series." In *The Television Genre Book*, ed. Glen Creeber, 41–43. London: BFI.

Moy, Suelain. 1999. "Girls Who Fight Back." *Good Housekeeping* 228.4 (April): 86.

Mulvey, Laura. 1989 [1975]. "Visual Pleasure and Narrative Cinema." In *Visual and Other Pleasures*, 14–26. Houndmills, Basingstoke, U.K.: Macmillan.

Muntersbjorn, Madeline M. 2003. "Pluralism, Pragmatism, and Pals: The Slayer Subverts the Science Wars." In Buffy the Vampire Slayer *and Philosophy: Fear and Trembling in Sunnydale*, ed. James B. South, 91–102. Peru, Ill.: Open Court.

Nazzaro, Joe. 2002. *Writing Science Fiction and Fantasy Television*. London: Titan Books.

Neale, Steve. 1993. "Masculinity as Spectacle: Reflections on Men and Mainstream Cinema." In *Screening the Male: Exploring Masculinities in Hollywood Cinema*, ed. Steven Cohan and Ina Rae Hark, 9–20. London: Routledge.

Nelson, Robin. 2001. "*Ally McBeal*." In *The Television Genre Book*, ed. Glen Creeber, 45. London: BFI.

Nixon, Nicola. 1997. "When Hollywood Sucks, or, Hungry Girls, Lost Boys, and Vampirism in the Age of Reagan." In *Blood Read: The Vampire as Metaphor in Contemporary Culture*, ed. Joan Gordon and Veronica Hollinger, 115–128. Philadelphia: University of Pennsylvania Press.

Nochimson, Martha. 1992. *No End to Her: Soap Opera and the Female Subject*. Berkeley and Los Angeles: University of California Press.

Ogle, Tina. 1999. "Where the Stakes Are Deadly" [review]. *The Observer* 24 October: 2.

Olsen, Heather. 1999. "He Gives Us the Creeps." *Ms.* 15 September: 79.

Ono, Kent A. 2000. "To Be a Vampire on *Buffy the Vampire Slayer*: Race and ('Other') Socially Marginalizing Positions on Horror TV." In *Fantasy Girls: Gender in the New Universe of Science Fiction and Fantasy Television*, ed. Elyce Rae Helford, 163–186. Lanham, Md.: Rowman & Littlefield.

Owen, A. Susan. 1999. "Buffy the Vampire Slayer: Vampires, Postmodernity, and Postfeminism." *Journal of Popular Film and Television* 27.2: 24–32.

Page, Adrian. 2001. "Post-Modern Drama." In *The Television Genre Book*, ed. Glen Creeber, 43–46. London: BFI.

Parks, Lisa. 2003. "Brave New *Buffy*: Rethinking 'TV Violence.' In *Quality Popular Television*, ed. Mark Jancovich and James Lyons, 119–133. London: BFI.

Parpart, Lee. 2003. "'Action, Chicks, Everything': On-Line Interviews with Male Fans of *Buffy the Vampire Slayer*." In *Athena's Daughters: Television's New Women Warriors*, ed. Frances Early and Kathleen Kennedy, 78–91. Syracuse, N.Y.: Syracuse University Press.

Pasley, Jeffrey L. 2003. "Old Familiar Vampires: The Politics of the Buffyverse." In Buffy the Vampire Slayer *and Philosophy: Fear and Trembling in Sunnydale*, ed. James B. South, 254–267. Peru, Ill.: Open Court.

Penley, Constance, and Sharon Willis, eds. 1993. *Male Trouble*. Minneapolis: University of Minneapolis Press.

Playden, Zoe Jane. 2001. "'What You Are, What's to Come': Feminisms, Citizenship and the Divine." In *Reading the Vampire Slayer*, ed. Roz Kaveney, 120–147. London: I. B. Tauris.

Ramsland, Katherine. 1991. *Prism of the Night: A Biography of Anne Rice*. New York: Penguin.

Rapping, Elayne. 1994. *Media-tions: Forays into the Culture and Gender Wars*. Boston: South End Press.

Redman, Jessica H. E. 2003. "The American Happy Family That Never Was: Ambivalence in the Hollywood Family Melodrama." *European Journal of American Culture* 22.1: 49–69.

Rice, Anne. 1996 [1976]. *Interview with the Vampire*. London: Warner.

———. 1996 [1986]. *The Vampire Lestat*. London: Warner.

Richardson, Diane. 1996. "Heterosexuality and Social Theory." In *Theorising Heterosexuality: Telling It Straight*, ed. Diane Richardson, 1–20. Buckingham, U.K.: Open University Press.

Riess, Jana. 2004. *What Would Buffy Do?: The Vampire Slayer as Spiritual Guide*. San Francisco: Jossey-Bass Wiley.

Robinson, Victoria. 1996. "Heterosexuality and Masculinity: Theorising Male Power or the Male Wounded Psyche?" In *Theorising Heterosexuality: Telling It Straight*, ed. Diane Richardson, 109–124. Buckingham, U.K.: Open University Press.

Rogers, Adam. 1998. "Hey, Ally, Ever Slain a Vampire?" *Newsweek* 131.9 (March 2): 60.

Rose, Anita. 2002. "Of Creatures and Creators: Buffy Does Frankenstein." In *Fighting the Forces: What's At Stake in* Buffy the Vampire Slayer, ed. Rhonda V. Wilcox and David Lavery, 133–142. Lanham, Md.: Rowman & Littlefield.

Rowe, Kathleen K. 1997 [1990]. "Roseanne: Unruly Woman as Domestic Goddess." In *Feminist Television Criticism: A Reader*, ed. Charlotte Brunsdon, Julie D'Acci, and Lynn Spigel, 74–83. Oxford: Clarendon/Oxford University Press.

Sakal, Gregory J. 2003. "No Big Win: Themes of Sacrifice, Salvation, and Redemption." In Buffy the Vampire Slayer *and Philosophy: Fear and Trembling in Sunnydale*, ed. James B. South, 239–253. Peru, Ill.: Open Court.

Saxey, Esther. 2001. "Staking a Claim: The Series and Its Fan Fiction." In *Reading the Vampire Slayer*, ed. Roz Kaveney, 187–210. London: I. B. Tauris.

Sayer, Karen. 2001. " 'It Wasn't Our World Anymore. They Made It Theirs': Reading Space and Place." In *Reading the Vampire Slayer*, ed. Roz Kaveney, 98–119. London: I. B. Tauris.

Schudt, Karl. 2003. "Also Sprach Faith: The Problem of the Happy Rogue Vampire Slayer." In Buffy the Vampire Slayer *and Philosophy: Fear and Trembling in Sunnydale*, ed. James B. South, 20–34. Peru, Ill.: Open Court.

Shelley, Mary. 1994 [1818]. *Frankenstein*. London: Penguin.

Shuttleworth, Ian. 2001. " 'They Always Mistake Me For the Character I Play!': Transformation, Identity and Role-Playing in the Buffyverse (and a Defence of Fine Acting)." In *Reading the Vampire Slayer*, ed. Roz Kaveney, 211–236. London: I. B. Tauris.

Siemann, Catherine. 2002. "Darkness Falls on the Endless Summer: Buffy as Gidget for the Fin de Siècle." In *Fighting the Forces: What's At Stake in Buffy the Vampire Slayer*, ed. Rhonda V. Wilcox and David Lavery, 120–129. Lanham, Md.: Rowman & Littlefield.

Silver, Alain, and James Ursini. 1993. *The Vampire Film: From* Nosferatu *to* Bram Stoker's Dracula. 2nd ed. New York: Limelight Editions.

Simkin, Stevie. 2004a. " 'You Hold Your Gun Like a Sissy Girl'—Firearms and Anxious Masculinity in *Buffy the Vampire Slayer*." *Slayage* 11–12 (April), 27 pars. 12 August 2004 <http://www.slayage.tv/essays/slayage11/Simkin_Gun.htm>. Number references given in the text refer to paragraph numbers rather than page numbers.

———. 2004b. " 'Who Died and Made You John Wayne?—Anxious Masculinity in *Buffy the Vampire Slayer*." *Slayage* 11–12 (April), 36 pars. 12 August 2004 <http://www.slayage.tv/essays/slayage11/Simkin_Wayne.htm>. Number references given in the text refer to paragraph numbers rather than page numbers.

Simpson, Philip L. 2000. *Psycho Paths: Tracking the Serial Killer through Contemporary American Film and Fiction*. Carbondale and Edwardsville: Southern Illinois University Press.

Skwire, Sarah E. 2002. "Whose Side Are You On, Anyway? Children, Adults, and the Use of Fairy Tales in *Buffy*." In *Fighting the Forces: What's At Stake in Buffy the Vampire Slayer*, ed. Rhonda V. Wilcox and David Lavery, 195–204. Lanham, Md.: Rowman & Littlefield.

South, James B. 2003. " 'My God, It's Like a Greek Tragedy': Willow Rosenberg and Human Irrationality." In *Buffy the Vampire Slayer and Philosophy: Fear and Trembling in Sunnydale*, ed. James B. South, 131–145. Peru, Ill.: Open Court.

Spah, Victoria. 2002. " 'Ain't Love Grand?': Spike and Courtly Love." *Slayage* 5 (May), 18 pars. 4 August 2003 <http://www.slayage.tv/essays/slayage5/spah.htm>. Number references given in the text refer to paragraph numbers rather than page numbers.

Spicer, Arwen. 2002. " 'Love's Bitch but Man Enough to Admit It': Spike's Hybridized Gender." *Slayage* 7 (December), 24 pars. 1 May 2003 <http://www.slayage.tv/essays/slayage7/Spicer.htm>. Number references given in the text refer to paragraph numbers rather than page numbers.

———. 2004. " 'It's Bloody Brilliant!': The Undermining of Metanarrative Feminism in the Season Seven Arc Narrative of *Buffy*." Conference abstract. The *Slayage* conference on *Buffy the Vampire Slayer*, Nashville, Tenn. 8 February 2004. <http://www.slayage.tv/conference/Proposals/S/Spicer.htm>.

Stevenson, Robert Louis. 1994 [1886]. *Dr. Jekyll and Mr. Hyde*. London: Penguin.

Tasker, Yvonne. 1993a. *Spectacular Bodies: Gender, Genre and the Action Cinema*. London: Routledge.

———. 1993b. "Dumb Movies for Dumb People: Masculinity, the Body and the Voice in Contemporary Action Cinema." In *Screening the Male: Exploring Masculinities in Hollywood Cinema*, ed. Steven Cohan and Ina Rae Hark, 230–244. London: Routledge.

Thomas, Lyn. 1997 [1995]. "In Love with *Inspector Morse*: Feminist Subculture and Quality Television." In *Feminist Television Criticism: A Reader*, ed. Charlotte Brunsdon, Julie D'Acci, and Lynn Spigel, 184–204. Oxford: Clarendon/Oxford University Press.

Thompson, Robert J. 1997. *Television's Second Golden Age: From* Hill Street Blues *to* ER. Syracuse, N.Y.: Syracuse University Press.

Tjardes, Sue. 2003. "'If You're Not Enjoying It, You're Doing Something Wrong': Textual and Viewer Constructions of Faith, the Vampire Slayer." In *Athena's Daughters: Television's New Women Warriors*, ed. Frances Early and Kathleen Kennedy, 66–77. Syracuse, N.Y.: Syracuse University Press.

Tonkin, Boyd. 2001. "Entropy as Demon: Buffy in Southern California." In *Reading the Vampire Slayer*, ed. Roz Kaveney, 38–52. London: I. B. Tauris.

Topping, Keith. 2002. *Slayer: An Expanded and Updated Unofficial and Unauthorised Guide to* Buffy the Vampire Slayer. London: Virgin.

———. 2003. *Slayer the Next Generation: An Unofficial and Unauthorised Guide to Season Six of* Buffy the Vampire Slayer. London: Virgin.

Torres, Sasha. 1993. "Melodrama, Masculinity, and the Family: *thirtysomething* as Therapy." In *Male Trouble*, ed. Constance Penley and Sharon Willis, 283–302. Minneapolis: University of Minneapolis Press.

Traube, Elizabeth G. 1992. *Class, Gender, and Generation in 1980s Hollywood Movies*. Boulder, Colo.: Westview Press.

Turner, Graeme. 2001. "Genre, Hybridity and Mutation." In *The Television Genre Book*, ed. Glen Creeber, 6. London: BFI.

Udovitch, Mim. 2001. "Buffy: On Set with Sarah Michelle Gellar" [interview]. *Esquire* 11.1 (January): 165.

Vint, Sherryl. 2002. "'Killing Us Softly'? A Feminist Search for the 'Real' Buffy." *Slayage* 5 (May), 26 pars. 4 August 2003 <http://www.slayage.tv/essays/slayage5/vint.htm>. Number references given in the text refer to paragraph numbers rather than page numbers.

Wall, Brian, and Michael Zryd. 2001. "Vampire Dialectics: Knowledge, Institutions and Labour." In *Reading the Vampire Slayer*, ed. Roz Kaveney, 53–77. London: I. B. Tauris.

Warhol, Robyn. 1999. "Making 'Gay' and 'Lesbian' into Household Words: How Serial Form Works in Armistead Maupin's *Tales of the City*." *Contemporary Literature* 40.3 (Fall): 378–402.

West, Dave. 2001. "'Concentrate on the Kicking Movie': *Buffy* and East Asian Cinema." In *Reading the Vampire Slayer*, ed. Roz Kaveney, 166–186. London: I. B. Tauris.

Whelehan, Imelda. 2000. *OverLoaded: Popular Culture and the Future of Feminism*. London: Women's Press.

Wiegman, Robyn. 1993. "Feminism, 'The Boyz,' and Other Matters regarding the Male." In *Screening the Male: Exploring Masculinities in Hollywood Cinema*, ed. Steven Cohan and Ina Rae Hark, 173–193. London: Routledge.

Wilcox, Rhonda V. 1999. "There Will Never Be a 'Very Special' *Buffy*: Buffy and the Monsters of Teen Life." *Journal of Popular Film and Television* 27.2: 16–24.

———. 2002a. "'Who Died and Made Her the Boss?': Patterns of Mortality in *Buffy*." In *Fighting the Forces: What's At Stake in* Buffy the Vampire Slayer, ed. Rhonda V. Wilcox and David Lavery, 3–17. Lanham, Md.: Rowman & Littlefield.

———. 2002b. "Pain as Bright as Steel." Unpublished paper, "Blood, Texts and Fears" conference, Norwich, U.K.

———. 2003. Foreword. In *Athena's Daughters: Television's New Women Warriors*, ed. Frances Early and Kathleen Kennedy, ix–xii. Syracuse, N.Y.: Syracuse University Press.

Wilcox, Rhonda V. and David Lavery. 2002. "Introduction." In *Fighting the Forces: What's At Stake in* Buffy the Vampire Slayer, ed. Rhonda V. Wilcox and David Lavery, xvii–xxix. Lanham, Md.: Rowman & Littlefield.

Williams, J. P. 2002. "Choosing Your Own Mother: Mother-Daughter Conflicts in *Buffy*." In *Fighting the Forces: What's At Stake in* Buffy the Vampire Slayer, ed. Rhonda V. Wilcox and David Lavery, 61–72. Lanham, Md.: Rowman & Littlefield.

Williams, Tony. 1996. *Hearths of Darkness: The Family in the American Horror Film*. Cranbury, N.J.: Associated University Presses.

Williams, Zoe. 2001. "The Lady and the Vamp." *The Guardian Weekend* 17 November: 30–36.

Wilson, Steve. 2001. "'Laugh, Spawn of Hell, Laugh.'" In *Reading the Vampire Slayer*, ed. Roz Kaveney, 78–97. London: I. B. Tauris.

Wilton, Tamsin. "Which One's the Man? The Heterosexualisation of Lesbian Sex." In *Theorising Heterosexuality: Telling It Straight*, ed. Diane Richardson, 125–142. Buckingham, U.K.: Open University Press.

Wisker, Gina. 2001. "Vampires and School Girls: High School Jinks on the
Hellmouth." *Slayage* 2 (March). 1 May 2003 <http://www.slayage.tv/
essays/slayage2/wisker.htm>.

Woloch, Nancy. 2000. *Women and the American Experience*. 3rd ed. Boston:
McGraw-Hill.

Wyman, Mark. 1999. "Buffy's Master." *Starburst* (London) 245 (January):
46–50.

FILMS CITED

Alien (TCF/Brandywine, 1979). Dir. Ridley Scott, 117 min.

Aliens (TCF/Brandywine, 1986). Dir. James Cameron, 137 min.

The Attack of the 50 Foot Woman (Allied Artists, 1958). Dir. Nathan Hertz,
72 min.

Blade (Amen Ra/Imaginary Forces/New Line Cinema, 1998). Dir. Stephen
Norrington, 120 min.

Blade Runner (Warner/Ladd/Blade Runner Partnership, 1982). Dir. Ridley
Scott, 117 min.

Bram Stoker's Dracula (Columbia Tristar/American Zoetrope/Osiris, 1992).
Dir. Francis Ford Coppola, 128 min.

Buffy the Vampire Slayer (TCF/Sandollar/Kuzui, 1992). Dir. Fran Rubel
Kuzui, 94 min.

The Craft (Columbia, 1996). Dir. Andrew Fleming, 100 min.

Falling Down (Warner, 1993). Dir. Joel Schumacher, 112 min.

The Hunger (MCM-UA, 1983). Dir. Tony Scott, 99 min.

I Know What You Did Last Summer (Entertainment/Mandalay, 1997). Dir.
Jim Gillespie, 101 min.

In the Heat of the Night (UA/Mirisch, 1967). Dir. Norman Jewison, 109 min.

The Lost Boys (Warner, 1987). Dir. Joel Schumacher, 92 min.

Mamono Hunter Yôko (Toho, 1991). Dir. Tetsuro Aoki, 45 min.

Nadja (ICA/Kino Link, 1995). Dir. Michael Almereyda, 100 min.

Near Dark (Entertainment/Scotti Brothers/International Video
Entertainment, 1987). Dir. Kathryn Bigelow, 94 min.

Rebel without a Cause (Warner, 1955). Dir. Nicholas Ray, 111 min.

Scream 2 (Miramax/Dimension/Kourd, 1997). Dir. Wes Craven, 120 min.

Silence of the Lambs (Rank/Orion/Strong Heart/Demme, 1990). Dir. Jonathan
Demme, 118 min.

The Terminator (Orion/Helmdale/Pacific Western, 1984). Dir. James
Cameron, 108 min.

Terminator 2: Judgment Day (Guild/Carolco/Pacific Western/Lightstorm,
1991). Dir. James Cameron, 135 min.

Terminator 3: Rise of the Machines (C-2/Intermedia/ IMF/MostowLieberman, 2003). Dir. Jonathan Mostow, 109 min.

Three Men and a Baby (Touchstone/Silver Screen III, 1987). Dir. Leonard Nimoy, 102 min.

EPISODES OF *Buffy* AND *Angel* CITED
Dates given are original U.S. airdates.

Angel 1999–2004 (WB)

"Five by Five." 1018. Writ. Jim Kouf. Dir. James A. Contner. 25 April 2000.

"Sanctuary." 1019. Writ. Tim Minear and Joss Whedon. Dir. Michael Lange. 2 May 2000.

"Darla." 2007. Writ. and dir. Tim Minear. 14 November 2000.

"The Trial." 2009. Writ. Doug Petrie and Tim Minear (story David Greenwalt). Dir. Bruce Seth Green. 28 November 2000.

"Reunion." 2010. Writ. Tim Minear and Shawn Ryan. Dir. James A. Contner. 19 December 2000.

"Disharmony." 2017. Writ. David Fury. Dir. Fred Keller. 17 April 2001.

Buffy the Vampire Slayer 1997–2001 (WB), 2001–2003 (UPN)

"Welcome to the Hellmouth." 1001. Writ. Joss Whedon. Dir. Charles Martin. 10 March 1997.

"The Harvest." 1002. Writ. Dana Reston. Dir. Stephen Cragg. 10 March 1997.

"The Witch." 1003. Writ. Joss Whedon. Dir. Charles Martin. 17 March 1997.

"Never Kill a Boy on the First Date." 1005. Writ. Rob Des Hotel and Dean Batali. Dir. David Semel. 31 March 1997.

"The Pack." 1006. Writ. Matt Kiene and Joe Rinkemeyer. Dir. Bruce Seth Green. 7 April 1997.

"Angel." 1007. Writ. David Greenwalt. Dir. Scott Brazil. 14 April 1997.

"I, Robot—You, Jane." 1008. Writ. Ashley Gable and Tom Swynden. Dir. Stephen Posey. 28 April 1997.

"Out of Mind, Out of Sight." 1011. Writ. Ashley Gable and Tom Swynden (story Joss Whedon). Dir. Reza Badiyi. 19 May 1997.

"Prophecy Girl." 1012. Writ. and dir. Joss Whedon. 2 June 1997.

"When She Was Bad." 2001. Writ. and dir. Joss Whedon. 15 September 1997.

"Some Assembly Required." 2002. Writ. Ty King. Dir. Bruce Seth Green.
22 September 1997.

"School Hard." 2003. Writ. David Greenwalt (story Joss Whedon and
David Greenwalt). Dir. John T. Kretchmer. 29 September 1997.

"Reptile Boy." 2005. Writ. and dir. David Greenwalt. 13 October 1997.

"Halloween." 2006. Writ. Carl Ellsworth. Dir. Bruce Seth Green.
27 October 1997.

"Lie to Me." 2007. Writ. and dir. Joss Whedon. 3 November 1997.

"The Dark Age." 2008. Writ. Dean Batali and Rob Des Hotel. Dir. Bruce
Seth Green. 10 November 1997.

"What's My Line? Part 1." 2009. Writ. Howard Gordon and Marti Noxon.
Dir. David Solomon. 17 November 1997.

"What's My Line? Part 2." 2010. Writ. Marti Noxon. Dir. David Semel.
24 November 1997.

"Ted." 2011. Writ. David Greenwalt and Joss Whedon. Dir. Bruce Seth
Green. 8 December 1997.

"Bad Eggs." 2012. Writ. Marti Noxon. Dir. David Greenwalt. 12 January
1998.

"Surprise." 2013. Writ. Marti Noxon. Dir. Michael Lange. 19 January 1998.

"Innocence." 2014. Writ. and dir. Joss Whedon. 20 January 1998.

"Phases." 2015. Writ. Rob Des Hotel and Dean Batali. Dir. Bruce Seth
Green. 27 January 1998.

"Bewitched, Bothered and Bewildered." 2016. Writ. Marti Noxon. Dir.
James A. Contner. 10 February 1998.

"Passion." 2017. Writ. Ty King. Dir. Michael Gershman. 24 February 1998.

"Killed by Death." 2018. Writ. Rob Des Hotel and Dean Batali. Dir.
Deran Sarafian. 3 March 1998.

"I Only Have Eyes for You." 2019. Writ. Marti Noxon. Dir. James
Whitmore Jr. 28 April 1998.

"Go Fish." 2020. Writ. David Fury and Elin Hampton. Dir. David Semel.
5 May 1998.

"Becoming Part 1." 2021. Writ. and dir. Joss Whedon. 12 May 1998.

"Becoming Part 2." 2022. Writ. and dir. Joss Whedon. 19 May 1998.

"Anne." 3001. Writ. and dir. Joss Whedon. 29 September 1998.

"Dead Man's Party." 3002. Writ. Marti Noxon. Dir. James Whitmore Jr.
6 October 1998.

"Faith, Hope and Trick." 3003. Writ. David Greenwalt. Dir. James A.
Contner. 13 October 1998.

"Beauty and the Beasts." 3004. Writ. Marti Noxon. Dir. James
    Whitmore Jr. 20 October 1998.

"Homecoming." 3005. Writ. and dir. David Greenwalt. 3 November 1998.

"Band Candy." 3006. Writ. Jane Espenson. Dir. Michael Lange.
    10 November 1998.

"Revelations." 3007. Writ. Douglas Petrie. Dir. James A. Contner.
    17 November 1998.

"Lover's Walk." 3008. Writ. Dan Vebber. Dir. David Semel. 24 November
    1998.

"The Wish." 3009. Writ. Marti Noxon. Dir. David Greenwalt. 8 December
    1998.

"Amends." 3010. Writ. and dir. Joss Whedon. 15 December 1998.

"Gingerbread." 3011. Writ. Jane Espenson (story Thania St. John and Jane
    Espenson). Dir. James Whitmore Jr. 12 January 1999.

"Helpless." 3012. Writ. David Fury. Dir. James A. Contner. 19 January
    1999.

"The Zeppo." 3013. Writ. Dan Vebber. Dir. James Whitmore Jr.
    26 January 1999.

"Bad Girls." 3014. Writ. Douglas Petrie. Dir. Michael Lange. 9 February
    1999.

"Consequences." 3015. Writ. Marti Noxon. Dir. Michael Gershman.
    16 February 1999.

"Doppelgangland." 3016. Writ. and dir. Joss Whedon. 23 February 1999.

"Enemies." 3017. Writ. Douglas Petrie. Dir. David Grossman. 16 March
    1999.

"Earshot." 3018. Writ. Jane Espenson. Dir. Regis B. Kimble. 21 September
    1999.

"Choices." 3019. Writ. David Fury. Dir. James A. Contner. 4 May 1999.

"The Prom." 3020. Writ. Marti Noxon. Dir. David Solomon. 11 May 1999.

"Graduation Day Part 1." 3021. Writ. and dir. Joss Whedon. 18 May 1999.

"Graduation Day Part 2." 3022. Writ. and dir. Joss Whedon. 13 July 1999.

"The Freshman." 4001. Writ. and dir. Joss Whedon. 5 October 1999.

"Living Conditions." 4002. Writ. Marti Noxon. Dir. David Grossman.
    12 October 1999.

"The Harsh Light of Day." 4003. Writ. Jane Espenson. Dir. James A.
    Contner. 19 October 1999.

"Fear, Itself." 4004. Writ. David Fury. Dir. Tucker Gates. 26 October 1999.

"Beer Bad." 4005. Writ. Tracey Forbes. Dir. David Solomon. 2 November
    1999.

"Wild at Heart." 4006. Writ. Marti Noxon. Dir. David Grossman.
   9 November 1999.

"The Initiative." 4007. Writ. Douglas Petrie. Dir. James A. Contner.
   16 November 1999.

"Pangs." 4008. Writ. Jane Espenson. Dir. Michael Lange. 23 November
   1999.

"Something Blue." 4009. Writ. Tracey Forbes. Dir. Nick Marck.
   30 November 1999.

"Hush." 4010. Writ. and dir. Joss Whedon. 14 December 1999.

"A New Man." 4012. Writ. Jane Espenson. Dir. Michael Gershman.
   25 January 2000.

"The I in Team." 4013. Writ. David Fury. Dir. James A. Contner.
   8 February 2000.

"Goodbye Iowa." 4014. Writ. Marti Noxon. Dir. David Solomon.
   15 February 2000.

"This Year's Girl." 4015. Writ. Douglas Petrie. Dir. Michael Gershman.
   22 February 2000.

"Who Are You?" 4016. Writ. and dir. Joss Whedon. 29 February 2000.

"Superstar." 4017. Writ. Jane Espenson. Dir. David Grossman. 4 April
   2000.

"Where the Wild Things Are." 4018. Writ. Tracey Forbes. Dir. David
   Solomon. 25 April 2000.

"New Moon Rising." 4019. Writ. Marti Noxon. Dir. James A. Contner.
   2 May 2000.

"The Yoko Factor." 4020. Writ. Douglas Petrie. Dir. David Grossman.
   9 May 2000.

"Primeval." 4021. Writ. David Fury. Dir. James A. Contner. 16 May 2000.

"Restless." 4022. Writ. and dir. Joss Whedon. 23 May 2000.

"Buffy vs. Dracula." 5001. Writ. Marti Noxon. Dir. David Solomon.
   26 September 2000.

"Real Me." 5002. Writ. David Fury. Dir. David Grossman. 3 October
   2000.

"The Replacement." 5003. Writ. Jane Espenson. Dir. James A. Contner.
   10 October 2000.

"Out of My Mind." 5004. Writ. Rebecca Rand Kirshner. Dir. David
   Grossman. 17 October 2000.

"No Place Like Home." 5005. Writ. Douglas Petrie. Dir. David Solomon.
   24 October 2000.

"Family." 5006. Writ. and dir. Joss Whedon. 7 November 2000.

"Fool for Love." 5007. Writ. Douglas Petrie. Dir. Nick Marck.
14 November 2000.

"Shadow." 5008. Writ. David Fury. Dir. Daniel Attias. 21 November 2000.

"Into the Woods." 5010. Writ. and dir. Marti Noxon. 19 December 2000.

"Triangle." 5011. Writ. Jane Espenson. Dir. Christopher Hibler. 9 January
2001.

"Checkpoint." 5012. Writ. Jane Espenson and Douglas Petrie. Dir. Nick
Marck. 23 January 2001.

"Blood Ties." 5013. Writ. Steven S. DeKnight. Dir. Michael Gershman.
6 February 2001.

"Crush." 5014. Writ. David Fury. Dir. Daniel Attias. 13 February 2001.

"I Was Made to Love You." 5015. Writ. Jane Espenson. Dir. James A.
Contner. 20 February 2001.

"The Body." 5016. Writ. and dir. Joss Whedon. 27 February 2001.

"Forever." 5017. Writ. and dir. Marti Noxon. 17 April 2001.

"Intervention." 5018. Writ. Jane Espenson. Dir. Michael Gershman.
24 April 2001.

"Tough Love." 5019. Writ. Rebecca Rand Kirshner. Dir. David Grossman.
1 May 2001.

"Spiral." 5020. Writ. Steven S. DeKnight. Dir. James A. Contner. 8 May
2001.

"The Weight of the World." 5021. Writ. Douglas Petrie. Dir. David
Solomon. 15 May 2001.

"The Gift." 5022. Writ. and dir. Joss Whedon. 22 May 2001.

"Bargaining Part 1." 6001. Writ. Marti Noxon. Dir. David Grossman.
2 October 2001.

"Bargaining Part 2." 6002. Writ. David Fury. Dir. David Grossman.
2 October 2001.

"After Life." 6003. Writ. Jane Espenson. Dir. David Solomon. 9 October
2001.

"Flooded." 6004. Writ. Jane Espenson and Douglas Petrie. Dir. Douglas
Petrie. 16 October 2001.

"Life Serial." 6005. Writ. David Fury. Dir. Nick Marck. 23 October 2001.

"All the Way." 6006. Writ. Steven S. DeKnight. Dir. David Solomon.
30 October 2001.

"Once More, with Feeling." 6007. Writ. and dir. Joss Whedon.
6 November 2001.

"Tabula Rasa." 6008. Writ. Rebecca Rand Kirshner. Dir. David Grossman.
13 November 2001.

"Smashed." 6009. Writ. Drew Z. Greenberg. Dir. Turi Meyer.
20 November 2001.

"Wrecked." 6010. Writ. Marti Noxon. Dir. David Solomon. 27 November
2001.

"Gone." 6011. Writ. and dir. David Fury. 8 January 2002.

"Doublemeat Palace." 6012. Writ. Jane Espenson. Dir. Nick Marck.
29 January 2002.

"Dead Things." 6013. Writ. Steven S. DeKnight. Dir. James A. Contner.
5 February 2002.

"Older and Far Away." 6014. Writ. Drew Z. Greenberg. Dir. Michael
Gershman.12 February 2002.

"As You Were." 6015. Writ. and dir. Douglas Petrie. 26 February 2002.

"Hell's Bells." 6016. Writ. Rebecca Rand Kirshner. Dir. David Solomon.
5 March 2002.

"Normal Again." 6017. Writ. Diego Gutierrez. Dir. Rick Rosenthal.
12 March 2002.

"Entropy." 6018. Writ. Drew Z. Greenberg. Dir. James A. Contner.
30 April 2002.

"Seeing Red." 6019. Writ. Steven S. DeKnight. Dir. Michael Gershman.
7 May 2002.

"Villains." 6020. Writ. Marti Noxon. Dir. David Solomon. 14 May 2002.

"Two to Go." 6021. Writ. Douglas Petrie. Dir. Bill L. Norton. 21 May
2002.

"Grave." 6022. Writ. David Fury. Dir. James A. Contner. 21 May 2002.

"Lessons." 7001. Writ. Joss Whedon. Dir. David Solomon. 24 September
2002.

"Beneath You." 7002. Writ. Douglas Petrie. Dir. Nick Marck. 1 October
2002.

"Help." 7004. Writ. Rebecca Rand Kirshner. Dir. Rick Rosenthal.
15 October 2002.

"Selfless." 7005. Writ. Drew Goddard. Dir. David Solomon. 22 October
2002.

"Him." 7006. Writ. Drew Z. Greenberg. Dir. Michael Gershman.
5 November 2002.

"Conversations with Dead People." 7007. Writ. Jane Espenson and Drew
Goddard. Dir. Nick Marck. 12 November 2002.

"Never Leave Me." 7009. Writ. Drew Goddard. Dir. David Solomon.
26 November 2002.

"Potential." 7012. Writ. Rebecca Rand Kirshner. Dir. James A. Contner. 21 January 2003.

"First Date." 7014. Writ. Jane Espenson. Dir. David Grossman. 11 February 2003.

"Get It Done." 7015. Writ. and dir. Douglas Petrie. 18 February 2003.

"Lies My Parents Told Me." 7017. Writ. David Fury and Drew Goddard. Dir. David Fury. 25 March 2003.

"Dirty Girls." 7018. Writ. Drew Goddard. Dir. Michael Gershman. 15 April 2003.

"Empty Places." 7019. Writ. Drew Z. Greenberg. Dir. James A. Contner. 29 April 2003.

"Touched." 7020. Writ. Rebecca Rand Kirshner. Dir. David Solomon. 6 May 2003.

"End of Days." 7021. Writ. Jane Espenson and Douglas Petrie. Dir. Marita Grabiak. 13 May 2003.

"Chosen." 7022. Writ. and dir. Joss Whedon. 20 May 2003.

INDEX

Entries marked with an asterisk are *Buffy the Vampire Slayer* episodes, characters, or institutions.

fan fiction, 119, 138, 163, 169, 202
n. 2

fans, 1, 7–8, 17, 58, 138, 142

fantasy genre, 1, 8, 12–13, 16, 56, 82, 112, 172, 192, 196

Farscape, 20, 196, 206 n. 1

*"Fear, Itself," 38, 125

femininity: and class, 85; as masquerade, 42, 71, 81, 90; in the 1950s, 48; in opposition to feminism, 6–7, 19; traditional qualities of, 27, 57, 119, 124, 134

feminism: and families, 167; and girl power, 18–19; influence on popular culture of, 18, 21, 119; and romance, 29–30, 123; second wave of, 3–8, 20, 42, 95, 174–175; Whedon on, 21

Femme Nikita, La, 30

Finn, Huckleberry, 108

*Finn, Riley. *See* Riley

*"First Date," 89, 138, 140–142

*First Evil, the (the First), 14, 28, 56, 67, 89, 116, 141, 189, 192

*First Slayer, the, 41, 116, 174, 201 n. 4

*"Flooded," 40, 113, 187, 203 n. 9

*Flutie, Principal, 189

*"Fool for Love," 27, 47, 75, 77, 79, 140, 158, 161–162, 202 n. 8

*Ford, 121–122, 145

*Fordham, Billy. *See* Ford

*"Forever," 177, 182–183

*Forrest, 105, 108–110, 115, 123, 146, 148–149, 203 nn. 4, 5, 6, 7

Frankenstein complex (Isaac Asimov), 110

Frankenstein's monster, 96, 110, 114, 175

*"Freshman, The," 135, 175–176, 182

gay rights movement, 3

Gellar, Sarah Michelle, 1, 50, 199 n. 1, 200 n. 3

gender: binaries of, 95–96, 98, 109, 142, 187; and genre, 20, 44, 193; and romance, 29–30, 120; as social construction, 2, 120, 144. *See also* femininity; feminism; masculinity; women

generational conflict, 16, 54, 167–168, 174, 189

Generation of Vipers (Philip Wylie), 131

genre, 10, 13, 20, 44, 60, 63, 193, 196

*"Get It Done," 26, 36, 165, 205 n. 5

*"Gift, The," 93, 133, 165

Gilda Stories, The (Jewelle Gomez), 72

*Giles, Rupert: accent of, 129–130, 160; age of, 127, 131, 172, 182, 184; and Angel/us, 99, 128–129, 204 n. 10; as British, 127, 204 n. 4; and Jenny Calendar, 127–129, 131, 173, 175; and class, 130–131; as demon-Giles, 132, 186; as father to Buffy, 127, 132, 169–171, 179–180, 182, 184–187, 190, 206 n. 9; gendered language of, 132, 185; heroism of, 128; as heterosocial, 128; and Joyce, 128, 131, 178–180, 184–185, 189, 206 n. 8; and killing of Ben, 67, 93, 133; as librarian, 127–128; as mentor, 132, 186–187, 193; names of, 127; and Olivia, 128, 131, 182, 184–185; as patriarch, 128, 186, 189, 193; as provider, 128–129; as Ripper, 129–131, 130 fig., 142, 160, 195; Scooby Gang position, 26–27, 112, 127–129, 131, 133, 178, 183, 187–188, 193; and sex, 131–132, 175, 182, 204 n. 5; sexuality of, 129, 131–133, 138; and viewing pleasure, 129, 131, 193; and violence, 67, 129, 132–134; and Professor Walsh, 132, 186; as Watcher, 19, 24, 26, 88, 128–129, 133, 148, 178, 184–186; Whedon on, 204 n. 5; and Willow, 38–41,